# MORAL EDUCATION

## A Teacher-Centered Approach

**Joan F. Goodman**

*University of Pennsylvania*

**Howard Lesnick**

*University of Pennsylvania*

PEARSON

Boston   New York   San Francisco
Mexico City   Montreal   Toronto   London   Madrid   Munich   Paris
Hong Kong   Singapore   Tokyo   Cape Town   Sydney

**Executive Editor and Publisher:** *Stephen D. Dragin*
**Senior Editorial Assistant:** *Barbara Strickland*
**Marketing Manager:** *Tara Whorf*
**Senior Production Administrator:** *Deborah Brown*
**Composition Buyer:** *Linda Cox*
**Manufacturing Buyer:** *Andrew Turso*
**Electronic Composition and Layout:** *Galley Graphics*

For related titles and support materials, visit our online catalog at
www.ablongman.com

*Library of Congress Cataloging-in-Publication Data unavailable at time of printing.*

Printed in the United States of America

10  9  8  7  6  5  4  3  2  1      08  07  06  05  04  03

*To the spirit of aspiration among educators*

# BRIEF CONTENTS

# CONTENTS

**CHAPTER FOUR**

# Moral Education Inservice   59

**CHAPTER FIVE**

# Moral Education and the Home   78

**CHAPTER SIX**

# Moral Discipline    103

**CHAPTER SEVEN**

# Whose Values? Relativism and Pluralism    133

# PREFACE

■ ■ ■ ■ ■

At a recent gathering of principals, vice principals, and experienced teachers we asked the following three questions:

"Are schools in the business of moral education?" (all hands raised).
"Should schools be in the business of moral education?" (all hands raised).

"Are *your* schools asking questions about the what and how of moral education?" (no hands raised).

What this tells us (and you) is that these teachers find the "call" for moral education at school paper-thin. It is easy to be in favor of moral education, and polls indicate that most of us are. It is slightly less easy, but still rather obvious, that school personnel make moral decisions moment by moment all day long; "shoulds" and "shouldn'ts" are the air they breathe. Yet despite exhortations from parents, government leaders, and the public at large to "do" it, thoughtful analysis of what we should be teaching and how we should engage the topic is meager. There appears to be an implicit message that morality, though obviously important, is intuitive; off-the-cuff responses suffice. Yet it is also obvious that there is widespread social disagreement on the nature of our moral obligations, on who is responsible for instructing the young, and on how moral education should be carried out. The whats and hows of this subject are hotly and persistently contested. Grasping the complexity of morality in our intricate society requires an intellectual sophistication that is anything but intuitive; an off-the-cuff pedagogy hardly suffices.

This book reflects our "calling" to reveal the richness (and divisiveness) of moral education, as well as its centrality and pervasiveness, and to provide an instructional approach that respects the diversity of viewpoints. That approach focuses on the role of teachers. If there is any chance at all that schools can seriously affect the moral orientation of students, the king- and queen-pins of this effort must be our nation's teachers. It is they who must aspire to the mission and be supported with some know-how.

But vesting responsibility in teachers will fail without substantial encouragement from administration and parents. If the "higher-ups" (including parents) feel entitled, in the name of accountability, to report and admonish them for their every action, teachers cannot do more than docilely enforce the rules. We cannot expect them to make a stir—as moral matters often demand—in the face of an almost certain reprimand. If teachers are to engage children in serious moral discussions and moral decision making; if they are to take a stand (on a classroom incident) or question a practice (a school rule they find unfair); if, in short, they are to act as moral agents and encourage students to do likewise, then the overseers of their practices must clear the space and grant them authority. This is not to say they should be autonomous; on the contrary, collective thinking is essential in moral education. But their professionalism must be privileged.

Our previous book, *The Moral Stake in Education: Contested Premises and Practices* (2001), carried a similar message. That work, however, is oriented more to college and university students than to practicing educators and is therefore recommended for those interested in pursuing the theoretical roots of school practice. Here, while we borrow extensively from *The Moral Stake,* particularly in the vignettes that form the core of each chapter, we reach out not only to readers in college classrooms but beyond to those in the trenches—teachers, administrators, parents—who most powerfully mold the consciences of children.

We are indebted to two groups of students at the Graduate School of Education, University of Pennsylvania. The first group, who took the course, Values and Education, read *The Moral Stake in Education* critically. Their reactions were formative in designing this more applied book. The second, a group of practitioners returning for a doctoral degree in the school's mid-career program, read a draft of this book and alerted us to plausible and implausible school happenings. They may be displeased that we retained some of the implausible—e.g., teachers engaged in extensive ongoing conversations—as an aspiration for the future, even if not generally today's reality.

We are also grateful to the teachers of the Merion Elementary School, Merion, Pennsylvania, with whom Professor Goodman met for an ongoing biweekly discussion over two years. Those talks gave us a deeper sense of life in an elementary school and a more palpable grasp of the typical incidents, large and small, that create ordinary moral tensions to be considered and resolved. A few of those incidents have been adapted for this book.

On an individual level, we thank Daniel DiCenso, a doctoral student and schoolteacher, who read the entire manuscript with insight and humor. Jeff Johnston, of the University of California at Irvine, unique in having read and commented on both the prior and present books, was continually helpful in giving us additional student reaction as well as his own. We also thank Frances Kreimer, who carefully read the text for clarity of ideas and language usage. Thanks as well to Jonathan and Frank Goodman. The former, a public school teacher, did his best to preserve realism at the classroom level; the latter pressed for clarity at the conceptual level. Finally, our appreciation to Joan Shapiro, Temple University; Steve Jay Gross,

Temple University; and Jeff Johnston at the University of California, Irvine, who reviewed the manuscript for the publisher and gave us exceptionally helpful chapter-by-chapter comments.

Joan F. Goodman
Howard Lesnick

Philadelphia, Pennsylvania
February, 2003

■ ■ ■ ■ ■

# CHAPTER 1

# THE MORAL COMPLEXITIES
# AT SCHOOL

Imagine yourself a teacher on lunch duty in an elementary school. You notice that Melissa, a fifth grader, while chatting intently with friends, drops a used Kleenex on the floor; it is not the first time she has done this. You are infuriated by the act and have an impulse to go after her, but you realize that in any group of teachers there would be many with other impulses. Some of the following options might appeal to your colleagues:

1. Do nothing and leave it to the janitorial staff to collect; she is not one of your pupils and you can't be watching over the behavior of every child in the school.
2. Pick up the Kleenex and properly dispose of it; set an example.
3. Go to her and say gently, "Melissa, perhaps you don't realize that you dropped your Kleenex again. Please pick it up before you get into the lunch line;" give the child a kindly reminder presumes she was merely inattentive.
4. Pull Melissa out of the lunch line, tell her to throw the Kleenex in the receptacle, and talk to her briefly about trash disposal and hygiene;, make no assumption about motive.
5. Pull Melissa out of line and say firmly, "Melissa, you know we have a rule against littering. Because you repeatedly ignore it, after school today I want you to take a plastic bag and pick up all the lunchroom debris;" impose a punishment premised on the belief in a character flaw.
6. Store the observation until class-meeting time and then make it the focus of a general discussion on littering; treat it as a group (civic) problem.
7. Report your observation (assuming this is not the first time) to her teacher or a student committee with responsibility for advising on minor infractions; delegate the decision-making process.

Assume that you decide to report the incident to Melissa's teacher, who chooses to follow option 6. Not wanting to embarrass Melissa by singling her

1

out, she raises the general question in class: "What do you think we should do with our trash?" Melissa's buddy, perhaps reacting to the minimal veiling of the teacher's point of view, boldly starts off, "How 'bout we collect all of it and leave it outside the third-grade classroom?" Other children jump on the bandwagon:

"Use it for a marshmallow roast after school."
"Put it under the climbing structure for a soft landing when we jump."
"Get the first graders to pick it up."

The children's trivialization of the question provokes Melissa's teacher to cut the conversation short, but she is left with her own doubts. *Her* judgment on this affair is clear: Melissa's habit of repeatedly dropping Kleenex in the corridor is offensive. Littering is not to be tolerated, especially when it carries the risk of spreading germs. It should be stopped by school personnel, if not gently then sternly. If this is not obvious to the children, they need another rule to make it clear.

She recognizes, however, the likelihood and legitimacy of different reactions. What is obvious to her and many others—that waste should be thrown into proper disposal receptacles—may not be obvious, or at least compelling, to all. Some would find this beyond the school's purview and too insignificant for yet another rule. Not every behavior, after all, can or should be monitored. Where do we draw the line? What about food spilled on the cafeteria floor or on the table? Others might think the throw-it-away solution inadequate. How about making waste disposal part of a recycling plan? How about collecting the waste around the school? How about substituting cloth handkerchiefs, which can be washed and reused, for Kleenex? How concerned are we about "doing something" to protect the environment? How concerned are we about hygiene, especially where the well-being of others is involved? What should those at school ask of Melissa, the other children, themselves?

We open with a pedestrian occurrence that may strike the reader as trivial, certainly not the stuff of moral education. You may have expected us rather to plunge into one of the "hot button" issues—violence, drugs, teenage pregnancy, condom distribution, prayers in the school, censorship—that so dominate newspaper accounts of the moral climate in schools. Why Kleenex?

First, this ordinary moment of an ordinary day, which might pass by without a teacher's notice, is not as simple as it appears. Our response— whether to ignore, scold, or punish the child or to broaden responsibility from her to the group and from Kleenex to the environment—marks our moral orientation. We need to understand those orientations and the moral messages they convey to children.

Second, the very ordinariness of the Kleenex incident illustrates how morality crops up constantly in our dealings with children. It is not restricted to those occasions when we focus on violence and drugs, or even cheating scandals. The pervasiveness of morality calls upon us to look closely at what we are doing on a daily basis, and to take advantage of all these "teachable moments."

Third, it is in the simple interchanges of everyday life that we develop our moral makeup. These responses compose our character. A person's morality is displayed less by the position he or she argues in the condom-distribution debate than by how he or she responds to an individual pregnant teenager. While we do not believe there is always one true moral response—teenage pregnancy is a legitimate topic of disagreement—morality is developed and revealed "on the street," not in policy positions.

Finally, although the Kleenex incident, like those in the scenarios that follow, may be prosaic, it triggers deep questions about what we expect of children, how we justify our expectations, and why we differ. It draws us inevitably into pedagogical and moral intricacies that cannot be dodged. We have on the one hand a set of questions related to instruction: How do we influence children to comply with rules that adults see as proper? How do we make sense of the different answers to this question? How do we determine whether or not our rules are right? Beyond compliance, how do we help children form personal convictions and a sense of personal obligation? We believe it is impossible to prescribe the right response to the Kleenex incident without getting into these issues.

All of us who spend time with children, both in and out of school, constantly monitor and direct their actions, sometimes intuitively, sometimes with forethought. When these actions have moral significance, in this case insufficient respect for other members of the community and the school environment, our reactions are products of a moral judgment; like it or not, we are in the business of moral education. And while this business is too important to relinquish to "gut" reactions, the sophistication of educators in dealing with the challenge of teaching academic subjects has not been matched by a parallel depth in addressing moral questions. Gut reactions may be their sole recourse.

There are multiple explanations for this failure. Some educators believe that morality is just not an appropriate topic for school—too controversial, too religiously infused, too private. Others, although recognizing that they are moral monitors of children's behavior, see teaching right from wrong as a simple matter. We disagree with both of these positions. We see classroom rules as grounded in moral questions, however much they may be treated as merely technical (as conveyed by the term "classroom management"). Educators Theodore and Nancy Sizer (1970) have put the points well:

> Morality is embedded in all formal education. The experience of schooling changes all children, some for the better, some unhappily. Often the changes are hardly the ones planned by the teacher or even apparent to him. Nonetheless,

teachers must carry a major burden, along with the family, in helping children to meet and deal justly with moral problems. . . .

There is no "morality-free" school, no valueless teaching. Any interpersonal experience contains a moral element, virtually by definition, and a classroom is no exception.

There was a time when "moral problems" were recognized as the core of formal schooling. These problems were cast in sectarian religious molds, and youngsters were "taught" moral conduct. . . . There was an appealing simplicity to [the] task: "right" and "wrong" were clear and undisputed and were to be learned directly. If one could recite righteous precepts, one would practice them—or so the crude pedagogy of the day implied. The nineteenth-century teacher sermonized, and his charges listened (sometimes) and learned (some things). Crude and philosophically simpleminded though the sermonizing tradition may be, it had its effect. . . .

While abstract morality is surely no more or less complex than it has always been (God knows that Dickens' slums were no better than ours), teaching toward it in any profound way is far more complicated than earlier schoolmasters may have believed. [Teachers] must approach their task vigorously and yet carefully, aware of all its intricacies and dangers. . . . The "morality" to be taught is more than a litany from McGuffey and infinitely more subtle and complex (pp. 3–4).

Reactions to children's behavior (especially their misbehavior), while often fairly automatic, are complexly determined. How we address the Melissa incident will be influenced, in varying degrees, by the following considerations:

our notions of good instruction (the effectiveness of examples, reminders, discussions, punishments)

our own value hierarchies and the depth of our personal commitments (just how wrong was dropping the Kleenex?)

our reading of Melissa's awareness and intentions

our broader reading of the child's character

our beliefs about the "calling" of an elementary school (the importance of Melissa's and the school's handling of trash to its mission).

## OBJECTIVES OF THE BOOK

One purpose of this book is to help educators recognize the many dimensions of the moral issues they confront and to become more limber in their reflections upon them. So armed, we believe, they will make considered choices among options, both about the values they teach and the pedagogy they use. To think that moral education is a simple matter is not merely a harmless failure of perception, for it opens the door to practices that are actually immoral in intention or effect. In the Melissa episode, for example, had the lunch-duty teacher raised the issue in a class meeting (recall she was not the child's teacher), one can imagine Melissa, upon hearing she was the subject of a group discussion, recoiling with humiliation, fear, and antagonism. Alternatively, if her teacher gave a lecture on ecology, Melissa might have responded with sneers, while a punishment from the teacher could have precipitated resentment and deliberate, if more secretive, littering. A certain perplexity in one's response to moral questions is itself an ingredient of moral judgment.[1]

Our ambition, however, is to go further than attending to the inherent difficulties of moral decision making, whether with respect to minor issues like Melissa's or more serious ones such as countermanding requests from parents and administrators. For we think it insufficient for a teacher to "cope" skillfully with misbehavior. A second purpose, then, is to make clear that moral education must go beyond classroom management and social skills training; it must reach deeply into the consciousness of the children, teachers, and school community. It needs to be a prism through which choices and decisions are screened; the "should I?" imposed upon the "I want."

A third objective is to convince the reader, largely through teacher conversations, that disagreements, even strong ones, are productive. Contested ideas, we believe, do not merely sensitize a class to diversity, they further the development of a moral community. Unity and agreement are not necessarily what hold people together; conflict may be more of a glue and lead to a more sustained connection (Sennett, 1998). The British philosopher Mary Midgley (1991) puts it concisely: "To get near to people is to collide with them" (p. 43). Too often we purchase tranquility at the price of conflict avoidance. Such suppression may well produce indifference rather than genuine agreement.

---

[1]We are mindful of using such words as "morality" and "moral education" without supplying definitions. We do so deliberately. These terms are elusive and, like beauty and intelligence, inevitably subject to various readings. As we discuss in our earlier book, *The Moral Stake in Education: Contested Premises and Practices* (Chapter 3), the attempt to define morality objectively, with adequate inclusiveness and exclusiveness, falls prey to the same controversies that are intrinsic to the entire subject. What to one person is a significant matter of morality, for example rules of courtesy, is to another a trivial, non-moral convention or, worse, an act of subjugation. For some, morality covers a broad realm of behavior including that which may hurt the self (health maintenance, entertainment, eating) as well as hurt others. For the broadband interpreters, morality may demand acts of benevolence, not just refraining from harm. Those more reluctant to pass moral judgments prefer a restricted definition. In Chapter 5 we elaborate on the distinctions between the moral and non-moral realms and on what is entailed in making a moral claim. Until then, we follow the thinking process of the school players as it might unfold in their school lives. They would not, we assume, stop for a definition of morality when determining what to do about Melissa.

However, to be productive, disputes must be handled skillfully. Listening openly to the other side, trying on the other's shoes, bending toward a position are as essential to argumentation as asserting one's own opinion. If schools, as they proclaim, want to encourage "critical thinking," there is no better venue than pondering moral problems.

## TWO PERSPECTIVES

There is no shortage of support for moral education. School administrators and teachers, with varying degrees of enthusiasm, are likely to tell you that they believe in it, maybe that they're "doing" it. According to polls, schools and parents alike believe that given the problems of youth today, moral education is a topic we cannot ignore. (To review the opinion polls on community support for moral education, see summaries by DeRoche and Williams, 1998; Ryan and Bohlin, 1999).

Most programs in morality, like those in sex and drug education, are designed to reverse the perceived moral laxity of our youth. The goals are to decrease rudeness, uncooperativeness, nastiness, aggression, even cruelty to fellow students and teachers, and instead to teach children to be respectful, courteous, conscientious in their work, orderly in their behavior, and decent to one another. The means for accomplishing these ambitions vary but usually include clear rules, rewards for virtuous behavior, sanctions for immoral behavior, involvement of students in establishing a moral climate (which includes dispute resolution), curricular attention to issues (and exemplars) of character, direct virtue instruction, and service learning. Such programs are generally subsumed under the rubric of "character education" (elaborated in Chapter 4).[1]

Another perspective, in partial antagonism to the above, revolves around the building of the student's individual conscience. This perspective sees the school's job as creating in children an inner taskmaster. It is less about accommodation to the school culture and more about students' construction

---

[1]The word *character,* like *morality,* is elusive. Literally it derives from a Greek word meaning to engrave. In modern usage it refers to the distinctive characteristics that mark a person inclusive of the non-moral. Someone's character could include a sense of humor, musicality, or inventiveness. In the context of moral education, however, character is restricted to moral traits. Character is closely associated with, and sometimes indistinguishable from, virtue. Ryan and Bohlin (1999), for example, describe virtue as the "disposition to think, feel, and act in morally excellent ways, and the exercise of this disposition" (p.45), but character too is defined as knowing, loving, and doing good. "Virtues" would seem to be a more restricted term. The Greeks identified four cardinal virtues: courage, temperance, wisdom, and justice. Unlike character traits these are clearly meant to be beneficial, even essential, for a thriving human community. See Foot (1978) for an extended discussion of virtues.

of an autonomous value system. It favors asking questions over asserting answers, emphasizing context rather than rules, considering values as fluid and uncertain, and affording hospitality to conflicting values. Such approaches are often billed as "developmental" or "constructivist" (also elaborated in Chapter 4).[1]

These reactions, in turn, emerge from our differing world views—those fundamental beliefs about human freedom and responsibility, about the role of authority and the nature of learning, that shape and explain the positions we take on so many questions. Educators themselves have varying perspectives on the nature of morality, the objectives of moral instruction, and how to teach. While conflicting in complex ways, which to some extent defy neat dichotomization, there is a pair of fundamentally opposing outlooks, which can usefully (if carefully) be labeled "conservative " and "liberal."

Conservatives tend to emphasize obedience to authority and habit formation because they perceive morality as composed of certain "right" responses. Although there are gray areas, for the most part they see the moral good as clear, absolute, transcendent, and universal. It consists of the traditional values handed down across generations. The primary objective of moral education to conservatives is the inculcation of character in children through insistent and directive teaching. They *tend* to be more concerned with the child's actions than with his or her reasoning, which, they suspect, easily falls prey to rationalization. Although not wanting the child simply to obey mindlessly, they believe that steady adherence and devotion to morality develops through the constant practice of performing moral duties. Given this mindset, they are predisposed to favor character education programs.

Liberals begin with a more suspicious stance toward authority, and toward the fundamental justice of the prevailing social order. Tradition is not necessarily a good source of morality. Tending to see significant *immorality* in conventional norms, and perceiving morality as proceeding largely from critical inquiry, they are less committed to habit building. They claim moral good is not clear, but rather contingent and variable, reached by taking into account the complex set of competing interests in each morally relevant situation. The liberal's primary objective is that children learn to think about their actions, especially to reflect on how they impinge on the interests of others. Generally, they are less concerned with the acts of the child than with

---

[1]The terms *developmental* and *constructivist* are even more resistant to definition than character and virtue. They refer to a set of beliefs regarding children grounded in the psychology of Jean Piaget and Lawrence Kohlberg. In a nutshell, proponents of this orientation believe that morality, as so much else, is built (constructed) by children over the course of the developmental stages as they interact with the social surround. For instance, when children press against one another for a favored position they learn, over time, the need to give and take and to establish rules. With the support and encouragement of adults, they come to construct (accept) such rules. For an extended discussion of moral constructivism, see DeVries and Zan (1994).

the care taken in deciding on them. Powerful commitments to the moral life, they believe, depend on this practice of vigorous reflection and will emerge from it. So they tend to favor the developmental/constructivist approaches.

We believe, and therefore argue thoughout this book, that a good moral education program must embrace both perspectives, despite the tension between them. By describing the uphill but persistent efforts of fictional teachers with highly divergent "world views," as they construct their moral education program, we ask the reader to think about why balancing both perspectives is essential and how it can be done.

In one sense this is a prescriptive book. It outlines a collaborative process through which a school community can get on with planning a moral education program and highlights essential ingredients that will ensure the inclusion of both major perspectives. But it is not prescriptive in the narrower sense of providing a blueprint. It is *our* perspective that blueprints for moral education, like blueprints for parenting, are inadvisable. Teachers, parents, and communities will vary their approach depending upon the values they hold most dear and the instructional methods they find most comfortable.

What we do believe is that moral education is essential in these times and all times. One does not become moral without being taught. To ignore the centrality of moral education, or to carry it out haphazardly, is to fail in our custodial task; we do so at the peril of our society and the lives of our children. As will become apparent in the following chapters, we believe that fundamental to good moral education are vigilant attention to the moral dimensions of schooling, a self-conscious involvement of the entire school community, and clear rules and expectations for children *along with* careful ongoing questioning of those rules and expectations.

## OVERVIEW OF THE BOOK

Each chapter begins with teacher conversation around a school or class issue. We employ this method because we believe that moral instruction must grow out of lived concerns rather than abstract formulations handed down. While there seem to be general moral principles (not always explicit) that govern school affairs, children are unlikely to "hear" them except when their interests confront those of others. Such confrontations happen throughout the day, for they include seemingly banal issues—Who gets to lead the line? Why must one raise a hand to speak? What's wrong with telling secrets?—as well as the familiar problems of lying, cheating, stealing, and fighting. When moral questions arise, the teacher is the likely point person to identify them and intervene.

In every chapter teacher reflections are followed by a more analytical section titled "A Deeper Look." Finally, we ask you, the reader, having absorbed the issues and points of view, to do your own analysis in the final section, "Your Turn." In three instances we shift to a more directed pedagogy: the two reports from Jan Bonham, an adviser to the teachers (pp. 41–43, 127–131), and the faculty report outlining a moral education program (Chapter 9). They are the "how to" pieces of the book, and might be particularly useful for inservice training.

After reintroducing a cast of characters from *The Moral Stake* and the controversial topic of moral education (Chapter 2), we proceed as a school might. The principal, having been asked to come up with a moral education program, assigns the task of developing a set of proposals to a faculty committee. The committee members quickly agree that the class meeting, a practice used by many elementary school teachers, might serve as a central component of moral education. It turns out that holding a class meeting involves more than just asking kids to address a problem together. The teachers find that they disagree on how much to lead the children to a desired outcome and how much to front the children's own reactions by allowing them latitude in making moral choices. The friction is partially resolved when a consultant offers a taxonomy of ways in which teacher authority can be calibrated to the nature of the moral issue (Chapter 3).

The teachers, caught up in the complexities involved in the familiar class meeting, recognize the need to go further. They participate in an inservice session on the topic and are exposed to existing programs that are generally subsumed under the rubric of character education. Once again they are at odds with one another in their responses (Chapter 4). It becomes apparent that their judgments of the programs, and of children, depend heavily on whether they choose to emphasize the character (virtues) of the person, her actions, her motivations, or her thinking. This moral elephant has many angles, and they are drawn to different ones.

The faculty committee meetings continue. An incident in one classroom raises the question of service learning. Is it good to devote some school time to community work? Should it be required? Against parental opposition? The group realizes that it cannot just stack components (class meetings, service learning) like blocks and call it a program of moral education, because the shape and content of the "blocks" depend on, and are responsive to, deep-seated attitudes toward the "reach" of the school as it expands into realms where families also are stakeholders (Chapter 5). The guidance counselor raises questions about the boundaries between home and school, when parents should defer to schools, and when the reverse.

Not surprisingly, the class meeting strategy does not eliminate classroom disruptions. One teacher believes that a troublesome child should be handled as a troubled child—sympathetically, caringly, reflectively. Her colleague is inclined to close down the misbehavior without getting into the "talking cure" business (Chapter 6). This leads into a discussion of the meaning and rightful role of discipline and the teachers' moral priorities.

As the teachers move further away from compiling morally educative activities and look more deeply into value systems, their own and others', they trip upon the hardest question of all; "whose values?" Many find this question so intractable as to negate moral education altogether. One cannot "do" this work without addressing two thorny issues: First, how can we respect the diversity of values across different segments of our school population and still give a moral message? Second, even within an agreed set of values (such as equality and freedom), how do we make selections when they clash? As our teachers take on these questions (Chapter 7), it is apparent that threading one's way between a position of full tolerance on the one hand and a strict code for all on the other may be their most difficult, and an ongoing, task.

In Chapter 8, we switch from the moral concerns that teachers confront with students to those they face with administrators and school board members. We do this not only because the ethical teacher will have to make difficult decisions when pressured from these sources but also because the decisions they make, and the process they go through in reaching their decisions, will powerfully affect the students' moral learning environment.

With the academic year drawing to a close, the committee finds itself deeply committed to the centrality of moral education in the school curriculum. The teachers are convinced that the worth of a moral education program consists in keeping alive the intrinsic complexities and conflicts of the field. However much they would like to offer a six- or ten-step program, such a document would nullify the insights they have accumulated. The goal of their plan (Chapter 9) is to convince children (as well as faculty, administrators, and parents) that becoming a moral person is a lifelong and deeply worthy process. To accomplish that goal, they have come to believe, a packaged program of "character education" marketed first to teachers and then to children may be minimally helpful, but one should not rely on it. Rather, what is needed is an ongoing program of collective moral inquiry *by* teachers, facilitating a decentralized, pervasive focus on the moral sides of students (and schools) to foster the development of the moral identity of both students and teachers.

# CHAPTER 2

# IS MORAL EDUCATION A SCHOOL'S RESPONSIBILITY?

## *Scenario*

The Friday before Labor Day found Maria Laszlo at school, as she had been most of the week preparing her fifth-grade classroom for the following Tuesday, her first day as a fully credentialed teacher. Preoccupied now with arranging books on the shelves and creating attractive, useful material for the walls, she had, at least temporarily, lost the feelings of dread and agitation that were her steady companions during the summer months. Yet she could not throw off an acute uncertainty about herself: Will the children like and respond to her? Will they be turned on to learning? Will she be able to mold them into a cooperative, mutually supportive group of friends and learners?

While lost in these thoughts, she was startled by the loud ring of her telephone and still more startled to hear the voice of the principal, Fred Helter.

"Hello, Maria, and welcome," he began genially. "When I passed by your room and saw you hard at work I didn't want to interrupt, but how about a few minutes later this morning for a brief chat? There's something looming on the horizon that I need to talk with you about."

Maria would have liked Helter to name the "something," so as to avoid her tendency to catastrophize: Was he about to—*could* he—cut her salary? It did seem on the generous side, given what she had heard about the school's pay scale. Was he going to change her teaching assignment on the eve of opening day? Would there be new, not-yet-disclosed nonteaching duties?

"No time like the present," she answered him, and without any further musing walked the long hallway to the front office.

After preliminary pleasantries he got to his point.

"Maria, I wanted you to know about a new initiative announced at our last principals' meeting by the superintendent, Ralph Senter. Given your freshly minted status, I thought you might have some ideas about it. As a student, you may have gotten wind of the growing movement across the country for schools to do something in the field of character education. The pressure comes largely from parent groups, the media, and grandstanding politicians, but it is also being felt by folks in the state ed departments, who are passing it on to the school districts. As I hear it, while parents know their kids aren't likely to shoot up a class—that's more a dark but distant fear—they just don't have any confidence that they can control the kids, even at the elementary school level. They've lost influence, they don't feel in charge any more, and they want us—it's *always* us!—to fix the problem, to make sure their kids will become decent human beings."

"So what's the plan?" a much relieved Maria asked.

"That's just it, Maria. I don't have a ready-made program, I don't even know if I support the super's idea that we get involved in character education, and I certainly have no knowledge of the 'field,' if there is such a thing. While the matter may come down to us as a mandate, right now Senter is asking the principals for their reactions. It's a serious issue, and I want us all to give it careful deliberation."

What a good guy, Maria thought to herself; he really meant what he said at my job interview about being inclusive. Emboldened by his openness she pushed past her caution and spoke frankly. "I don't know, Mr. Helter, er, Fred, (he had invited all the teachers to call him by his first name, but this was the first time she was actually doing it) whether I'll have much to contribute, although I did take a course on moral education at the university from Jan Bonham, and she is enthusiastic about helping schools develop programs of that sort."

"Do I take it that you're not?"

"Well, it's not that I don't believe children should learn right and wrong; obviously, they should. My own parents, very religious people, pushed moral lessons all the time. But I wonder if it's the teacher's job."

"Why not, Maria?" Fred Helter asked.

Reading genuine curiosity behind Helter's question, she went on. "As I see my job, it's to teach academics, especially reading and math. I know way back schools thought moral education should happen in the classroom; maybe it was that way when you went to school. But that's not how it has been recently, and with all we've got to do nowadays, it's a task I can't imagine pursuing. Morality is best handled in the home or church. I just don't see it as central to our educational mission. Do you?"

Letting pass Maria's evident bracketing of him in antiquity with Abe Lincoln and the McGuffey readers, the principal pursued his own uncertainties. "You know, Maria, until recently your words could have been mine, but having sat in this office for a few years, I'm beginning to wonder if your agenda, critically important though it is, may not be too narrow. The students who walk in here are bright enough, but they aren't learning what we dole out. They don't see the point of it. I suppose that was true of many of us too in the good old days. But unlike back then, I now see a lot of students with "attitudes," sometimes explicit, more often implicit. We buckled down at school because it was expected, because we respected those expectations, because we wanted to please teachers and parents. Today a lot of kids are indifferent, even hostile, to such expectations; they are rude to teachers, sometimes even confrontational with us. Maybe what you see as your job can't be done without some of the moral training Senter appears to be advocating."

"I know, Fred. What you're pointing to is a real problem. I saw that indifferent and even insolent behavior in my student teaching, but I mostly thought it was the teachers who had an 'attitude' problem. The way I look at it, I'm going to try my hardest to get the kids to care about our work and one another. I'm going to use books that I think are exciting and absorbing. I'm going to have a few classroom rules, the same ones everyone else has. I'm going to be kind and caring toward the children; provide a good model; and expect them, with occasional reminders from me, to be kind to, and caring of, one another. All that's obvious, right? It doesn't require a new 'program.'"

"I appreciate knowing where you stand, Maria. I think you'll find many on the faculty who more or less agree with you, while others don't. I'm thinking in particular of your fifth-grade colleague, Hardie Knox, whom you probably know because he's an alum of your school. I suspect he'll greet this initiative with a sense of relief; finally 'downtown' is paying attention to his concerns.

"As a faculty we'll be devoting more time to this topic over the year. Senter will want a written response from us and will probably ask each of us principals to speak about the issue at a district meeting. I'd like to ask your mentor, Jan Bonham, to help us come to grips with the issues, but before I do that I'd like a small group of teachers to brainstorm together about the question. I am asking Aggie Cerine, a veteran teacher—as wise as she is experienced—to act as informal convener of the group, and I'd be very grateful if you would join it."

"But, Fred," Maria responded with some energy, "I am as wet behind the ears as they come. I haven't even taught one day!"

"That will be a plus, Maria," Helter urged gently, "so long as we have a diverse group, which is what I have in mind. Hardie has a bit more experience, but not a lot, and if my guess is right he'll approach the subject a little differently than you do. I am rounding the group out with another "old hand," Connie Comfort, our guidance counselor, who has a perspective more oriented to the outside world, especially parents, than most of the staff. The four of you would be as powerful a package as I can think of, and I hope you will see your way clear to taking this on."

"What can I say?" Maria concluded. "Thanks for the expression of confidence. Even if I don't fully share it, I'll be happy to talk with Aggie."

"Great," said Helter, rising. "I've asked her to wait a couple of weeks before getting the four of you together. We all need to focus on our new classes at the outset of a semester."

"Amen to that!" Maria exclaimed, taking her principal's outstretched hand.

It was the third week of the semester before Agatha Cerine's invitation came. "Maria," Aggie began, "You know that Fred Helter has asked us to join Hardie Knox and Connie Comfort to think up some brilliant ideas about moral education. But, before we get into that, I've noticed lately that you sometimes walk the halls looking pretty droopy. By any chance is something going wrong that an old warhorse like me might understand?"

"Something! Lots of things are wrong, everything is wrong," Maria burst out, surprised by Aggie's keenness and pleased by her informality. "I'm turning into one of those 'don't smile-until-Christmas' monsters. I'm yelling at the kids. I'm totally confused about how to handle them. I can't figure out why they aren't responding. All my planning was useless. Do you know that, from the photos in the folders that Helter gave us, I had memorized the name of each child before school started? On the first day I greeted them at the door by name. I was so proud, but they couldn't have cared less. Many kids didn't even look me in the face, never mind shake my hand or answer my greeting."

"Is that it, no one clued you in on the little monsters we teach around here?" Aggie said a bit mockingly.

"It wasn't so much their rudeness, though I guess that startled me, as the flood of self-doubt it seems to have released. All my fantasies of 'I'll be nice, then they'll be nice' crashed as they entered the room. The ones who had been together last year separated themselves into a few small, *noisy* groups. They didn't even acknowledge the newcomers to the class. When I asked everyone to sit down so we could get started, a bunch of them immediately complained about the chair arrangements—three children around each small table. Four girls insisted they could not be separated. I suggested (on that first day I was still suggesting) that they accept this arrangement until we had an opportunity to discuss the matter as a group. Well, was that ever a mistake! Wait? Not these kids. They wanted to discuss it right then. So I backed down and started a class meeting on the spot. (In our Methods class, we were told that a class meeting is a good way to discuss problems). I presented my views to the children: Today they should take any available seat; in a few days we'd organize work groups that would change from time to time, and we'd plan future seating around the work groups. 'No, no, no,' the four insisted. They'd have none of it. Last year they were allowed to sit together, and they wanted the same treatment this year. Forget all the other stuff: what was fair to the class as a whole, the importance of getting to know the new children, thinking about who was being hurt by being left out."

"How did you handle all of that?" Aggie asked.

"Next day, you better believe it was assigned seats for everyone! The kids grumbled. I was stern and unyielding. But it didn't accomplish much. Now everyone reluctantly sits where he or she is assigned; however, they make constant eye contact, mouth words, whisper, and sometimes just plain talk. At first it was just the 'gang of four,' but after a few days other kids, especially the ones who had been together last year, began picking it up too. So, defying everything I believe, I've started a disciplinary system: one point each time they stare, whisper, or talk to each other out of turn. Three points and they miss recess. Five points, they go to the assistant principal. Would you believe that's already happened. I've already sent her a child! Now, even when they're quiet, I feel their resentment. So much for my wanting to be liked!

"These confrontations have really confused me. I'm not sure how much decision-making authority I should give the children and how much I should preserve. Maybe they *should* decide on where they sit. Perhaps eventually they'll develop some empathy for those who are ostracized, or maybe the rejected kids will find a way to survive. How flexible should I be, and how do I even think about that question? Once a decision is made, either by me or by the class, and some balk, what should be the consequences and who should determine them?"

"Great questions, Maria," said Aggie. "There aren't many new teachers who haven't confronted similar problems, although not all address them so thoughtfully. We could roll up our sleeves and dig right in, but something tells me you have more than seating arrangements on your mind."

"Yes, I wasn't sure if I should go further. Do you have the time?"

"Of course. Believe it or not, once upon a time I was a beginning teacher, and believe *this* or not, I still don't have all the answers. And it sounds to me as if what you have been experiencing will be grist for our committee's mill."

"If it were just the seating arrangements and my yelling at the children," Maria continued, "I wouldn't be so dismal. At least when assigning seats and insisting on quiet before starting a lesson, I had a sense of my own righteousness. But I've got another problem that has cost me even that.

"It has to do with a kid named Tony. He and his family dress and behave unconventionally—the kids say 'weird.' They live in an old house on a big lot near the edge of town, raise a lot of their own food, don't use a car at all. He always wears a cap, dungarees, and heavy shoes, and he has pretty wild hair—definitely not cool. When I told him it would be better to leave his cap at home because you can't wear hats in school, he just looked perplexed, or maybe hurt, who can tell? But he didn't change his behavior.

"I thought of calling his parents, but his teacher from last year told me not to do it. 'I know that family all too well,' she said. 'They'll just defend him. They don't believe schools have any business telling them how their child should dress. They don't care if Tony looks different from the others. They are loners, and so is he.'"

"You were right about what you said to Tony, Maria," said Aggie. "I'm sure Helter would tell you that. We once had a kid who wore a hat for religious reasons, and he said to allow it. But I'm pretty sure he'd draw the line there. Tony needs to know there's a rule against hats and fall in line."

"But it's not as if he is being rebellious or defiant. It's not an in-your-face gesture. You say the school has already agreed to give a kid a pass if he wears a hat for religious reasons. Suppose Tony were African American? We read a lot in our classes about how symbolic actions like keeping a hat on might be a cultural thing, and refusing to take it off might be what the authors called a 'counter-hegemonic' act, expressing opposition to assimilation. And—

"*Is* Tony black?" Aggie broke in. "I know several African American teachers who are quite firmly *against* the kind of response you are talking about. They . . ."

Now it was Maria who interrupted. "Yes, I know, and anyway Tony is white. But is his resistance to me any less an aspect of his identity, just as entitled to be respected by a school, as it would be if triggered by his being part of a group? The presence of the cap is not bothering anyone else."

Maria went on, breathlessly. "And what about Tony and his clothes not being tip-top clean? As long as he is disease-free (the nurse checked him along with all the others when school began, and she told me he is fine), who gets hurt but himself? Can we even say that he's hurting himself? Einstein had pretty wild hair; most people thought it added to his distinctiveness. Those dungarees (like the hat) seem to be part of who he is, part of his and the family's identity.

"As for the other kids calling him weird, I'm uncertain about how to handle that as well. Isn't the problem that the other children are being intolerant? Shouldn't I be after *them?* Still, I see why they are annoyed by him. Even when invited to join in, he's aloof, preferring to go off and read. That would have bothered me too as a youngster, and I wonder if it's right for me to expect much tolerance and sympathy for deviancy from ten-year-olds. At this age they're intensely focused on friendships, 'best friends,' and the major criterion for a friend is one who looks, says, and does just how or what you look, say, and do."

"Maria, when we started this conversation I had no idea you'd be into such deep stuff," said Aggie looking at her watch. "Believe me, I hate to cut this off. It's a pleasure to have a colleague who cares about her work the way you do. Fred certainly showed a great instinct when he fingered you for our moral education planning group. Let me set up our first meeting for next week sometime. That will also give me the chance to think hard about what you've shared. Meanwhile don't be timid about talking with other colleagues. We've all been there."

Maria walked away wondering whether she had said too much, and why Aggie had started out giving a pat answer about "rules" but had then left everything unresolved. Was it really a matter of limited time or, her encouraging words notwithstanding, was she reluctant to take Maria's concerns seriously?

As luck would have it, Hardie Knox was just emerging from his classroom as Maria rounded the corner of the hallway. He greeted her cordially and asked how the first weeks were going.

His friendly demeanor and the link of their common alma mater emboldened Maria to forgo a routine response.

"If you really want to know and have time to spare, I'd like to give you a straight answer and get your reactions."

Hardie readily agreed, and they began to walk along the now-quiet hallway. Rattled as she was after her talk with Aggie, Maria gave Hardie a detailed account of how her teaching was going.

"Maria, you are a new teacher trying to befriend all the children," he began (a bit condescendingly, she thought). "But that's not a teacher's job, at least not centrally. You are here to give them skills, cultivate their minds, influence their intellectual development, not primarily to *support* them. They have to see you as a person of status, a person to be listened to, a person who *knows* what is in their best interest, who is demanding and not one of them. When you let students decide who sits with whom, when you let one of them break a rule because it may not fit his idiosyncrasies, you lose your authority as a teacher as well as your moral authority. You appear wimpy and cannot be an effective instructor."

Maria winced at the word *moral* and was more than a little put off by Hardie's overly assured, lecturing tone. But she didn't let that keep her from engaging with him. "How do I lose moral authority, Hardie, when I listen to their views and try to individualize treatment? And how do I gain moral authority by enforcing rules that don't make sense?"

"Part of being a decent person, Maria, is bowing to group rules whether you like them or not. Societies, including classrooms, require rules that apply to everyone uniformly, and citizens who obey those rules. And it's good for children to submit to rules; submission is more important than what the rules are about, unless of course they are clearly unfair. So I don't much care if we have a rule to keep hats on or to keep hats off; I do care that kids obey the rules, willingly obey them out of respect for the importance of rules and for the school community of which they are a part.

"What they have to learn, first and foremost, is to do what the teacher tells them to do and not pick an argument over every little thing. What difference does it make why you want them to take off their caps, sit in groups of three instead of four, or dress the way everyone else does? The point is, once you tell them what you want, you should stand behind it. Otherwise, you're teaching them that they can whine or cajole their way out of anything that their little minds tell them is not fun or fair. That is a prescription for turning them into willful, self-indulgent brats—first little brats and then grown-up brats."

"Hardie, I can see why Fred Helter was eager for me to speak with you. He obviously thought you'd set me straight, harden me (no pun intended). I hear what you're saying. I've heard it, perhaps said less eloquently and passionately, before. I hear it but I can't quite buy it. And I confess that the word *wimpy* stings, probably because right now I do feel a bit wimpy.

"Yet wimp or not, I resist your approach. I don't want kids to follow rules willy-nilly. I want them to think about the content of rules, to question them, to figure out what rules we need, when there should be exceptions, what we should do when rules don't fit or are broken. Otherwise we are turning out obedient but mindless robots."

"Maria, I retract 'wimpy.' I'm not saying that no crazy idea of a teacher can ever be questioned by a kid, and I recognize that it's important to come across as a person who is fair. But what you are asking of the class is perfectly usual and reasonable. If children—and remember you are dealing with fifth graders; they're not yet budding philosophers—if children get their way over something like not wanting to take off their cap, how are they going to learn to deny themselves things that really matter to them later on, like getting an A by cribbing a friend's paper even though they didn't do any work, or cutting school when a 'real important' ball game is coming up?"

"I do get your point, Hardie," Maria acknowledged as they circled the halls for the third time. "Kids need the structure and boundaries, two important words in the ed business, that they get from rules. But they also need opportunities for choice and input, don't they? From choice comes responsible decision making. We give even two-year-olds opportunities for choice. We obviously disagree about a lot of basic stuff. Still everything you have said is important food for thought, and I appreciate your being so blunt with me."

"Maria," he replied, "You're the one who deserves praise and thanks— for coming to me in the first place with so many challenging questions, and for being willing to 'take me on.' I know I often sound pretty sure of myself. But I never fail to learn from a disagreement with a thoughtful colleague, and it looks as I have just found myself one. Working with you in Aggie's group is going to be a great experience for me."

## A DEEPER LOOK

Maria Laszlo's discussions with her principal and two teaching colleagues raise several fundamental questions about the role of schools in moral education. Maria came to her work disposed to believe that "moral education" was not an appropriate subject of a school's curriculum. Morality should be taught, she believes, at home and in religious communities. Of course, the teacher-student relationship has an implicit moral grounding and great moral significance, but it requires neither lengthy inspection nor searching introspection. Teachers need to be well-motivated, caring people who want the best for their students. If that is true, it is sufficient; if not true, a greater focus on morality won't help.

After just a few weeks of school, however, Maria's convictions are somewhat shaken. She now realizes that it is not enough simply to be a person of goodwill. Matters that she previously saw as concerned only with classroom management—how children greet a teacher, how decisions are made about where they sit, what to do with a child who objects to a school's rules—now trip her up; they appear to be saturated with moral values that are not easily resolved.

Hardie Knox, an experienced teacher, disagrees with Maria. He believes that school *is* saturated with moral questions, and that teachers *are* obligated to help students live up to moral standards. But recognizing the importance of moral goals hardly warrants a "fall into perplexity."[1] Schools require strong leadership and a decorum suitable to the task. Just as we would not expect a new intern to express her wishes regarding surgical procedures, so too we should not tolerate students making or strongly influencing decisions about seats and hats. Knowledgeable and experienced about his or her work, the teacher, like the surgeon, knows how to pass on a body of knowledge and create a moral atmosphere. To become moral beings, children need most of all to learn to place their own desires second to the rules of society, and they learn that by *doing* it, not by discussion.

The tension between the teachers has three strands: Is school a setting saturated with morality? Should moral issues be foregrounded by teachers or remain part of the implicit (hidden) curriculum? If foregrounded, what is the best way to address them?

## Schools as Morally Saturated Institutions

Notwithstanding our brief consideration of this question in Chapter 1, the reader may resist thinking of schools as thoroughly morally infected environ-

---

[1]In *The Meno* (1961, p. *84c), Plato has Socrates note that it was only through being "thrown into perplexity" that the slave-boy became able to understand the solution to the problem of doubling the size of a square.

ments rather than simply places for learning. But note what's involved in the ordinary event of assigning seats. The children in Maria's class want to make their own decisions and believe they are entitled to do so; the teacher must decide whether to grant or override their autonomy. Since autonomy and freedom are generally perceived to be moral goods, on what basis does the teacher exert her authority? One might reply, obviously in the name of order. Order is a dominant value at school because, presumably, learning requires it. But does the need for order override all other values? Is it so absolute that it always preempts choice and autonomy?

Rules, generally inhibitions of self-expression, are certainly an area for moral scrutiny. Because they touch upon concerns of fairness, justice, and equity, they often require thoughtful justification. Even those rules that are best described as procedural (homework should be dropped off in this bin, we walk along the left side of the hall when in a group) become moral issues at the level of enforcement. What is a morally justified response to a child who moves out of line or places her homework in the wrong bin? One can consider these infractions along the same lines as Melissa's disposal of Kleenex.

The moral saturation of schools is not limited to the exercise of teacher authority. For Jackson, Boostrom, and Hansen (1993), it includes all condoned and condemned behavior, what we teach, how we teach, the ceremonies and rituals of school, the visual displays (and lack of them) in a classroom, even the facial expressions of a teacher. This book is more restrictive in identifying the moral, for to turn every situation into a matter of morality is, perversely, to deprecate morality. (A moral distinction needs to be made between bringing backpacks into a classroom—bad because of the clutter they cause and perhaps the danger of tripping over them, but not morally wrongful—and stealing a backpack.) Nonetheless, it is as clear to us as it is to Maria and Hardie that making moral judgments is a major school activity.

## Exposing the School's Morality

Even granting the moral saturation of schools, does it follow that teachers should put their judgments under a microscope? Perhaps leaving values to the implicit (hidden) curriculum is reasonable, more reasonable than leaving undisturbed assumptions such as "The task of the elementary grades is to teach the 3 Rs" or "Schools should be governed by locally elected boards."

The benign neglect theory might be justifiably applied to the morality of classrooms in an era of uncontested values. Turn the clock back to the mid-nineteenth century and enter a world in which there is no question about the content and centrality of giving children a moral education. To raise a moral child was then the primary mission of schooling, surpassing all other educational priorities. Schoolbook heroes were admired for their morality and patriotism, not their intellectual standing; George Washington was lauded in

American mythology more for his honesty than for his political or military judgment. Moral lessons permeated texts, spellers, and arithmetic books, as well as readers.

Schools operated under a national moral consensus. Textbook authors "painted good and evil in stark, absolute terms and left no gray areas in their moral education—no room for interpretation, no flexibility to apply values as shifting contingencies might dictate. Only absolute rules rigidly adhered to, they believed, could provide a reliable guide to behavior and protect against the enormous temptations of the day" (McClellan, 1992, p. 26; see also Kaestle, 1983). Binding rules governed every aspect of life: decorum (appropriate dress manners, and etiquette), personal habits (frugality, cleanliness, and punctuality), work habits (thrift, persistence, honesty, diligence, perseverance), recreation (health, fair play), and citizenship. The last was particularly stressed until it became what, to a modern sensibility, appears chauvinistic: A good person was a good American, aware of the special privileges of living in this singularly blessed and singularly virtuous land.

The above sounds very quaint and dated. It surely is not applicable to the educational word of today, in which there is controversy over the fittingness of all our inherited traditions—the content of curriculum, the forms of instruction, the governance of schools—as well as moral judgments and moral instruction.

The morality of classrooms is an inherently controversial subject, which our nation's diversity has not created but brought to light. Not to recognize and deliberate over the controversies is as wrong as not exposing children to a diversity of political or historical judgments. It is deceptive.

Morality needs to be reclaimed as a vital topic of conversation. Its centrality to our individual and collective lives must be acknowledged through diligent study. Limiting it to classroom management techniques, disciplinary codes, or occasional outreach activities is insufficiently attentive. In the end our objective must be to build, in fellowship with families and other institutions, the consciences of children—what we often refer to as a moral identity.

Try an experiment. Ask a group of children what they would like to be when they grow up. How many of them tell you, "a good person"? Not good at x, y, or z, but good, in and of itself. The moral desires of children—so palpable in the early years when good and bad fills the minds of parents, the stories they read, and their play—get buried in the distractions of our society unless they are cultivated by the adults on whom they depend for guidance. Hidden messages are insufficient to the task.

## Addressing Morality at School

Once morality is "outed," how does a teacher address it? We have noted significant pedagogical differences between Maria and Hardie over whether children do or do not learn to act morally if their teachers insist that they cultivate habits of obedience to rules. For Maria, learning to do as one is told has far less to do with being a good person than learning how to identify and decide moral questions. This exploration is a large part of what being moral *is*. The habit that Maria wants to encourage is that of conscious reflection on choice, including the decision to follow or question the preferences of those who speak in the name of society. To do that, of course, requires a more interactive, less impositional teacher stance than Hardy advocates.

The incident of Tony and his hat provides a telling example of the teachers' differences. To Fred (the principal) and Hardie, the "bare your head" rule is designed to establish a modicum of uniform appearance and, more important, to symbolize respect for the educational enterprise. Both men would have yielded to Tony if a religious conviction had been at stake, for wearing a hat out of respect for (submission to) God takes precedence over doffing it out of respect for (submission to) the school, and in contemporary society there is widespread acceptance of the idea that people manifest their submission to God in differing ways.

To Maria, the principle involved is a broader one, hinging on respect for difference, even if a particular manifestation concerns only lifestyle or family norms. Moreover, she is less willing than her colleagues to accept with full seriousness the importance of the "hat" act as an expression of respect for school, teachers, and the enterprise as a whole. Children can be taught to express respect for their school in more meaningful ways.

Hardie recognizes that wearing or removing a hat has no intrinsic moral valence, but it is *derivatively* moral, for in our society wearing a hat in class is *taken* as a signal of lack of seriousness or respect. Part of learning to act morally is learning to accept the guidance of societal norms and not be overly insistent on preferring individual norms that differ. Tony needs to learn to set aside his own desires and views about the meaning of wearing or removing a hat; to defer to the judgments, of teachers, peers, and "society." He should learn this cognitively, as a norm ("Remove your hat in class," or "Do as your teacher says") and also as a habit not requiring conscious thought.

The choices one comes to make, Hardie believes, are contingent upon habits built in the early years. An adolescent is more apt to put principles of equity into practice if she has previously developed the habit of repressing greedy impulses. Having practiced restraint, she is also more likely to value it, for we are biased in favor of the behaviors we possess. A neat person believes that a person's mind is only as ordered as her desk, while a sloppy person rejects the analogy, finding no merit in order. As the British educational philosopher R. S. Peters (1974) noted: "Habituation may . . . help to lay down a pattern of response that may be used in the service of more appropriate motives at a later stage," when the screws are put on and the child is called to resist "social threats and pressures such as ridicule, disapproval, ostracism" (p. 328). It is then that Hardie's training in obedience will come in handy; habits become duties, and they too foster voluntary obligations.

Many educators advocate habit training as a virtually exclusive induction into morality, especially in a child's early years. Because young children tend to identify rightness with authority, they accept, perhaps even seek, Hardie-type rules without needing (or understanding) their rational justification. Joel Kupperman (1991), a thoughtful character education philosopher, advocated dogmatic instruction as the dominant form of moral education in the primary grades:

> The central norms should be presented as assuredly correct; this does not mean, of course, that teachers need be heavy-handed, should refuse to take questions seriously, or refuse to regard what is taught as subject to reflective thought. [But] it is absurd to suppose that very young children generally are in a position to understand, and to weigh reflectively, justifications for considering, say, murder and theft to be wrong. . . .
>
> . . . To suppose that there can be effective moral reflection without a first stage in which categories are learned and habits and attitudes are formed is . . . naive. . . . (pp. 175, 176).

## Finding the Balance

Which side is right? Each seems to include some basic truths and ignore others. While there is certainly merit in Kupperman's analysis, we take issue with his advocacy of dogmatic instruction as the *exclusive* form of early moral training. Too many rules, too much authority, quash spontaneous empathy, just as too few rules and too little authority cheat the child of moral direction. Maria appreciates the superiority of self-selected to imposed values, but she exaggerates children's reasoning skills and their capacity for objectivity.

Hardie is apt to overrate habit training because he is convinced that submission to rules, any rules, is a step toward self-discipline. But we know intuitively, and research supports the intuition, that excessive authority is less likely to promote self-direction than defiance or a calculated obedience responsive only to the actual presence of a credible threat of sanction (see Kohn, 1993, 1998 for summaries). Hardie also underestimates the propulsion that fellow-feeling gives to moral behavior. He believes that one "crafts" caring children by requiring the performance of good deeds; he is excessively skeptical of natural empathy mutating into social responsibility.

Those of Hardie's persuasion should acknowledge that the value of inculcating the habit of respect by enforcing the hat rule is undermined when enforced solely as a matter of the teacher's authority. For then all that Tony learns is that he had better not cross his teacher. Those sympathetic to Maria in turn need to acknowledge that the capacity for moral reflection is a factor of the child's maturation, and that it is good for children to learn to inhibit impulses, postpone gratification, follow an etiquette, and show respect to others, including those in authority. Only through such training will they cultivate strong habits of self-discipline that later on can be put to moral purposes. The courage and steadfastness often demanded of morality are not options for those without self-control.

We agree with Hardie that courage and honesty are virtues to be taught, but they must be conceptualized and situated if they are not to become mere slogans. It takes courage, after all, to rob a bank, and the kindness that leads one to withhold an honest comment is sometimes morally preferable to blunt outspokenness. We agree with Maria that deliberation over options is morally preferable to mindless obedience, but such a preference should not lead us to discard longstanding traditions. We recognize the value, depending on a child's age and circumstances, of cultivating a certain amount of rule-ordered behavior. At the same time we recognize incipient dangers in enforcing submission to a do-it-because-I-say-so ethic.

In subsequent chapters we elaborate further on these controversies, trying whenever possible to find a way across the disagreements so that schools can "take a stand" without undue concern that the stand they take is offensive to large segments of the public. At the same time, it needs to be recognized that ambiguity and disagreement are at the heart of morality. We do not all hold the same values; even when we share a value system we have different priorities; even when we agree on the priorities we have different approaches to instruction. As we will see, values that seem simple—respect, fairness, obedience—when closely inspected are not. But this is not a fact of life to bemoan. When issues are unresolved, when multiple alternatives exist, when context is a significant determinant of decision making, we stay more sensitive and attentive than when answers are predetermined. Consider the contrast between playing a game in which the strategy is settled and the logical sequence of moves fixed (tic-tac-toe) versus one in which strategy is still contested and evolving (chess). The friction seeds our alertness. Moral unsettledness keeps us self-consciously engaged, able to appreciate its subtleties, wanting to be permanent apprentices and aspirants.

For the moment, two thoughts—divergent though they are—need to be borne in mind. First, it seems apparent that however one might try to integrate both poles, agreement is not easily achieved and perhaps should not be expected. Second, we should not lose sight of their considerable common ground. Most fundamentally, for both sides the moral dimension of life is critical, and its diminished presence in contemporary society is profoundly disturbing. For both viewpoints, morality provides a framework for human aspirations, without which life dissolves into the pursuit of pleasures that inevitably fail to satisfy while seriously marring the fabric of social life.

## Your Turn:
## What Are Your Leanings?

1. When a child has personal habits (dress, speech, social patterns) that deviate from the norm but are harmless, is your reaction to ignore the situation? Alternatively, are you inclined to "help" the child either by urging him to adopt the more conventional style or by trying to develop more tolerance in the other children? What do you think is the basis for your leanings?

2. Consider Maria's problem of assigning seats: Which of the following appeals to you and, more important, why?
   a) Assign the children seats alphabetically.
   b) Assign seats according to your perception of classroom dynamics (who would do best next to whom).
   c) Jointly decide with the children who sits where, but first explain to them the criteria for choice.
   d) Allow self-selection but reserve the right to interfere if behavior becomes too disruptive.
   e) Don't interfere at all with self-selection and turn the problem of disruptiveness over to the children.
   f) Other?

3. Your school has a number of rules regarding decorum that cover dress, language, bathroom privileges, and touching. You notice their range and detailed specification. What would you do?
   a) Follow them closely because they are the rules and unless clearly injurious should be obeyed.
   b) Follow them partially, playing them down, preferring wherever possible to discuss them with students.
   c) Speak to others of your objections to the rules and attempt to gather support for altering them.
   d) Tell the principal that as a matter of personal integrity you cannot enforce particular rules.
   e) Other?
   f) Regardless of what you *would* do, what *should* you do?

**4.** Select a few typical classroom rules—where to put homework, when not to talk, no pushing, no shoving, no fighting with other children, etc. Consider alternative ways of responding to a child who has broken one of the rules. Would your sanctions differ depending upon the rule, and if so, how? In reaching your decision, ask yourself (and others) why you are lenient about (or disregard) one infraction and not another.

# CHAPTER 3

# A CLASS MEETING

## *Scenario*

"Welcome, friends," Aggie began, smiling at Connie, Hardie, and Maria as they shuffled into the small, crowded, stuffy, and by this time of day littered teachers' lounge. "I guess the time has come to roll up our sleeves. Old Fred has given us a tough task and wants to have at least a preliminary report from us by the end of the school year. To jump-start the project, he's considering inviting Jan Bonham to do an inservice. We need to register an opinion on that, but first, to get some ease with the subject, I thought it might help if we took up a very concrete topic. Last week Maria talked to me, and I believe to you, too, Hardie, about an incident that came up in her class. Without getting into the specifics and unnecessarily putting you on the spot, Maria, I was impressed that you dealt with it by holding a class meeting. Because that's a practice most of us use, I thought we could ask ourselves what a class meeting with a moral slant might look like.

"Well, as you already know, I actually did a bit more than *think* about it; I got inspired to write a mock teacher-led discussion and left copies in your boxes so that you could absorb it at leisure. I tried to make it a garden-variety example of the breed. I'd like to read it aloud, so that we all can hear it together, and then share reactions to the teacher's handling of a problem that was dumped on him one morning during recess. Agreed?"

"Go for it," Hardie replied. "I'm not a true believer when it comes to using class meetings to settle moral problems, but, hey, you've not only done a lot of thinking about it, you actually wrote something up. So I'm game."

Aggie looked at Connie and Maria and saw their nodding acquiescence. "I've no objections," Connie added, "But don't count on me for reactions at this stage. It's been a long time since I was a classroom teacher."

"I don't believe for a minute, Connie, that your reactions wouldn't be valuable to us, but OK, for now we'll give you a pass if you wish."

■ ■ ■ ■ ■ ▬▬▬▬▬▬▬▬▬▬▬▬▬▬▬▬▬▬▬▬▬▬▬▬

## PROBLEMS ON
## THE PLAYGROUND—Agatha Cerine

Don Downer, a fourth-grade teacher, had hoped to use his free period for paper grading, but ten minutes into recess he was interrupted by the noise of kids clashing on the playground. He decided to ignore it as best he could; students were supervised by aides, who had been instructed—oh, how many many times!—to behave as if he were on the premises. The students knew that they were to be civilized to one another, walk away from provocative encounters, and solve conflicts by themselves. Tattling was out. Still, Don was not surprised when Alfred burst into the classroom.

"Mr. D.," he panted, "I think you'd better come out; Peter and Mark are at it again, arguing and pushing each other around. The new aide is busy with another kid who had a bad fall and isn't doing anything about it."

"Alfred, you remember the recess rule," replied Don. "No tattling. Please go back and tell them that if they can't stop scrapping with each other, the aide will cancel recess and the whole class will have to come inside and sit silently."

"Well, umm, OK, but, ah . . ."

"What are you trying to say, Alfred?" asked the somewhat impatient teacher.

"It's just that they won't stop unless you come out. Peter is out to get Mark again. A lot of the kids think Peter is a big bully, and they'll probably try to join up with Mark. Me too. It's not fair the way Peter is allowed to get away with murder."

"Maybe Peter will surprise you, Alfred, or maybe you and your friends can interrupt them. See you later."

The squabbling continued and the aide did cancel recess. Don Downer brought the students back to class, where they sat at their desks for the remainder of the period. Several glowered in open anger at their teacher—for the punishment—and at one another.

When the bell rang to signal the end of recess, Don announced his disappointment with the students and told them that instead of holding their scheduled class meeting at the end of the week, they would have it immediately. Don began, as he always did, by asking the class to state the problem.

The children were quick to single out Peter as the villain and Mark as a helpless victim. Don asked Peter what he thought.

"I don't really want to talk about it," he said. "Whatever goes on between Mark and me has nothing to do with the class. We were having words. No one got hurt. I think the problem is making this into a big-deal problem. Why didn't everyone leave us alone?"

Turning to the class, Don asked, "Why didn't you leave Peter alone?"

"Because he pushes Mark around," said Alfred, "and besides, you told us we should stop fights; that's part of 'conflict resolution.'"

A chorus of agreement.

"I also told you no tattling," said the teacher.

"Right," said a girl named Ruby, "and because you tattled, Alfred, we all had to come in and get punished. I think *that's* part of the problem. Why do we all have to pay for those guys not getting along?"

"Hold on," said Don, "let's see where we are in identifying the problem. Most of you think the problem is Peter. Peter disagrees and thinks the problem is interfering with a dispute that was no one's business. That's related to the tattling issue, which is what caused everyone to suffer."

"No," said Alfred emphatically. "I was just trying to prevent a fight, like I'm supposed to. How did I get to be the bad guy? It was the aide who stopped recess. I didn't make up the rule that everyone should be punished when just a couple of kids are at fault."

"True enough," said Don. "That's my rule. If we are to be a community, we need to be responsible for one another and to one another. Before we get to solutions, I'd like to hear what Mark thinks the problem is."

"Dunno."

"Was Peter picking on you?"

"Sort of."

"Was he fighting with you?"

"Not really, just kind of."

"What was he doing?" Don continued.

"Oh, he pushed me. I pushed him back. Then he called me a name."

"And calling you a name, was that wrong?"

"Guess so."

"Was Alfred's interference a problem?"

"No, he was just trying to be a good friend."

"So what's the problem, Mark?"

"I think, well, actually the problem is that we don't have enough to do at recess now that they took the hoops down."

Don couldn't resist a grin, as he had lobbied for more equipment last year, to no avail. Nothing had, probably nothing would, change. He felt obliged, therefore, to say, "Well, Mark, the equipment issue is just a fact of life and we can't change it. If that's a problem, there's no solution, so let's put it aside."

"Well then, how about more aides?"

Again, Don felt Mark was reading his mind, but again he couldn't get the administration to ante up the funds for aides, so he replied:

"Same answer, Mark, there are not going to be any more aides. Now, how about solutions to the problems we identified that we *can* resolve?"

"Since Peter picks on Mark a lot, why don't we pick on Peter and swear at him too? That would teach him to quit," said a boy named Roger, with obvious relish at his ingenuity.

"Roger, if you guys started picking on Peter, do you think he *would* learn to stop?" the teacher asked.

*(continued)*

"Maybe," said Roger. "He would see it don't feel good to be picked on."

"But what else might it do to Peter? What does Mark do when he feels picked on?"

"Mark gets back at Peter. Is that what you mean, it might make Peter angry?"

"Yes, exactly," replied Don, "So it's probably not the greatest solution. Can you come up with other ideas, Roger?"

"Well, instead of tattling, Alfred could have asked Mark to come play with him or with a bunch of us."

"That's a good idea, don't you think so, Alfred?" Don queried.

"I asked him if he wanted me to help him," said Alfred, "and he said no."

"Yeah, but do you think *helping* in his conflict is the same as *inviting* him to join you and others?"

"What's the difference?"

"Seems to me," said Don, "that no self-respecting kid is going to accept an offer of help when he is in a one-on-one tussle. Makes him look weak. But an invitation to escape by doing something else, well that doesn't hurt his self-respect. Do you agree, Mark?"

"I guess so."

"Any other solutions?" the teacher asked.

"Maybe I shouldn't have come in to tell you about Peter. Maybe I just should have waited longer and minded my own business," said Alfred, eager to rehabilitate himself in the eyes of his teacher.

"It's not that Peter and Mark aren't your business," the teacher replied, chastened. "They are. It's just that you and all the others need to figure out when and how to intercede. Was this really a fight or just a fight brewing? If it wasn't yet a fight, could you be resourceful in finding a solution other than coming to me? There isn't always going to be an adult around to bail you out. But I know you were trying to keep the peace.

"Who else has an idea?"

Ruby tried once again: "Can we talk about why we all had to miss recess because of Peter and Mark?"

"Who can explain to Ruby why we have the whole-class responsibility rule for recess problems?"

After a longer-than-usual silence, José spoke up. "I think it's because when we're outside and you're here and there's trouble, you can't be sure who is to blame and so we all have to take the blame."

"Yes, but can you think of anything else, José?"

"Umm, because maybe if we know we're all going to get in trouble, we'll stop the trouble, is that it?"

"Well, that's true enough, but I'd say it more positively: The class is a kind of family. When good things happen, like a birthday, we share in the fun; when we have a chance for a field trip, we all decide together on a place we'd like to visit as a group. And on the trip, if one of you lags behind the others, we wait for you to catch up, or if the student assigned to bring the snacks doesn't, then we don't have snacks. We make decisions together, we share the consequences, and we share the responsibility."

"But we don't do everything together as a group," Ruby jumped in. "If someone doesn't do her homework and has extra work, we don't all have to do extra work."

"Now there's an idea I hadn't thought of," Don laughingly replied.

"But why isn't not doing your homework like having a fight, or whatever it was that happened between Mark and Peter? What's it got to do with the rest of us?" Ruby persisted.

"Mr. D. thinks that we'll act more like a family at recess if we share in the consequences," said Alfred.

"Yea, sure," muttered Peter under his breath to a neighbor. "Wonder what kind of freaky family he's got."

It was time to bring this discussion to a close. The teacher summarized:

"Because we have something else to talk about today, I'd like us to review what I believe we've agreed upon: When two kids start going at one another during recess you *all* have to think hard about the obligations of a responsible citizen. First, you need to recognize that although recess *is* your collective responsibility, that doesn't mean you need to interfere immediately in a squabble. You need to figure out when and how to intercede. One possibility is to ignore it, at least for a while. Or you could just remind the boys to quit, that their behavior spells trouble. Another is to break it up, or try to, by asking one of the combatants to come play with you. And don't forget to talk with one another about strategies. If two minds are better than one, think of how smart a group can be."

"Yeah, and how dumb too," Ruby whispered.

"Now, the other matter for us today," Don went on. "Summer will soon be upon us [cheers from the class], and because the reading scores in this school leave something to be desired, Dr. Helter has announced that there has to be a summer reading program for third through fifth grades. He is allowing the teachers to decide on the nature of the program and I am consulting with you. Two conditions, however, are not up for grabs. We must have some way of being 'accountable.' That means students have to 'prove' that they have completed, and absorbed, the readings; and everyone must complete four books.

Compared to the previous discussion, the children participated vigorously in this one. The first option was that the same four books, selected by the teacher, be required of the whole class and that they all take a test on them at the beginning of the fall. Most of the kids were content with this until a second option came up. Why not give more choice in the accountability measure? Students could either opt for the test or instead submit journal summaries of a specified length. A chorus of objections followed.

Journal entries weren't as hard as a test.

*(continued)*

Well, then, that was the choice most would make.

But they were more demanding of time and thinking.

Well, then, maybe some would prefer the test.

The children who liked choice came up with a third option. It was stupid, they claimed, for the whole class to read the same books. Why not have everyone submit books of interest? Mr. D. could compile an inclusive list and each student would select four that interested him or her.

That wasn't fair, a minority protested. Some kids would list and select books that they had already read, so they wouldn't really be doing any work; others would list baby books.

Those who did such dumb things were only cheating themselves, the pro-choice group replied, and anyway they still had to prove they knew the books. Under this option, accountability would have to mean individual reports.

The teacher decided to take a vote. There was no majority for any of the options. The second option had a plurality, but the third lagged by only a couple of votes. When the results were tallied, a few children argued in favor of having a choice between option two (teacher-assigned books with choice on the method of evaluation) and option three (student-driven list). Mr. Downer rejected this request and went with the plurality.

## TEACHERS DISCUSS AGGIE'S CLASS MEETING

After Aggie had finished reading Don Downer's story, she asked, "OK, who wants to start us off? What did you all think of Downer's direction of the class meeting?"

Hardie was eager to step up to the plate.

## Hardie

"Poor Mr. Downer! He is trapped. Someone has fed him the notion of group responsibility, group participation, and group consensus, but you can tell he only half-believes in it. He has instincts, better instincts I think, that pull against so much child consultation. He would like to rule with a firmer hand. He knows that's what these children (fifth graders only) need, but the word is out that his success depends on getting 'buy-in' from the students, so he is valiantly following the school line. It's pretty clear to me that he doesn't share the school's enthusiasm—which to me, too, is exaggerated—for class meetings as a way of community building.

"It's not that inviting student viewpoints is always misguided, but he has gone off the deep end. Let me be more specific. The first big mistake was to assign *group* culpability for indiscretions that were not group-related. The analogy of a class to a family gets you only so far. What family requires the punishment of all for the wrongdoing of one? I think Peter was on to this; Ruby also. In fact, I doubt whether the family analogy took hold at all. Look how he had to quiz José repeatedly—"Can you think of anything else, José?"—to get an explanation for group sanctions. Sometimes, when you are the solitary caregiver for several children, group sanctions are required. You can't send one kid to her room and go off with the rest. But that's just pragmatic. If you could, you would punish the offender, period. What went on between Mark and Peter is clearly not the concern of the other children, or at least not very much their concern. And, more important, they are not sufficiently mature to handle the conflict. Mr. Downer must know it is beyond their current capacity 'to figure out when and how to intercede.' Group sanctions do have a role, but only when it is the group that is *directly* affected, for example, the kid who forgets to bring a snack for the class trip obviously makes it impossible for anyone to have a snack. Mr. Downer needs to distinguish offenses *between* children and offenses *against* the group.

"There is also a big downside to saddling the class with such a heavy responsibility. We saw how poor Alfred was caught in a bind: The instructions were to keep the peace, but no tattling. He failed at the first (offering his help) and resorted to the second; he saw no other alternatives except to let the 'fight,' as he perceived it, continue, with him as a helpless bystander—clearly not a 'responsible' behavior. Mark was entirely right. What was needed for an improved recess was better equipment and/or more aides. You can't ask kids to assume responsibilities that belong to the school. How often *we* are irresponsible in asking them to make up for our lapses!

"Moreover, by allowing the children to persist in discussing matters they couldn't handle, the teacher (inadvertently, I am sure) had to keep suppressing or 'redirecting' the conversation. I see teachers doing this all the time, and it must feel very coercive or at least confusing to the children. For example, Mr. Downer flat-out rejects Roger's suggestion that the group retaliate by picking on Peter. Well, maybe he doesn't reject it flat out, but he does a heavy-handed redirection, asking Roger several times for the likely outcome of such a tactic—'Can you come up with other ideas, Roger?'—He does not explain why retaliation is wrong; he just says, implicitly, it won't work. Surely that is not a very thoughtful response to what is the most commonplace and most practiced form of justice: You tease me, I tease you; you hit me, I hit you.

"On the other hand, he applauds the suggestion to distract Mark by inviting him to play with other classmates, but again he doesn't say why that's preferable. To a child of this age—and to many adults—it's not obviously a more constructive way to go. He pays little attention to the views of the main contestants: Peter (the most important player and one who is completely soured on the meeting), Alfred (who is put on the spot), and Mark (who is talked about as if he weren't around but does not talk freely himself).

"Asking for opinions, but only accepting the 'right' ones, does not a good discussion make. Better just to state the policies, or problems and solutions, if you like that framework, and elaborate on why they are better than the alternatives. Sometimes Downer does that, as when he stated the foolish rule on community punishment. Apparently the kids had previously agreed on what makes for civilized behavior at recess. He should simply have reviewed those commitments (rules) and perhaps found out where the slip-ups occurred, though I think it's obvious—they need more supervision.

"Another error he makes is to have so many matters off the table. He will not permit discussion on why the conflict is a matter of group responsibility, inadequate equipment, too few aides, or tattling. The children are frustrated by the fact that conversation about so much, and much that they have not accepted, is prohibited. Of course, I agree that we shouldn't invite discussion on topics that we've determined *aren't* discussible. But that being the case, Mr. Downer should have narrowed the subject for the meeting at the outset—if indeed any meeting was called for. At most, I would have opened the agenda to suggestions for good recess activities and methods for ensuring full and fair participation in these activities. Then I would have tried to persuade the class, not discuss with them, why it's important to make the activities work for everyone, why it's right to play fair and square and not let personal disagreements get in the way of the class spirit, and why the school won't obtain more aides or equipment.

"He did a much better job with the summer reading assignment, which was a more appropriate topic. There, he carefully explained the limitations of the discussion before it got started by stating clearly that the requirement was four books and an assessment. The students had a chance to consider important issues: how equality (everyone reads the same book) conflicts with individual freedom, an issue we confront daily at school, and how we make decisions in the face of disagreement. In the end he took a vote and let the majority, or plurality, prevail. That's a good lesson in democracy for the class."

## Maria

"Hardie, great job! We agree on so much: It *was* a mistake to 'invite' a conversation but then substantially restrict the topics. The teacher asked children for *their* description of the problem, then discounted many of their assessments (equipment, aides, common sanctions, tattling); he asked for *their* solutions, then either rejected them (Roger's solution to pick on Jack) or evaluated them (a play invitation to Mark was a 'good idea'). Don was better when he encouraged a child to think through the likely consequences of a suggestion (an invitation to play rather than an offer of help), but even then I felt the child was trying to psych out the 'right' answer rather than reflect on his own.

"Of all the kids we heard from, I most pitied Alfred. He's clearly (and unfortunately) a teacher-pleaser. He tried to do the right thing by reporting the recess squabble and got put down by Don as a tattler. He defended himself—'How did I get to be the bad guy?'—but I guess he was feeling pretty disparaged. Yet Don, insensitively I think, kept at him by asking (really telling) whether it wouldn't have been better to *invite* Mark to join in play rather than *offer* to help. Another put-down. And then, pathetically, Alfred again tries to please the teacher: 'Maybe I shouldn't have come in to tell you about Peter. Maybe I just should have waited longer and minded my own business.'

"As for holding the meeting in the first place, I'm still unsure about that. On the one hand, as Hardie said, the issue does seem circumscribed to the two kids involved. On the other hand, it really isn't. Many of the children had views on the fighting. They knew the personal histories behind the conflict, cared about the participants, and at least a few wanted to help. Maybe they could have been useful. Furthermore, on another day it won't be Peter, Mark, and Alfred but three other children. Similar incidents will recur; so too the options for resolution.

"If we are to build community—and I don't think that word is overused or overemphasized—and agree upon ways of resolving disputes, then we have to reduce the barrier of the private. Classmates *are* like family in the sense that we should be able to trust them. But I grant you it didn't work in this instance.

"I'm wondering if part of the failure wasn't Don's confused motives. By the way, Hardie, I don't see why we need to assume he was holding the meeting against his better judgment. Perhaps his thinking is in some sort of transition. I assume he is accustomed to announcing rules and punishing disobedience. Now he is trying to get the kids to figure out their relationships. Only he can't quite let go of the reins, or he hasn't figured out how much to loosen them. And that's a problem. He has a rule against tattling and a rule to punish the group for problems at recess. Then, after enforcing the rules, he asks the students for their thoughts. Well, I don't see how you can do anything productive faced with surly kids under a punishment that they don't see as just. Even as a listener, I felt the class meeting was part of the punishment. I wonder why Don didn't forgo the threat and just hold the meeting after recess bombed. Why the silent treatment? If there was uncertainty about the problem—and I guess there was, since he asked them to define it—what were they being punished for? I also don't get the idea of a *rule* against 'tattling.' Seems to me sometimes kids need adult help, sometimes they don't, and the teacher's job is to help them clarify the distinctions. In any case did the kids 'buy into' these rules about group punishment and tattling? It didn't seem that way from the conversation.

"While we're on the subject of motives, Don was so focused on what happened, what he called the 'problem' (assessing and stopping the fight, bullying, and tattling) that he failed to capture the children's (like his own) confused motives. Many of them clearly don't like Peter and identify with Mark. Alfred hinted that they'd really like to join the fight against him. That's why he came to Don in the first place. Others, like Roger, would settle for picking on Peter. On the other hand, they've been told that's all wrong—and I don't know whether this is what they *believe* or think they *should* believe —so they make other suggestions for ending the fight. But I wasn't convinced that the idea of distracting Mark, which Don loved, was sincere. After all, it didn't happen during recess; it was an afterthought. Maybe the kids don't much like Mark either. It's one thing to identify with the victim of a bully—if that's a fair indictment of Peter—another to want to include the victim in your play. Victims are not usually the most popular kids on the block. Right? We need to know so much more about what's going on here, who feels what about whom, including Don."

Maria pressed on despite Hardie's low moan. "And another thing. This gets back to the silencing of children. Why is Don so protective of the school? He too believes that there should be more equipment and aides at recess, but when the children bring up these complaints ('read his mind,' he puts it), they are told the topics are off limits. I guess he doesn't want to fritter away time discussing issues that are out of his control. I don't think I agree. Why would it be so terrible if he acknowledged these external problems as contributing to the recess debacles? I'd go further. Why can't he say he agrees with the kids, that he has tried to get the school to do more and has been told there are no funds, or children shouldn't be spoiled, or they should learn to play unsupervised? I guess he doesn't want to take sides with the children against the school, but I wouldn't frame it that way.

"The school, like the class, should be a community. The school is not some abstract entity; it's *us*. What I'd want to do, if only I dared, would be to join the kids in bringing these concerns to the principal. But first I'd help them think through what it is they are requesting, maybe even what it would cost. If money is tight, perhaps they could come up with other solutions. How about a drive to get funds from the parents or the community? Couldn't we appeal to the marketing instincts of a sporting goods store to contribute solid hoops for the kids? Perhaps volunteers could assist during recess. The children might even try to recruit some of the retired folks in the area. If all their efforts failed, and I know that's a real possibility, the children (hopefully) at least would learn something about budgetary constraints (and human constraints), and feel that they were participating in an effort to improve their school lives.

"In listening to the scenario, I felt Don just couldn't relax and join the kids wholeheartedly. He seems prematurely discouraged. Yes, he wants their views on problems and solutions, but only select views. He sort of believes that the children can rise to the occasion, but he also seems to distrust them and has a strong urge to manage and control them. He keeps pressing for the answers he wants—'Can you think of anything else?'—rather than allowing a genuine interchange among the kids. As a result of his ambivalence about the class meeting the kids are uncomfortable, and I sense they too have low expectations. Mark won't divulge his feelings, Alfred has probably determined to keep a low profile hereafter. The conversation, at least the first one, doesn't flow freely; there is no enthusiasm for the discussion or for the notion of collective responsibility. Given how Don feels, it's no surprise that they haven't been too successful in forging a community.

"Having said all this, my own feelings of guilt are now on the rise. My efforts at 'We're all in this together,' 'We're all one happy family' failed, and in just weeks I became a 'Do as you're told' teacher. We've dumped and dumped on Don, and that's no way to treat even a hypothetical teacher. Aggie must think he didn't do too poor a job, because she designed him as a prototype. So how about your views, Aggie?"

## Aggie

"I'd rather be playing tennis!

"Speaking of complexity, you guys have nailed so many nuances that never occurred to me, the inventor. Here I had naively thought Don Downer did a reasonable job under the circumstances. True, I assumed he was 'charged' with holding class meetings, and they were novel for him. That will be true for the faculty too, if they are charged with a similar undertaking. Maria put her finger on it; he was moving from one style of teaching to another, so yes, he dragged some of his old ways with him. But Hardie was right too; like many of our faculty, he was reluctant to join the new initiative. Still, I didn't think the new and the old were as contradictory as both of you implied. Hardie sees Downer as bending too far forward, Maria sees him as leaning too far backward. I'm getting a backache just from swaying back and forth!

"What is emerging from your reactions, at least for me, is that if we are to engage children in discussing moral issues and give them some decision-making authority—and why else have the discussions?—we need to think very carefully about the constraints we place on the conversations. Both of you were displeased by Downer's tendency to invite comments and then either reject them or redirect them down routes that met with his prior approval—or perhaps it was his comfort. Something slightly deceptive there; it's the illusion of consultation.

"You disagree, as I see it, on just what the boundaries of discussable issues should be. For example, Hardie thinks that Don should have been more explicit about what is wrong with retaliation, while Maria thinks he failed to encourage the kids to inquire more deeply into whether retaliation may actually be OK in some instances. Hardie appears to believe that the more one can contain a problem the better. Let the two boys sort it out, or sort it out with them alone. Maria is into expanding issues, 'Who feels what about whom.' I don't find these differences problematic, as long as teachers rationally review their positions. There could be teachers who pose narrow topics for the class, others who pose broad ones. We probably also need to think about what we mean by a discussion. Hardie says often that he wants to 'persuade' the kids about a particular policy. Well, persuade doesn't mean just lecturing, persuasion also admits of some form of conversation, but I guess that a persuasion-oriented discussion is different from a more open-ended one. Maria wants the kids to 'buy in.' To me that doesn't come from a single conversation. So what sorts of discussion formats move gradually toward buy in?

"Another thought, which may amount to the same thing: What is the relationship of group discussions to responsibility? Over what kinds of matters should children actually make decisions, experiment with their own ideas, and reflect on the consequences? You wouldn't get much support for children deciding on the school calendar or dismissal time, but what about input into homework? Maybe. We clearly need to go further with this exploration of class meetings.

"But my head is spinning right now. You know, Fred wants to ask Dr. Jan Bonham to hold an inservice with the faculty. He's authorized me to consult her as our group works. How about we call a halt now and I talk this over with her before we get together again? Maybe a preview covering just class meetings would help her plan the broader meeting with the whole faculty and help the four of us move our discussions along too. Meanwhile, I hope each of you will give me your thoughts about next moves."

## AGGIE'S MEETING WITH JAN BONHAM

Aggie followed through with a visit to Dr. Jan Bonham. She summarized the trouble they were having figuring out a format for class meetings because of their differing notions about when and how to invite children's input. When

Jan asked for more specifics, Aggie went through the entire Downer scenario and Hardie's and Maria's reactions. While doing so, she was impressed, and a bit surprised, by Jan's hunger for details and her obvious fascination. The surprise was short-lived.

"This is remarkable," Jan began. "You have gone through exactly the sort of uncertainties that I've imagined teachers experience. More than once I've left a fall inservice with a gnawing feeling because the programs I offer to schools have a patness that doesn't fully capture the ambiguities of teaching morality. In puzzling over these inadequacies, it occurred to me that we need a document to guide us through these waters. I don't mean a detailed guide for discussion topics and outcomes—we would want to leave it very flexible— but something that alerts teachers to the decisions they need to make about running meetings.

"Most of us, like Hardie, probably want children to adhere to the legitimate rules of the school. But like Maria, we also want children to buy into the rules and contribute to their formation. Lurking in the scenario are additional strains. For one, fairness is not always obvious. What looks fair—no bullying—may change once we learn more about the particular context (e.g., the prior history between these boys, facts not known to the observer that precipitated the "bullying" response). For another, we also disagree on what is fair. School rules of dress, greetings, seating arrangements, and forms of speech touch on many values that prompt considerable discord among teachers and between schools and families. The disagreements extend to more significant matters. For example, Maria seems less persuaded than the others that 'retaliation' is always to be termed wrongful. From this less condemna-tory moral stance, she will more readily want the teacher to be careful not to lead the class meeting immediately into the question of the best means of preventing or redressing certain conduct. She will encourage an open explo-ration of the prior question, that is, whether the conduct ought to be allowed. It is these concerns that underlie Maria's preference for a more facilitative, less directive teacher role in managing a class meeting.

"Of course, most educators 'want it all': children who are obedient, have good habits, are sensitive to the concerns of the group, and simultaneously make rational decisions, resist peer pressure, override personal interests, and speak truth to power. In short, they want children who are obedient, caring, and autonomous. Any specific approach is likely to be good for what it includes and deficient for what it slights. Teachers need complex strategies for encouraging a moral outlook. They must be able to exercise authority and to release it. To do that, they need to be aware of their own individual bias—their particular orientation toward a more directive or a more facilita-tive approach—and hold on to it *lightly*, able to lean against it from time to time.

"To accommodate these complexities, Aggie, I've been working on a model that describes and illustrates what I've termed '*Levels of Teacher Authority*.' It is designed to encourage the teacher (reader) to locate his or her own general position on matters of authority and understand how that position might vary in response to different, though familiar, contexts. As we've seen, some teachers, like Hardie, are clear on matters of right and wrong. They generally want children to toe the line; 'tell, don't ask' is the philosophy. They believe in imposing sanctions when children stray, with or without explanations. Others, like Maria, are more uncertain about right and wrong, less inclined to apply sanctions, and more open to a variety of outcomes. Still, there are issues about which Hardie is flexible and Maria is rigid. Don Downer, now he's hard to place. I sense confusion [Aggie shudders. Like me, she thinks]. He opens up a broad discussion, but then closes it when the children raise what he believes are nondiscussable issues. He solicits their ideas but won't air those he finds objectionable.

"It was my intention, hopefully not a utopian one, to construct a model that accommodates the varying positions teachers take. At the same time, it should help them become more aware of their options and preferences. But I've not yet exposed it to anyone, so I may be way off the mark. Perhaps you'd be willing to kick it around with your group and give me some feedback. One of its functions, after all, is to stimulate dialogue and reflection, and you all seem primed to go."

"I've obviously come to the right place at the right time," Aggie acknowledges with genuine relief. "Why don't I take it with me, and the four of us will look it over carefully. Then, if you're willing, you could meet with us and get everyone's reactions firsthand while we have the benefit of a discussion with you."

"That would be a great opportunity for me," replied Jan Bonham.

# SIX LEVELS OF TEACHER AUTHORITY—Dr. Jan Bonham[1]

Each of the six levels initially offers a justification for a particular degree of teacher authority and then illustrates its application. For purposes of clarity, the same specific content is used at each level. Some educators may find very few issues that fit a level-6 discussion; others will want to be mostly at level 6. The level selected for a class meeting is less important, however, than a willingness to consider just where an issue fits and the potential contributions made by each of the levels.

The justification for the first three levels is that they contribute to the development of habits, acculturation into traditional virtues, and the notion of obligation. The justification for the next three levels is that they contribute to appreciation of the complexity and ambiguity of morality, tolerance and a pluralistic understanding of values, ongoing moral vigilance and attentiveness to the moral implications of life, and an internalization of moral identity.

1. *Rule imposition by authority.* In our society there are certain accepted obligations and conventions that all children must follow regardless of their personal and contrary opinions. The teacher is justified by the position she holds in society in imposing these traditional values.

Examples:

It is wrong to exclude another child from play; no one may do so.

Trash must always be thrown into proper receptacles.

Children must never tease other students.

Everyone must always be courteous to substitute teachers.

2. *Rule imposition with attempt at moral persuasion.* All of us should abide by a set of obvious virtues: respect, responsibility, sharing, caring, trustworthiness, fairness. But these virtues are elusive, and children need to understand the underlying principles that make them mandatory.

Examples:

To exclude another child is wrong because it causes pain that may have long-term consequences.

Trash should be thrown into proper receptacles out of consideration for the community's welfare, so that it can be recycled and the premises kept clean.

Children may not tease other students because doing so is hurtful and intolerant even if not so intended.

Substitute teachers deserve the same respect as all others, because they are doing their best in a difficult situation and often cannot be expected to know the regular teacher's plans thoroughly.

[1]As first appeared in *Education Week,* March 20, 2003. Reprinted with permission of Joan F. Goodman.

*(continued)*

3. *Rule imposition with encouragement of children's moral engagement and agreement.*   Often, children will come to the right decision when given the chance to consider an issue thoughtfully. The teacher is confident that through reflection and empathy good answers will emerge. However, questions are not open-ended.

Examples:

Why do you think it is wrong

to exclude another child?

not to throw trash into proper receptacles?

to tease children?

to be discourteous to a substitute teacher?

4. *Slight modification of adult rules based on listening to disagreements and then finding common ground.*   There are instances in which a rule fits imperfectly with an event and admits to exceptions. Children's views on contextual variations (that include a prior history, motives, and consequences) are relevant in such instances.

Examples:

Are there times (and was this a time) when it is not wrong

to exclude another child?

to fail to throw trash into proper receptacles?

to tease children?

to treat a substitute teacher discourteously?

5. *Joint construction of rules.*   If we want children to bind themselves willingly to prescriptive rules, they must have the opportunity to make their mark on those rules through genuine discussions in which opposing positions have been respectfully considered. If we want children to become participatory citizens, then they need to experience democracy in action. However, the teacher, with her broader perspective and larger responsibilities, may exert more than a single vote.

Examples:

How should we figure out what rules, if any, are required around the following issues?

exclusion of children from activities

throwing trash into proper receptacles

teasing each other

behavior toward substitute teachers

6. *Child-generated topics, construction of rules, and resolutions.*   The rationale is the same as in level 5, but with the added recognition that children should be allowed to make the "wrong" decisions and learn from them, and that the "right" decision is not always obvious. The decisions must be open to regular reconsideration as experience leads to new perspectives.

Examples:

Are there moral matters you recently confronted that you wish to discuss?

X has just complained to her teacher about being excluded. Is this a problem, and if so, how should it be resolved?

X suggests we have a rule that everyone throw away the trash they see on the floors. Should we?

X didn't think it was funny when you joked with him. What should we do?

We are having a substitute teacher. Are there any issues we should discuss?

## TEACHERS MEET WITH DR. BONHAM

The group reviewed Bonham's *Six Levels of Teacher Authority* with interest, hoping this might become the crux of their program, and reassembled to talk with her. Hardie and Maria greeted their former teacher warmly. All agreed that Aggie would open the discussion with her own reactions.

### Aggie

"I've been chewing this over for a few days and think it has some real potential for us. As I understand Dr. Bonham's model, the first three levels all *assume* wrongfulness. Level 1 relies on authority: It is wrong to hit another child because I say so, or the school says so, or our society prohibits it. It is such a self-evident truth that no explanation is required; indeed, the explanation lessens the imperative. The second level *tells* why something is wrong: Using force to get your way is wrong because it violates the sanctity of another person; it's an unacceptable mode of coercion. The third level still assumes a right answer, but *asks* why something is wrong. The expectation is that the child will have assimilated, and will give, the proper response, not that she will engage in a discussion of alternatives.

"The next three levels are willing to focus on the *whether* of wrongfulness. The fourth level opens the door just a crack. It admits the possibility that sometimes it may be appropriate to engage in violence and welcomes the children's input into that crack. Level 5 broadens the opening. Should we have rules that describe the circumstances under which certain kinds of aggression may be permissible? The teacher at this level must genuinely believe that mild aggression—a shove, angry words, a threatening fist—can sometimes be tolerated, or is at least open to that possibility. At the more restrictive end, perhaps she is willing to consider a broader rule against aggression, one that goes beyond hitting to include insults. The teacher might welcome a discussion that compares verbal to physical aggression. Finally, at level 6, the door is wide open. The teacher takes an entirely agnostic view of aggression and grants children permission to come up with their own policies (or no policy). To be at level 6, when the subject is violence, requires faith that the children will naturally see, or eventually come to see, that violence is largely unacceptable.

"Sometimes it's hard to think of topics that a teacher can 'release' to children (levels 5 and 6), but I've culled a few examples that I can recall from my own recent teaching. I have had several boys who, whenever they get a chance to write creatively, choose gory topics such as killing people, chopping them up, and then feeding them to animals. This is a topic we could talk about at levels 5 and 6 because I do not see a clear right/wrong answer: Does the class find such stories acceptable? Why? Why not?

"I have a girl who frequently comes to class with new (and very elaborate) hairdos. She is greeted with frowns and 'yuks' from her classmates. In a class discussion we could explore respect for others' aesthetics, ask why and at what cost children are delivering their judgments, and consider when limiting honest reactions is and is not advisable.

"Because a number of children are forever 'losing' their pencils, I have to keep (and replenish at my own expense) a supply. Do the children think that is fair?

"You obviously have your own topics to contribute, and so may the students. I suspect that with practice we'll find lots more high-level topics and a rapid increase in the quality of thought and of trust in the process. That growth will then permit an 'upgrading' of topics we'd now assign to levels 1 and 2. I suspect, too, that such conversations will lead students to assume more responsibility for themselves and one another.

"To conclude this lengthy reaction (I was turned on by the paradigm), what Jan's proposal does for me is to join the, what shall we say, importance, obviousness, centrality of a moral value with how you teach it; the more major the wrong, the more impositional the teaching. When it comes to inflicting serious harm, there is total prohibition. But when the value is disputable she invites the children's input or even cedes authority to them; they become proprietors of their own morality. I like that range.

"What are your reactions?"

## Connie

After a period of silence Connie began. "I'm not a classroom teacher, so perhaps I lack authority to speak, but speak I will. I appreciate the innovative idea that we need a mix of methods for a mix of issues and am impressed, Dr.

Bonham, with your attempt to make the match. But tell me who decides (and how) what is a contestable or incontestable issue? If all aggression isn't clearly a no-no, what is? It seems to me we are taking what's obvious and making it obscure. In the process we're opening a Pandora's box. I can just imagine a parent phone call: 'Ms. Comfort, I understand that today the children discussed when hitting was permissible. Could I possibly have heard right? I want to be assured that did not happen.' What do I say next?"

"I am also concerned that these discussions will quickly break down the firewall we try to erect between home and school. My impulse has always been to bury the clash of values between home and school, to protect family privacy and to have an expansive view on what is private. I normally would have said, for example, 'What you and your family do outside school is none of my business; in school there will be no hitting, shoving, or hostile language.' But I have to admit that I'm beginning to have doubts about my firewall. It seems just like saying to a child caught smoking, 'If you want to smoke outside school, fine; inside school we won't allow it.' I know I wouldn't say that. What sort of adult tells a child it's OK to smoke elsewhere when it's illegal and unhealthy? Is shoving any different?"

Hardie smiled in apparent agreement, but Maria was obviously perplexed and preoccupied. "What are your thoughts?" Aggie asked her.

## Maria

"I too am drawn to the *Six Levels of Teacher Authority*, but bothered by this seemingly orderly progression you've described. Dr. Bonham, I'm wondering if this attempt to match teaching method with content is realistic. I could imagine a kid doing something clearly wrong—capturing a fish from the tank and throwing it on the table—and horrifying all the kids. That could be a level 6, even though a serious wrong, because the peer group would do the sanctioning. Often children know the big do's and don'ts and teachers can be silent. Alternatively, there could be something fairly trivial, morally speaking, such as speaking only when recognized, and that could be at level 1 or 2 because the teacher just can't tolerate it.

"But even if we went along with the formula that the more serious the infraction, the more directive the intervention, how does one judge the infraction? Unlike Connie, I'm in the cloudy vision camp. To me, it's hard to judge the Peter and Mark imbroglio. Did they cross the line into unacceptable aggression? Isn't it worth noting that neither of the boys asked for help and neither seemed to believe that what went on between them merited group attention, never mind a punishment? True, the other kids in the class all piled onto Peter, but are we certain they weren't just a chorus trying to please the teacher? Peter apparently had a bad rap, so everyone assumed he must have been a bully. But even accepting the bully attribution, which I wouldn't given the scant evidence, should he be punished? Will that change him or possibly, by mortifying and angering him, make matters worse? And come to think of it, is changing Peter necessarily what Don (or we) would want to do? Maybe Don was just plain meting out justice. If you're bad, you should be punished. I can imagine Hardie taking such a position. Right, Hardie?"

## Hardie

"You bet your britches," Hardie jumped in. " 'Meting out justice' doesn't sound too bad to me. But like you, Maria, I wouldn't take the kids' view on fault very seriously. If I'm going to be judge and jury, I'd better have clear evidence. As all of you perceptive colleagues have surmised, I lean to the first three levels. Unlike Maria, I'm not afflicted with 'cloudy vision.' Serious aggression is clearly wrong; a mild push or shove, a swear word at recess, can be overlooked. The latter falls into the boys-will-be-boys category. Yet I recognize that Connie, who has never complained of cloudy vision, thinks *all* aggression is plainly wrong, so I have to agree, reluctantly, that even two such clear-sighted folks as we may not have the same moral take on behavior.

"The truth is that I am unenthusiastic about class meetings. I might use them occasionally, but only as a means of explaining why I took a particular action, not to solicit opinions. Student reactions are welcome *after* a child has demonstrated resistance to temptation or persistence in a difficult task, not before. Otherwise, talk just degenerates into self-serving rationales for rejecting essential moral obligations."

Maria was about to return fire but Aggie, looking at her watch, broke in. "In the time we have left, Jan, I think it would be good if you would give us *your* thoughts about our differences."

## Jan Bonham

"I think I can," began Jan, "and some pretty basic stuff is involved. This very rich conversation makes it apparent that it is easier to accept the principle of holding class meetings for moral questions than it is to agree on the what and when of them. Here, as elsewhere in moral education, the details are bedeviling.

"Because, as he told us, Hardie is clear about his own judgments and clear that they are largely right, he tilts strongly toward the first three levels of authority. He also believes that foisting a lot of responsibility on a child, or on the class, for establishing and enforcing behavioral standards is more than their ten years of life can manage. Such an enterprise, he believes, will fail. It's sufficient if children responsibly carry out their assigned tasks and do so in accordance with established, time-honored codes of behavior.

"For her part, Maria welcomes open-ended meetings, open both in content and approach. That which concerns the child, whatever its nature and source, should concern the class. If the issue between Peter and Mark originates outside school, or if it has to do with parental disagreements, it is nonetheless a welcome topic, for it affects life at school. To her, Connie's firewall surrounding school is unrealistic and unnatural. One does not shape a child's school behavior while remaining indifferent to his home behavior. Children should not be encouraged to segregate their school selves from their regular selves.

"Maria is also clearer about the problems than the solutions, so she finds the last three levels of authority much more palatable. Not giving children a fair degree of responsibility for decision making (and the consequences of their decisions) is treating them as instruments of adult power. That she finds unconscionable and ineffective. They will not be convinced of those rules they had no role in establishing, and it is their *convictions* that concern her.

"Aggie, backed by considerable teaching experience, wants to reconcile the two positions. From prior contacts, I know she is drawn to experiments in peer dispute resolution, to giving student councils greater authority for codes of behavior and discipline, and to involving children in the daily operations of the school. Such activities, she believes, promote their loyalty to one another and to the purposes of the academic enterprise. She is also concerned, however, about the possible boomerang. Give children too much opportunity for input and the output will be a litany of complaints. How much authority, at what ages, and under what conditions? Of that she is uncertain.

"Connie would just as soon have moral education keep a low profile, remain part of the 'hidden curriculum.' She worries that seepage from home to school and the reverse will create conflagrations that the school, with its limited resources and authority, cannot handle. Peter and Mark's parents, for example, cannot reconcile their differences under school auspices. The teacher situated in a classroom is highly constrained and possesses a limited charge from the community, which includes not interfering in child-rearing practices. Yet Connie worries that without more 'parent involvement'—a constant mantra of our times—the school's effectiveness in both the academic and moral domains is extremely weakened."

Aggie consulted her watch and brought the session to a close. "Thanks very much, Jan, for that helpful glimpse into each of our presuppositions. It's obvious that we have to think through some of our instinctive priorities in light of the differences among us. It looks as if we will have to dig deeper."

"Aggie," Bonham responded, "You and your colleagues here have already done some very important digging. With the four of you so obviously invested, I strongly suspect that something quite remarkable is in the works."

## A DEEPER LOOK

Aggie, in scripting the class-meeting scenario, intended to portray an ordinary conversation over a run-of-the-mill conflict. In the telling, however, neither her protagonist, Don Downer, nor the "audience" found it simple. The teachers had multiple concerns: What are appropriate topics for class discussion? Under what conditions should they be held? How do the children interpret them? At the heart of the matter they disagreed over the extent to which children should determine the mores (from which the word moral is derived) of their mini-society, essentially, how authority is to be distributed. Should the squabbles of children be regulated by adults, children, or both? If both, how *does* power get distributed? Bonham's six-level schema suggests that the more serious the moral issue, the more authority the teacher retains. And it accepts the fact that teachers will not agree on the question of "how serious." Does this mean that the giving and taking of authority is arbitrary, up to the teacher's subjective opinion? Her personality? Her upbringing?

Not quite. The extent to which children should have a voice in their own schooling is conditioned by one's views in three areas: pedagogical, moral, and developmental. A dip into each hopefully will deepen the reader's judgment on how to conduct class meetings and the wisdom of doing so.

### Class Discussions and Pedagogy

Under the influence of such luminaries as Jean Piaget, John Dewey, and Lawrence Kohlberg, it is conventional wisdom to many educators that children attain cognitive and social knowledge through active participation in resolving the problems and conflicts of everyday life. Because, according to this view, knowledge is "constructed," not received, the belief is often referred to as "constructivism." According to Piaget, for example, a child knows the properties and functions of an object only when she acts upon it; mere looking does not make it hers (Piaget, 1952). Knowledge simply "laid on" by teachers (or parents) is thought to wash away because it fails to bring about an active change in a child's thought patterns. Authoritative instruction of adult-chosen values, be they moral or arithmetic, is, therefore, not an effective pedagogical tool; absent a child's active collaboration, there is no learning.

The teacher's role, then, is not to give instruction, impose rules, and coerce obedience, but instead to facilitate construction, to guide the development of a child's autonomous meaning making. The effective educator stimulates inquiry (rather than giving the right answers) and encourages reflection and rational discourse by allowing students to clash, experiment, compromise, and finally reach cooperative decisions about their moral lives.

It is in a group situation that children rub up against the desires of others and are stimulated to inspect their actions against those desires. And it is through democratic classroom discussions that an enlarged perspective, critical to enhancing moral reasoning, occurs. Through such discussions, so the theory goes, children will move beyond their specific conflicts. They will formulate and voluntarily bind themselves to that which serves the greater good. The discussions also encourage more complex analyses of dilemmas (hypothetical or real) in which values compete, for example, telling a lie versus helping a friend, injuring one to save many, stealing goods that will otherwise be used for bad ends.

An opposite belief system maintains that every culture, rather than evoking children's ideas and engagement, is responsible for selecting the knowledge children must acquire and transmitting it to them. Indeed, such advocates argue, children do not have "ideas" independent of their culture, they do not have any innate propensity to acquire moral understanding, and they do not take intrinsic satisfaction in resolving problems. This orientation, associated with the pedagogy of behaviorism—a theory that stretches from John Locke to B. F. Skinner—holds that all learning comes from positive and negative reinforcement of emitted behaviors and that reinforcement is the most powerful inducement to learning. Morality, involving as it does severe inhibition and restraint of self-serving desires, is a hard sell and should not be left to open-ended discussions. According to advocates of this more impositional approach, it is the difficulty of moral attainment that particularly justifies the use of strong incentives.

Educational theorists Edward Wynne and Kevin Ryan (1997) argued that because successful moral instruction requires rigorous behavioral incentives, schools should thoughtfully and generously reward children for their pro-social conduct through means such as the following:

1. *Conspicuous praise*: notes or phone calls to parents; announcements over the school public-address system; names listed on the blackboard or the class or school bulletin board; photographs prominently displayed; mention in the school paper; notations on report cards; certificates on award occasions; bumper stickers for parents ("My child is a character-award winner at the _____ school"); invitations to a special party; names on a plaque or poster place on the school wall.
2. *Symbolic recognition* (like athletic letters): pins, ribbons, badges, jackets, medals, trophies.
3. *Publicly recognized titles*: school president, team captain, member of the honor society (where character is one requirement for membership).
4. *Contacts with prominent people*: breakfast with the principal (p. 67, italics in original).

## Class Discussions and Moral Certainty

A like difference in orientation influences the level of a teacher's confidence in the right and wrong of a given situation. Teachers sympathetic to "constructivism" tend to see moral issues as complex and elusive. The tendency of those in the "cultural transmission" camp is to the contrary. When a teacher running a class discussion is morally certain of the right outcome, he or she has two choices: impose it on, or extract it from, the children. What such a teacher cannot do is sanction the morally wrongful decision (see Chapter 5 on moral obligation). A teacher who is uncertain of the right outcome obviously has more room for maneuvering.

It was difficult for Don Downer to hold an open discussion with children in view of his moral certainty. The initial confrontation, you will recall, revolves around Peter and Mark's conflict. Roger, in trying to stop Peter from beating up on Mark, suggested a solution: "Since Peter picks on Mark a lot, why don't we pick on Peter and swear at him too? That would teach him to quit."

The idea does not sit well with Downer; he pushes on: "Roger, if you guys started picking on Peter, do you think he *would* learn to stop?"

Roger doesn't take the clue: "He would see it don't feel good to be picked on."

Downer, still dissatisfied and hinting ever more strongly asks, "But what else might it do to Peter? What does Mark do when he feels picked on?"

This probe does the trick. Roger answers, "Mark gets back at Peter. Is that what you mean, it might make Peter angry?" To which a relieved Downer replies, "Yes, exactly."

On the heels of this interchange, Ruby confronts Downer with an objection undoubtedly shared by others: Why must they have a meeting and miss recess just because two children are not getting along? They hadn't signed onto, and do not fully understand, the "whole-class responsibility" rule that Downer endorses. Queried for the rule's justification, José answers that "you can't be sure who is to blame." When Downer seeks a more apt response, José makes another attempt: "[M]aybe if we know we're all going to get in trouble, we'll stop the trouble, is that it?"

In both examples the children advocate notions of justice that Downer rejects. Roger's attitude, "do unto him what he does unto others," expresses a primitive, retributive morality. Adopted, Downer believes, it will escalate into harsher and harsher vendettas between individuals and children who want to "get even." Pursuing such an ethic might even foreshadow gang behavior and, writ large, exemplifies the lethal ethnocentrism that contaminates international relationships. Don believes it is his job to help Mark, and through him others, to find a more productive alternative—one that will extricate him from the fight and allow him the experience of pro-social gratifications.

We are left with two questions: Was Downer clearly right either in his moral certainty or in his conduct of the discussion? Those of "cloudy vision" would argue that the childrens' proposals deserved more vetting. Retributive justice, after all, not only has a hallowed place in sacred texts and is followed in many "undeveloped" cultures where if you wrong my family I will wrong yours, it is at the core of our own legal system. While we do not endorse personal vendettas, if you injure someone, society (admittedly not the victim) will inflict punishment, not rehabilitation; the greater your wrong, the greater your deserved pain. Furthermore, it might be argued, retribution works. The most effective means of stopping Peter is for him to learn, through experiencing Mark's retaliation, that bullying has no long-term payoff. Roger's idea, then, may not have been so obviously wrong. As for Downer's conducting of the class meeting, it too becomes suspect given these other moral considerations. If the children reject collective responsibility and support tit-for-tat punishment, they will justifiably view the meeting as an unfair restriction, not an opportunity.

Given all this ambiguity, those afflicted with cloudy vision might want to let the children experiment with (and then revise) their own moral decisions. They would allow this as good constructivists.

The heavy use of leading questions, however, is problematic for both teachers. Hardie finds fault with Downer's habit of "asking for opinions but only accepting the 'right' ones." Maria labels Alfred a "teacher-pleaser" when, in response to Downer's persistent questioning, he rather pitifully acknowledges, "Maybe I shouldn't have come in to tell you about Peter. Maybe I just should have waited longer and minded my own business." Look at two of the children's statements quoted above.

Roger: "Mark gets back at Peter. *Is that what you mean*, it might make Peter angry?"

José: "[M]aybe if we know we're all going to get in trouble, we'll stop the trouble, *is that it*?"

Both illustrate children trying to guess what's on the teacher's mind rather than their own.

Attempts to infiltrate a child's mind through suggestive questions aimed at promoting the "just solution" is a frequent school maneuver. Who in the education community has not heard a teacher say to her class, "We're all friends here, aren't we?" or "I'm sure Johnny didn't mean to hurt Samantha, did you, Johnny?" The child, listening to such subtle suggestions *may* adopt them willingly, that is, *may* be genuinely convinced. More likely, however, he or she will go along with the teacher's statement because that's what's expected; one is supposed to think and say (not easily distinguished by the young child) what the teacher suggests. The mind twiddling that occurs when an adult suggests (or tries to extract) the "right" answer from the child is bothersome to both our teachers because it feels deceptive. The presumed objective—for Maria genuine autonomy of thought, for Hardie obedience to an external truth—is eroded by subtle yet insistent suggestiveness. The apparent autonomy that comes from getting the right answer is illusory, for the collective decisions are not genuinely discovered or truly accepted by the children.

Consistent with their orientations, however, both Maria and Hardie can hold a meeting and sidestep the problem of leading. Downer, probably a more typical teacher, cannot. Maria, with her moral uncertainty, avoids leading by asking questions openly and trying to accept the group's decisions. She might in some circumstances even let the children experiment with retaliation and use the experience for further reflection. As long as playground problems do not involve serious injury, why interfere with the children's resolution? She trusts that with sufficient experience of being the revenged upon as well as the revenger, they will find more productive solutions to their disagreements. An added benefit of such a policy is that it discourages tattling, a source of confusion for Alfred. Most significantly, it fits with her genuine commitment to constructivism.

Hardie avoids leading because he combines moral certainty with a nonconstructivist pedagogy. In the service of morality, he is quite comfortable wielding undisguised authority when persuasion is likely to fail. If Hardie had been at the helm when Roger suggested picking on and swearing at Peter, he would simply have asserted that there were better solutions and named them.

For Downer, a morally certain teacher who is (at least on this occasion) acting as a constructivist, the problem is more acute. Given confidence in moral truths (retribution is wrong, period) he cannot just leave the decision to the children. He feels obligated to lead them to the right answers, despite the possible compromise to their autonomy. To justify the probing, he would likely say that because the right solution is obvious and will eventually become obvious to the children, hinting ("scaffolding" in today's lingo) does not corrupt their thinking; rather, it's a process of unearthing latent knowledge. It's the same process as extracting the right answer to an arithmetic problem. Meanwhile, getting children to engage a moral problem and securing their consent to a solution, even when they are led to it by the teacher, is preferable to either a wrong decision or an authoritarian proclamation.

In real life, of course, the belief systems of teachers are more blurred than those of Maria, Hardie, and Downer. In real life it is hard to distinguish genuine questioning, persuading, suggesting, and discussing. A question such as "How do you think we should behave when we have a visitor?" can be a genuine inquiry, an order, or an infiltration. However, the teacher probably knows the differences, knows if he is truly interested in what the children think or is merely trying to elicit the right answer. When he is determined that children come to the "right" decision, even when it is clearly not on their trajectory, then better, Hardie would argue, that he decouple his ideas from theirs and simply make the demand.

A teacher like Maria, who is comfortable with open class discussions and glad to experiment with higher levels of Bonham's schema, will reverse herself when the children reject her critical bottom-line values. Although for a while she might tolerate the conflict between Peter and Mark and permit retaliation by Mark or accept the bullying by Peter, eventually she would override either, if one was repeatedly or seriously being harmed. If the children held on to other views, she would either impose a solution or lead them to the right answer. As much as she values democratic practices, she believes that there are limits to the children's self-rule resulting from the nature of schools and their own immaturity. And so we come to the third peg that conditions our notions about children's participation in moral decisions: their developmental maturity.

## Class Discussions and Child Development

If instead of fifth graders, Downer had had a class of four-year-olds, neither he nor the others would grant them substantial authority over the resolution of conflicts. Obviously, the extent of children's emotional and cognitive maturity bears upon *any* moral education approach. In particular, the finding of developmental psychologists that the rational cognitive capacities of young children lag behind their emotions and are not independent of them will strongly influence a teacher's pedagogy.

Children habitually assemble experiences into emotional polarities: Good and bad are easy distinctions. As Kieran Egan (1988) observed, "Before children can walk or talk, before they can skate or ride a bicycle, they know joy and fear, love and hate, power and powerlessness" (p. 28). In the morality of the young, what becomes characterized as good or bad is closely tied to desires and fears. Anything we enjoy, are praised for, or aspire to, is a candidate to be regarded as good. Conversely, that which we dislike, are scolded for, or condemn is likely to be considered bad.

Empathy appears to be another "given" of the human mind. As a global reaction of distress to the distress of others, this response is apparent long before a child can appraise the basis of the distress.

With age, empathy is modulated by cognitive understandings; it becomes a more refined response, with more carefully chosen targets. Self-regarding distress shades into other-regarding sympathy. Further, a child comes to feel more empathy for those who suffer enduring rather than temporary life-insults, and for those who are close rather than remote. Empathy is, however, an inconstant force, frequently failing in competition with egoistic drives and dependent on pressure from the adult world for its robustness.

Another "given" of the human condition, fortunate for the socialization of morality, is the attachment that children develop to those responsible for their gratifications. Because they love and seek love from the hand that feeds them, they eagerly respond to parental approval and disapproval. Parents, aided by the leverage of attachment, can sensitize even the prerational child to what is morally most critical by meting out their strongest approbation and disapprobation for the values they most cherish.

At first the child is obedient in order to avoid disapproval or avoid jeopardizing the attachment. But accompanying a growing separation from parents is a deepening identification with them: The child comes to share and incorporate parental values as his or her own. Thus, around school-entry age, resisting the temptation to steal a cookie, hitherto motivated by fear of being caught and suffering the attendant disapproval, becomes to varying degrees, depending on situational forces (conspicuously, that of self-interest), a self-addressed directive against violating one's own conscience. Obeying out of fear becomes obeying out of guilt. Adults deepen guilt by drawing on a child's empathy. They point to the child's responsibility for harm caused to another— "You just pushed Billy, that wasn't nice"—and stress the feelings of the injured party—"How would you feel if Sally took your toy, if Sally didn't give you a turn?"

Until approximately ages seven to nine, young children are prelogical, in the state that Kohlberg calls "preconventional" and Piaget calls "moral realism."

What is the problem with younger children's reasoning? According to Piaget, the limitation lies in the self-centered or "egocentric" nature of their thinking. This is not a conventional self-centeredness, which presupposes knowing others' interests but privileging one's own. It is rather a simple inability to see the world through the eyes of another, to understand the likeness between other minds and one's own. Although acts such as stealing and lying are perceived as wrong, the wrongness lies in rule-breaking, not in the harm inflicted. The younger child treasures her own property, but simply isn't aware of the property interests of others, and a lie is not understood as injuring the lied-to.

The younger child is above all a literalist. She judges the seriousness of an offense by its material results, not by the perpetrator's intentions. For example, the young child believes that the rule "don't bite" doesn't mean "don't hit," the rule "don't lie to a parent" doesn't mean "don't lie to a friend," and that breaking one dish on purpose isn't as bad as breaking a lot of dishes by accident. These views fade only gradually, hanging on under some circumstances until late in elementary school.[1]

As for lying, the bigger the discrepancy and the more *unlikely* the false statement, the more evil the perceived lie. Thus, saying you saw a dog twice the size of a cow is, to a six-year-old, worse than saying you got a good grade when you got no grade. Because there is nothing unusual about receiving good grades, the lie about grades is insignificant; such an event could happen and parents are likely to believe it is true. "It is therefore only a little lie, all the more innocent because a mother is taken in by it," whereas there is no such thing as a dog bigger than a cow (Piaget, 1952, p. 151).

By age ten a reversal has occurred. The very credibility of the lie is now a reason for condemnation rather than exculpation; the naughtier child is he who deceived his mother by saying that the teacher was pleased with his work. "*Why is he the naughtiest? Because the mother knows quite well that there aren't any dogs as big as cows. But she believed the child who said the teacher was pleased*" (Piaget, 1952, p. 154).

To the younger child, morality is obedience. As autonomous thinking increases, children begin the process of critical rationality; they move from a view of obedience as an inherent obligation to a growing concern for fairness, first recognizing that although the command is unjust, obedience nonetheless trumps fairness, and finally believing that fairness trumps obedience.

A parent or educator may respond with skepticism to the notion of a child's long apprenticeship in moral rationality. After all, we urge quite small children to give way (turn over a toy, let pass an act of aggression) to younger ones on the ground that the smaller child cannot understand rules of fairness, which we presume the slightly older child does understand. When we get compliance, we assume our argument was accepted. But this assumption may be wrong. A six-year-old probably does not understand why her parents get angry when she throws an object or hits another child while they tolerate the very same behavior from her three-year-old sibling. The child obliges because she is obedient to authority, perhaps also because she has empathy for the younger child. Only later will she come to understand that compensation for age differentials is a form of equity; even then, she might resist unless being fair is becoming part of her emerging moral identity.

The young child, then, largely *feels* his way into an early quasi-morality. He starts with a strong tendency to slot experience into moral-emotional polarities. In his own mind, the good is what feels good. It is what he desires

---

[1]The impact of this "realism" on judgments of culpability is illuminated through Piaget's inquiries of children's responses to clumsiness, stealing, and lying. For a full treatment of this work, see Goodman and Lesnick (2001).

and admires, what is desired from him and admired in him, what nurtures his empathic feelings and avoids generating feelings of guilt. It is a start to his moral journey, but without benefit of more cognitive maturity, it is a whimsical and unpredictable start.

That the young lead with their feelings is not a matter for regret for early feelings are suffused with moral sentiments, however diffuse. Over the years, what start as fleeting sentiments become transformed into an independent self-conscious component of the self—call it moral identity—with the cognitive element growing in importance. There are obvious hazards on the journey: The child's morality, undernourished by caretakers, may fail to develop altogether or, insensitively nourished, may grow askew, tilting excessively to the cognitive or emotional. Why is tilting a hazard? Because, if one only *knows* the interests of another without *feeling* them, there will be no will to act, whereas if one merely *feels* for someone else's interests, without *understanding* the basis of their call, there will be moral blundering. Blending the cognitive and emotional, therefore, is a prime objective of moral education; indeed, we think that the extent to which an adult persistently and consistently accentuates moral considerations in his or her life has much to do with the successful unification of these two sources, as well as the prominent residence of the moral in one's self-image.

## Class Discussions and Authority Reconsidered

Discussions of class discussions often center on facilitative procedures such as how to include all children, elicit all opinions, take turns, prevent interruptions, support classmates, organize suggestions, and plan for next steps.[1] Such advice is helpful, we believe, only *after* a teacher has rigorously considered her leadership role, that is, should the issue be submitted to the children in the first place? If so, to what extent will it be resolved by the children, mutually by the teacher and children, or indirectly or directly just by the teacher? These decisions, in turn, rest upon the teacher's preferred pedagogy (constructivist or behaviorist), her moral certainty, and her judgments as to the children's developmental status. The more you tilt towards constructivism, moral uncertainty, and a presumption of maturity, the more you will toss them the ball; the reverse is true as well. Once again, the particular leanings of a teacher, we believe, are less important than her awareness of them. "Know thyself" is a worthy goal here as elsewhere.

Those who know themselves well will avoid Downer's all-too-common plight: A teacher requests a class meeting to "discuss" a problem but closes off suggested resolutions that are distasteful, then grills the children until they come up with his preferences. It is crucial, we think, that the decision-making

---

[1]See, for example, Child Development Project, 1996; Lickona, 1991.

power one *gives* to children is no greater than one's willingness to *accept* their decisions. When it is *your* decision they must reach, and leading is the process to that outcome, the invasion of their minds can cloud the independence of their thoughts. Given the likelihood that young children will often come to the *wrong* decisions on such moral issues as aggression, responsibility, and retribution, this invasion will be frequent.

The ideal teacher will be flexible in her use of authority. In areas of moral certainty and with younger children it has an important role. Telling rather than asking is also *sometimes* more respectful of the child. It is an honest nondeceptive insistence that the child live by our rules, that she, for example, must respect the rights and property of others, even when she does not and cannot understand the reasons why. That will come. Building up habits of conformity to bedrock values, hopefully few in number, is a foundational process. With age comes the understanding, and perhaps productive disagreement.

At every age level there needs to be a balance between the teacher's exercise of authority and deference to children. In this effort, especially in the early grades, one appeals to the feelings of children — empathy, attachment, identification, and to their impressionability, so that the moral life is seen as warm, vital, splendid. Within a grade and from one grade to another, the processes of stepping forward to enforce rules and stepping back to give children decision-making power are themselves a complex mix of dogmatic, emotional, and rational appeals, with the rational lagging behind the emotional. The exercise of control depends as well on the actual issue (more control for more serious matters) and on the personality and comfort levels of the people involved.

## Your Turn:
## The When and How of Class Meetings

Class meetings have obvious merit in a moral education program. We do see them as core. However, managing the discussion wisely requires the teacher to examine closely the topic, the objective, and the roles of the discussants. The teacher must be clear on a number of factors:

- An incident to be discussed is not prematurely described as a "problem."
- The discussion is not meant or taken as punishment.
- The topic is appropriate for the teacher to raise with the group (rather than a few children, a single child, child and parent, or just parent).
- The topics are generated by children and adults. Those relating to a specific class issue are preferred over hypothetical dilemmas.

- Topics are ongoing and solutions understood as tentative.
- Topics that are basically directives should proceed at levels 1 to 3, those with more open endings should proceed at levels 4 to 6.

1. Bearing in mind the above constraints, pick an incident familiar to you (or one mentioned in this chapter) and conduct a dialogue with yourself or others imagining the flow of questions and answers. Be particularly attentive to how far you are comfortable "going" with the children, "leading" the children, "persuading" the children, or "directing" them. Ask yourself what is the *source* of your preference.

2. There is an upsurge of concern over bullying. It takes many forms: cliques, ostracism, assault, teasing, pranks, mockery, gossip, and so on. Imagine two girls in your class who are systematically excluded from the conversations and social activities of the larger group. They also happen to come from the "wrong side of the tracks," and you have heard remarks ridiculing their clothing.

    Would you consider addressing this topic in a class meeting? If so, at what level or combination of levels, and why?

3. A group of fifth graders asks you, as their teacher, to hold a class meeting about homework. The children have a number of complaints and suggestions: Some object to nightly homework and want to have assignments due every other day or even once a week. Others object to the class time that is taken up with correcting and reviewing homework and think it could be done more efficiently if they were just given answer keys. Some students find homework itself useless. They think it should be given only to those who are falling behind.

    What is your reaction to this appeal? Would you allow some but not all of the topics to be aired? How would you frame the discussion? How openly would you conduct the meeting? Who, in the end, would make the decisions?

4. Think of Melissa (of Kleenex infamy) acting as she did, only now she is in kindergarten rather than fifth grade. You will recall (see p. 1) that we raised seven response options for your consideration. Now that you are confronted by a younger Melissa, would you make a different choice? If so, what is your rationale (consider both your objectives and your assumptions regarding her understanding)?

# CHAPTER 4

# MORAL EDUCATION INSERVICE

## *Scenario*

Aware that there was more to moral education than class meetings, the teachers (reluctantly) gave Helter their consent for an inservice. Nonetheless, Maria was surprised, just a week following their discussion of class meetings, to hear the principal announce on the intercom a forthcoming inservice on character education by Dr. Jan Bonham. Spying Aggie in the hall, she asked, "Aggie, must we really have this Bonham inservice so soon"?

"You bet!" Aggie responded. Helter is moving quickly because he's been getting a lot of parent complaints. Nothing we don't already know: The cafeteria is bedlam, with kids talking rudely to food servers, saving seats for friends, discarding wrappers anywhere, and sometimes even leaving food on the floor. The school is a mess, with littered hallways, dirty bathrooms, and some graffiti on the walls. The children curse, shove, fight, interrupt teachers and one another, talk during class, and chew gum. They look awful, with some of the older boys sporting brightly dyed hair and a few of the older girls wearing eye makeup, nose rings, and some very tight skirts."

"So, is Jan Bonham supposed to descend from the ivory tower to tell us how to deal with this stuff?," Maria asked with irritation. "Don't get me wrong. I think her meeting with our group was really helpful because she was addressing a specific issue—the role of a teacher in leading a class meeting—and what she did helped *us* develop our thoughts and proposal. But laying out the ABCs of moral education to the faculty as a whole seems premature. Couldn't you have persuaded Helter to have a discussion among the faculty first?"

"Actually, I didn't try, Maria. I thought bringing Bonham here was better than the likely alternatives."

"Which were . . . ?"

"'Cracking down,' I think it's called. Assigning a fleet of monitors—you can guess who the monitors would have been—to the hallways, lunchrooms, bathrooms, and the grounds outside school."

"Well, thanks, I guess, for heading that off, but now we'll have a lesson on Aristotle's virtues and the kids will stop chewing gum, right?"

"Maria, let's give her a chance. I share your doubts. I told Helter we needed something practical, none of the airy-fairy stuff of the college classroom. But look, sometimes 'practical' doesn't cut it either. Cracking down is plenty practical, but neither you nor I could stomach too much of it. Some of the teachers and parents, I strongly suspect, would advocate going beyond monitors. I've heard suggestions for bathroom passes, silence in the hallways, assigned seats in the cafeteria, parental sign-off on every piece of homework, more detentions, and. . . ."

"OK, Aggie, I get the picture. I'll come with an open mind. See you there."

Maria arrived early for the inservice to welcome her former teacher. Jan Bonham greeted her warmly.

"Hi, Maria. It's good to see you again so soon after our meeting with Aggie Cerine and your other committee colleagues. But after that meeting I was remembering some classroom discussions last year in which you were pretty skeptical about moral education. Now you're on a committee to develop a program in the area! You haven't become a convert, have you?"

Put at ease by Bonham's lighthearted manner, and flattered by her memory, Maria replied, "Well, I've got to admit I may be a little sadder but wiser than I was last May, but you don't quite yet have a convinced disciple on your hands."

"Perhaps today will turn the tide," Jan smiled. "Meanwhile, how about giving me a hand with these displays. I'd like to lay the booklets out on the table and tack the charts to the wall."

Maria began rummaging through the large well-stocked bags, pulling out posters, spiral notebooks, videos, handouts, articles. She vaguely recognized the materials. They came from the better known moral education programs—Character Counts Coalition, Character Education Curriculum, CHARACTER *plus*™, Child Project, Community of Caring, Heartwood Curriculum, Jefferson Center for Character Education, Just Schools, Second Step. Maria was pleased that it apparently wasn't going to be a heavy theory trip. But whatever relief that awareness gave her was overshadowed by her instinctive discomfort with the materials she was looking at. Objectifying the teaching of morality, all these how-to books, posters, catchy mottoes, songs, even public-address announcements—it just didn't sit right with her.

She thought back to her parochial school days. The nuns would have been appalled by this; her parents, too. It felt crude (even though it was slick), excessive, yet also insufficient—something like shopping for food in a huge supermarket with rows of products all overwrapped, overdecorated, and overpromising.

She also realized that the packaged approach offended her. It re-minded her of ads on how to succeed in love and marriage: five ways to please your significant other, or your money back! It was troubling enough when she had to attend workshops on how to teach reading. Even then, she had objections. The process was too various, complex, and individual-istic to be so prescriptive, but literacy is duck soup compared to teaching children to become decent human beings.

Decency, she mused, is a subtle accomplishment. You pick it up, mostly at home, in little ways. You notice how family members treat one another, how they express their care and expectations for you and others, what matters to them, and their reactions when they and you fall short. Learning to be decent *is* a lot like learning to love. It's about cultivating a generous spirit, embracing the other person's viewpoint, admitting to error, aspiring to be better, taking on worthy challenges. She was beginning to get a handle on her nagging misgivings. Morality was too precious, she revered it too much, to see it turned into concrete lesson plans. Maybe that was why she was wary of bringing it into the school curriculum in the first place.

Jan broke in on her reverie. "How's it going, Maria? What do you think of this stuff?"

Maria chose to respond only to the first question. "Sorry, Dr. Bonham, I got distracted by the materials. I'll get the job done quickly so you can start on schedule."

After briefly introducing the topic and its importance, Bonham fo-cused on the several aspects emphasized by different moral education programs and the varying ways they addressed each.

"Many programs," she began, "emphasize instruction in *moral charac-ter*. They enumerate a 'catalogue of virtues,' a list of qualities thought to be constitutive of good character. So, the well-known Six Pillars of the Char-acter Counts Coalition are trustworthiness, respect for others, responsibility (including accountability, excellence, and self-restraint), fairness, caring, and citizenship, while the Character Education Curriculum (CEC) identifies a full dozen so-called basic universal values: honesty, truthfulness, gener-osity, kindness, helpfulness, justice, tolerance, honor, courage, convictions, equality, and freedom. Neither program, however, can rest content with naming only six, or even twelve, virtues. Character Counts packs seven more virtues into the meanings it ascribes to several of the six, and the CEC adds eleven to its original twelve.[1]

---

[1]The Character Counts Coalition includes honesty, integrity, promise keeping, and loyalty within trustworthiness, and accountability, excellence, and self-restraint within responsibility. The supplementary list of the Character Education Curriculum specifies "good self-esteem, responsi-bility, drug prevention education, self-discipline for setting and achieving goals, critical thinking, decision-making skills, resisting negative peer pressure, respect for rules, laws, and authority, accepting individual differences, cooperative learning, and economic security."

"The Jefferson Center for Character Education focuses on honesty, respect, responsibility, integrity, courage, tolerance, justice, and politeness, while the Heartwood Curriculum promotes courage, loyalty, justice, respect, hope, honesty, and love. I suggest that you reflect less on the specifics of the lists than on their differences in tone and quality, the overall comprehensive message of each. Perhaps you will find it helpful to meet in small groups to generate your own catalogue.

"A second aspect of many of the programs is their desire to encourage what we might call *moral action*. This can be promoted through a variety of approaches, such as (1) urging students to participate in school governance (through student councils, peer mediation, and conflict resolution); (2) requiring students to keep their own space orderly, complete their work with high standards, and cooperate with others; (3) carrying on compulsory service-learning projects, inside the school and outside. Within the school, students may be asked to tutor or befriend other children, or help in the library, cafeteria, or office; outside, they might work with the elderly or disabled, help out in an animal shelter, mount drives (clothes, food, toys), or participate in environmental projects.

"A third aspect emphasized in some programs is the development of what we might term *moral thinking*. This is encouraged through group discussions of class issues that raise moral questions, the teacher's presentation of moral dilemmas, exploration of moral issues in the curriculum, or reflective decision making.

"The Jefferson program is an example of a highly structured version of this, featuring a decision-making model called by the acronym *STAR*, which stands for Stop, Think, Act, and Review,[1] while the Character Education Curriculum more simply uses everyday classroom issues as dilemmas for discussion: Should one give up his swing for another, and if so, when? What's the difference between tattling and honesty? Is it fair for children to exclude others from play groups? The Philosophy for Children (Montclair State) program promotes philosophical reasoning as a way to develop ethical thinking. The Heartwood Curriculum would enhance 'moral literacy and ethical judgment' through legends and folk tales drawn from the world's literature; and the Child Development Project stresses the importance of building 'caring classroom communities' through guided discussions designed to forward student involvement in decisions about such classroom issues as how to act with a substitute teacher.

"A fourth approach is to emphasize *moral feeling*. Second Step, for example, is designed to reduce aggressive and impulsive behavior by teaching children to empathize with the feelings of others rather than to

---

[1] Each word is more fully described: *Stop* ("Take the appropriate amount of time to think through the action about to be taken"), *Think* ("Make a mental list of options that are available in a particular situation"), *Act* ("Choose the best alternative and take appropriate action"), and *Review* ("Ask, 'Did my action get me closer to or farther from my goals and how did it affect others?'").

react precipitously. They have a series of lessons for elementary school students directed toward advancing these social-emotional skills.

"Finally, notice how some programs seek to develop *moral motivation,* and how their methods differ. These programs may single out specific virtues for a week or month and award children who have excelled through public recognition (announcements, awards, photographs in the school, articles in the school paper). Identified virtues become occasions of school pride and are included in logos, posters, back-to-school nights, parent-teacher conferences, sporting events, assemblies, and the strategic plans of a school. The Child Development Project, by contrast, takes a more intrinsic view of motivation, emphasizing cooperative learning as a means of cultivating children toward the desire to be kind and generous to each other.

"I've said a mouthful. Let's take a break, during which you can talk informally among yourselves and examine what is on the walls more closely before we come together again for some small-group discussion."

Engrossed by the presentation, Maria was forced to recognize not only the considerable variety among the programs in both content and method of delivery, but the fact that each was more complex than she had first noted. Her rush to judgment was, once again, too hasty. She was drawn to the programs that were less packaged and more process-oriented, to those that relied on intrinsic rather than extrinsic motives, and those that used words such as "constructivist," "collaborative," "caring."

Nonetheless, she remained skeptical. "Cooperative learning" sounded good, but she now knew of its fragility. She had witnessed how quickly cooperation is undermined by dominant kids who lord it over submissive ones and children who complain about one another. After her recent experiences, she thought it might be too utopian to bank so much on the natural emergence of goodness from a group of children.

While Maria was alternately struggling against her judgmental crabbiness and succumbing to it, Hardie, seated a few rows away, was beaming with enthusiasm. At the break, he beckoned her to the Character Counts Coalition table.

"Get a look at this great stuff, Maria. These folks really have their act together. The Six Pillars provide a terrific structure for what we should all be doing. And look what an impressive membership they've got! It runs the gamut from William Bennett to Marian Wright Edelman.[1] I'd like to order copies and have them displayed prominently in my room. Wouldn't you? Sure beats the maps and planets now up on the walls. I wonder if we can get Helter to pony up funds."

---

[1] William Bennett was Secretary of Education in the Reagan administration and is a leading conservative proponent of character education. Marian Wright Edelman is the founder and longtime director of the Children's Defense Fund, a liberal children's advocacy organization.

Maria's quizzical look was plain to see. "For God's sake, don't tell me Maria Laszlo disapproves of Trustworthiness, Respect, Responsibility, Fairness, Caring, and Citizenship?"

"Disapprove? No, Hardie, it's not disapproval. Just something in me says 'not so fast.' I'm not sure where these virtues get you or just what they mean. What's the difference between honesty and truthfulness, between generosity and helpfulness? Aren't there times when honesty is unkind, when generosity is unhelpful? And some of the 'virtues' don't seem to have much to do with character. How did self-esteem get on the list of moral traits? I also sense something dangerous lurking behind these seemingly noncontroversial attributes. Can't any demand be justified as a matter of respect and responsibility? Did you ever read the *Handbook for Schooling Hitler Youth* [Brennecke, 1938]? It talks a lot about promise keeping, courage, loyalty, responsibility, discipline, and unselfishness."

"That's absolute rubbish, Maria," said Hardie, obviously irritated by the Nazi reference. "Of course, any word or concept can be undermined, even 'love' and 'beauty.' I cherish the virtue words, and I can't fathom your distaste for them. Yes, they're old-fashioned, hardly a mark against them. They express who we are, we as a country, we as citizens who believe in playing by rules, in treating one another fairly and generously. They're about taking our responsibilities seriously. Frankly, Maria, if we don't have demanding expectations of children, we sell them short and undermine their potential."

"Hardie, I apologize for the crack about the Hitler Youth. I too am a proud American, if also a critical one, and that too is part of our grand tradition. Maybe we can have some reasonable discussion of the moral ed programs at the next break. I hear Bonham calling us back into session."

Bonham, noting the animated talk all around, suggested that for twenty minutes the participants break up into small groups to consider their reactions. "Choose what seems most salient for you to explore, but let me put out a few questions: What do you see as the relative value of each of what I have called 'aspects of a moral education program,' namely, generating lists of behavioral or characterological goals (virtues), engaging in moral actions, developing moral thinking, or fostering moral motivation? What about the means by which each of these is pursued in the various programs?"

As the teachers gathered in small groups, Hardie and Maria quickly sought out Aggie and Connie so that they could make use of this opportunity to talk together further. Connie was first to speak.

"I overheard you two going at each other during the break over virtue lists and the like. Can we backtrack to a more fundamental problem I have?"

Her three colleagues nodded, and she began. "Frankly, I just don't think the school is equipped to take any of this on. I mean, if we selected some small, very small, piece—say getting kids to greet the teacher in the morning, or walk in the halls when they go to lunch—OK, but this business of selecting various ingredients of an extended menu and putting them together into a whole-school program, I don't see how we can pull that off. Even if we could, the parents—that's my constituency—wouldn't stand for it: too big a cut into time that's supposed to be for academics (read preparation for high-stakes testing).

"Here's an example—perhaps an extreme one, but I'm not sure—of what I mean. I found this statement of "Eleven Principles of Character Education" on the display table. It's put out by the Character Education Partnership (1996) and written by Tom Lickona, Eric Schaps, and Catherine Lewis—some of the biggies in the field.

1. Character education promotes core ethical values as the basis of good character.
2. "Character" must be comprehensively defined to include thinking, feeling, and behavior.
3. Effective character education requires an intentional, proactive, and comprehensive approach that promotes the core values of all phases of school life.
4. The school must be a caring community.
5. To develop character, students need opportunities for moral action.
6. Effective character education includes a meaningful and challenging academic curriculum that respects all learners and helps them succeed.
7. Character education should strive to develop students' intrinsic motivation.
8. The school staff must become a learning and moral community in which all share responsibility for character education and attempt to adhere to the same core values that guide the education of students.
9. Character education requires moral leadership from both staff and students.
10. The school must recruit parents and community members as full partners in the character-building effort.
11. Evaluation of character education should assess the character of the school, the school staff's functioning as character educators, and the extent to which students manifest good character.

"That's just for starters," Connie continued. "Take number 10, about recruiting parents. Regarding that single criterion, the statement says, 'parents should be represented on the character leadership committee that does the planning, the school should actively reach out to disconnected subgroups of parents, and all parents need to be informed about—and have a chance to react and consent to—the school's proposed core values and how the school proposes to try to teach them.' It then goes on to advocate recruitment of the wider community in promoting the central values.

"I don't know how you guys react, but I ask myself, in what world can anything approaching this scale be done?"

"Now that's the voice of practicality we all need to keep in mind, Connie," Aggie said, "but I hear those eleven criteria as a statement of aspiration rather than an action plan. The question is whether, taken in that spirit, it points us in the right direction, or whether something more narrowly focused on student misbehavior is what's called for. Maybe, Connie, we should start with your idea of a few discrete changes and focus our attention on them."

"Not so fast," objected Hardie. "I'd like us to take a serious look at those criteria, along with others. I too think of these eleven principles as an invitation, what you call a set of aspirations. So even though I think they are pointing in the wrong direction, because they hardly focus on student misbehavior at all, as you suggest, Aggie, I wouldn't reject, out of hand, thinking about a moral education program in an ambitious way.

"Still," Hardie went on, "in the interest of practicality, so we don't feel overwhelmed prematurely, I'm willing to start modestly, but not with classroom greetings and running in the hall. Those are such small-ticket items and such obvious imperatives that they should be part of our regular expectations of children. I agree with Maria, we don't need a program for such matters."

"Good to be on the same side, Hardie," Maria replied. "But I suspect we have different reasons for rejecting their inclusion. I don't want a program for morning greetings and running in the halls, or for that matter removing hats, because I see them as mere conventions. There is nothing sacrosanct about them. To some extent they are administrative conveniences, though I guess you, Hardie, see them as indicators of respect."

"Just a minute, you guys," interrupted Aggie. "What do you think about Connie's issue? Should we reject the eleven-criteria approach as just too ambitious, regardless of what we think of its specific priorities? Perhaps we might look at the list and find just one to dig into?"

"Looking over Connie's shoulder and reading some of the small print," Maria jumped in, "I vote we discuss number 5, about how students need opportunities for moral experiences. In the small print it refers to students as 'constructive learners' who need to tangle with 'real-life challenges.' I take it that means working out the rules as a community, not just adhering to preordained edicts."

"Well, we're pretty much out of time for now, Maria," said Aggie, forestalling Hardie's predictable objection to Maria's approach. "But we shouldn't let all of this good energy evaporate. Let's check our appointment books right now, and see when we can get together again."

## TEACHERS' MUSINGS

### Hardie

All these skeptical women, how come? I feel so at odds with their objections and fears. The possibility of putting our energies into moral education gives me a marvelous jolt of excitement, a renewed sense of what might be possible, almost a sense of deliverance from school as it has become.

This is such important stuff. It's what schools should take on as their number-one priority. I find the virtues of the moral education programs inspiring, I even felt uplifted by the mottoes and songs that so disturbed Maria. If we, the faculty, rallied behind the spirit of the virtue lists, so would the kids. Awards fit fine with me too. Why not? They are effective. We award athletes and scholars. Imagine a character plaque claiming equal prestige with a football trophy. Now wouldn't that be something!

Of course Maria had a point. Dangling words like respect and responsibility at kids when what you're really after is obedience, yeah, that's a problem. But on the whole I just don't believe teachers abuse their authority. That Nazi reference was infuriating. It was an assault against our time-tested traditions and against our teachers who are simply asking kids to be well mannered and thoughtful of others. That accusation is what I would call disrespectful and irresponsible.

Anyhow, we could do with a bit more obedience. It would center the pendulum, which has moved too far toward individual self-chosen rights (around here that means automatic objections to school rules). Falling in line, doing what you're told—within reason—is the foundation of an ordered community. How else can the general welfare, as opposed to the individual's self-interest, prevail? And doing what you're told, followed by imposing those rules on ourselves, is the basis of self-discipline and self-denial, the means by which we protect the group against individualistic excesses. Even when the rules may not express big ethical principles, obeying them is a crucial form of demonstrating respect for the teacher and the educational enterprise. It seems a stretch in today's climate, but I think we need to build a reverence for schools as much as rituals build reverence in religious institutions.

I'd push hard on rules and the development of habits, especially habits that are difficult, whether or not the particular behavior has intrinsic merit. It's how you build character. The child who is taught to put pennies in the bank is more likely to become thrifty than the one who isn't. The child who is taught to save up his pennies and donate them to a good cause is more likely to become charitable than the one who is merely asked, "Would you like to save your money and give some of it away?"

In my class, from day one the children stand up first thing in the morning and in unison say, "Good morning, Mr. Knox." I guess that seems old-fashioned, but I think it's a good habit. It starts the day by forcing them to pay respect to me, and more than to me, to the role of a teacher who is leading them to a better place. More broadly, it gives them the habit of attending to those who are guiding them and, at least at the beginning, being gracious toward them. I suppose the greeting is fairly meaningless to many of the kids, as is saying the Pledge of Allegiance, or so I'm told (although I don't recall its being meaningless to me). But the meaning of the pledge will come along in time. *Then* the students will be glad they know it by heart, and I bet they'll recall with pride how each day they stood before the flag, a symbol of our great country, and expressed their commitment to something other than themselves. These days a lot of kids (and their parents) object to taking the pledge. OK, if it violates a prohibition on taking oaths, or if they are atheists I can excuse them, but if it's just because they have a disagreement with the politics of the moment, or just because they don't like the coerciveness of it, well that leaves me cold—angry, actually.

When I took Bonham's course, Emile Durkheim was the philosopher who most appealed to me. He talked about the "discipline of the school." Discipline included such conventional behaviors as being punctual, listening to and not interrupting others, and doing one's lessons and homework well. These disciplines are good not just in and of themselves but because they teach restraint, allow us to inhibit our impulses, and contribute to self-mastery. I believe that is more important than, or maybe essential to, the buzzwords of today—"self-confidence," "self-fulfillment," "a positive self-image." Without self-mastery there is only very limited freedom, because if we are driven by our passions, we can't emancipate ourselves sufficiently from them to make any thoughtful choices.

## Maria

Why am I such a curmudgeon about going forward with a moral education program? Now that I've seen how saturated the school day is with moral decisions, why don't I welcome the opportunity to think hard about how we handle moral problems? There is a sense in which I agree with Hardie. After all, look how upset I was when the children failed to greet me and were inconsiderate of the newcomers in choosing their seats. A little politeness and sensitivity would have made that first day, and subsequent ones, markedly better for me. Yet I balk. I balk at enshrining conventional rules into moral imperatives and I balk at the excessive use of authority.

To turn hall running into a moral issue just seems wrong. It diminishes the universal power of important values, such as the Golden Rule, and exaggerates the importance of a trifling behavior that is only *sometimes* inappropriate. Running in the halls is a problem only because of safety issues, but running elsewhere is fine. Of course we have to keep the halls safe but *that's* what should be emphasized, not the evils of running. Even worse are the rules of politeness. Why should children stand up when the teacher enters the room? If the children already respect me, it's an empty ritual; if they don't, standing up isn't going to achieve it. Empty rituals are a lot worse than no rituals.

The virtue words that so attract Hardie give me this gnawing sense of an unacknowledged and dangerous political spin. Respect and responsibility seem harmless enough, but are they? Responsibility to whom? For what? Do the demands of every teacher become the responsibilities of every student? Even when a demand conflicts with other obligations? Even when it is a meaningless chore? Are teachers expected to be responsible toward, and to respect, students? Do powerful people and institutions (teachers and schools, vis-à-vis students) have the "responsibility" to act so as to deserve respect? When I was a student, there was plenty of coercion latent in the idea of respect. I believe it blunted rather than enlarged my conscience. Respect is easily transformed into subservience (child to adult, woman to man, follower to leader). So the issue remains, respectful of whom and for what?

Hardie's goal is to have children take on the obligations of studenthood, to inhibit impulses, and to submit to school norms such as listening to the teacher, following her instructions, and completing work on time. It's right to speak of the *force* of character. An individual must be able to stand up and count for something. But you teach these goals by modeling responsible behavior at the same time as you encourage it. You listen to children respectfully, prepare for class carefully, get papers back to students promptly. You also encourage group work, embolden the shy, and restrain the belligerent.

Responsibility has less to do with conformity to the group and its rules than with developing a well-thought-out notion of who one is, how one should behave, and what it means to be faithful to the identity and commitments one makes. So to me, a teacher's job is to help children think rationally about the meaning, purpose, and effect of their actions (in ed-speak, becoming reflective and critical thinkers) and to support the kids, sometimes, when they dare to disregard the opinions of others, to be *un*conventional. Being a responsible person may mean speaking out *against* school rules and school loyalty. It may mean *resisting* the teacher's requests because the teacher is being unfair or because of other more pressing priorities.

## A DEEPER LOOK

In their initial stages of considering moral education, Aggie had hoped that the group would present a set of activities drawn from the field and that the faculty would then endorse a small number of them. She was aware of such possibilities as class discussions, student government, peer tutoring and mediation, service activities, moral dilemmas, character-oriented literature, and major virtues. Even this early on in their planning, however, she and the others had come to realize that morality is both obscure and multifaceted. They could not present a list of suggested activities without more thoroughly analyzing the purposes of this effort and the competing means to accomplish them. Underlying the activities were implicit assumptions that required exposure.

To appreciate these teachers' disputes more fully, *we* need to see the facets *they* see. A child steals lunch from another student. Bad? Yes, if you judge the act alone. But suppose that usually the thief is a wonderfully kind and reliable child and this action is "out of character"? Or what if he took it for a hungry friend, removed only one of two sandwiches, and returned the other? Or supposing he didn't know he shouldn't take the lunch box, doesn't grasp the notion of private property? These considerations would surely modify one's judgment. That's because morality is a mix of one's actions, character (virtues), motivations, and thinking (understanding). Our teachers place differing emphases on these facets.

## An Emphasis on Character (Virtue)

To some, morality is largely a matter of being a certain sort of person. What sort? One of good character. A person of good character has those reliable characteristics, those habitual ways of reacting, that are virtuous. The term "character" can, of course, include a fuller constellation of traits (being humorous, serious, introverted, extroverted), but here we limit it to traits of moral significance, such as benevolence, bravery, tolerance, steadfastness, persistence, self-restraint, temperance, loyalty, and generosity.

Virtue ethicists prioritize the actor (or agent, as philosophers like to call us) over the act on several grounds: First, they claim, our conduct is in fact derivative of who we are; who we are does not derive from our conduct. Second, it is intuitively obvious that for the most part, when judging people we appraise their character, their abiding dispositions, goals, and overall life patterns; we excuse the moral error made by the well-intended and are suspicious of the good deed displayed by the ill-intended. Third, the commingling of feelings and thoughts—moral will, moral sensitivity, and moral analysis—comprised in any virtue, reflect the real-life psychological messiness of moral behavior.

The virtue ethicists come in two variants—one traditional and conservative, the other contemporary and liberal—and they compete vigorously with each other in today's market place. To many character-oriented thinkers, moral virtues, such as those mentioned above, have in common their demand for mastery over what used to be termed our "appetites." Philosopher Philippa

Foot (1978) referred to virtues as "correctives," because they stand "at a point at which there is some temptation to be resisted or deficiency of motivation to be made good. As Aristotle put it, virtues are about what is difficult . . ." (p. 8).

So, Hardie Knox has a number of routines—daily greetings, rituals, chores—in his classroom. The point of them, to Hardie and his like-minded colleagues, is that although not of intrinsic importance, they "build character." Good character is linked to habit formation: Character refers to personal traits of moral significance, habits to patterns of action. Aristotle (1987), for example, who stressed the centrality of character and virtue, asserted that, just as one becomes a builder by building, a harpist by playing the harp, and a brave person by doing brave acts, one becomes virtuous by acting virtuously (Bk. 2, Chs. 3, 4).

To Hardie, morality is primarily about developing self-restraint over self-serving impulses. It is about becoming able and willing to regard the interests of other people with something other than indifference or competitive hostility. That is why he requires children to perform routines, even though the specific routine may have no independent moral valence. The children's growing self-control, he maintains, will benefit others and add value to the community's well-being. Thus, for Hardie, following reasonable rules is itself a moral matter, and it is a teacher's option to select the (reasonable) rules that he or she will prescribe. For the teacher, deciding whether to prescribe any particular rule is optional; for students, following a rule that the teacher has chosen is obligatory.

Maria views Hardie's "routines" as needlessly burdensome, even dangerous, specifically because she regards the making of morally sound decisions as more contextual, more nuanced, more difficult than Hardie acknowledges. Excessive emphasis on habit, in this view, may actually make children less likely to do the right thing, for it neglects what they most need to develop, their powers of reflection.

The other variant of virtue ethics owes its current visibility to feminist thinkers such as Nel Noddings and Carol Gilligan, who have advocated what is often termed an "ethic of care" (or an ethic of relation). These writers find moral significance in our disposition toward others, and a surer guide to action in the realm of affect than in habit. They de-emphasize a morality of rules, which would attempt to imprint maxims of behaviors on children (or adults). Such an approach is seen as both excessively binding and, where no rule is in sight, seriously deficient in its ethical strength. According to the ethic of care, the likelihood of pursuing one path or another has little to do with the dogged inculcation of habitual patterns of behavior or the "curbing" and "correction" of natural appetites. This approach also minimizes the value of rational reflection. In disputes between children it is not analysis of rights and wrongs that produces a just resolution of conflicts, but rather, the ability of each child to empathize ("receptive attention" in Noddings' language) with the other. "Caring-about," said Noddings (2002), "may provide the link between caring and justice. Chronologically, we learn first what it means to be cared for. Then, gradually, we learn both to care for and, by extension, to care about others. This caring-about is almost certainly the foundation for our sense of justice" (p. 22). To seek care and to care about are viewed as inherent human attributes, though certainly needing to be nourished and cultivated.

The ethic of care shares with more traditional character approaches the belief that a person faced with a moral decision will come to know the right response more or less immediately. This insight is brought home in a moving description of "righteous gentiles" who saved European Jews from extermination during World War II by hiding them in their homes (Oliner and Oliner, 1988). When these rescuers were asked why they risked their own lives for strangers, most cited affiliations with political, religious, or social groups that supported the rescuing efforts; others were moved by empathy for the Jews' distress. While thus coming to the decision "built" with virtues, at that moment their decisions were spontaneous. For them, "helping Jews was less a decision made at a critical juncture than a choice prefigured by an established character and way of life" (p. 222). Despite the obvious risks, most of the rescuers reported that they made the decision in "minutes." Indeed, many reported not experiencing a choice; they could not do otherwise.

Both variants of virtue ethics, then, while acknowledging that virtues must be nurtured in order to flourish, are skeptical about the rational component of moral decision making.

## An Emphasis on Action

We must pause before embracing fully the attractions of virtue ethics. Talk of virtuous traits may mean rather less than it appears to do. Lawrence Kohlberg (1981) spoke dismissively of a "bag of virtues," an arbitrary compilation of traits with only vague behavioral implications.

> One difficulty with this approach to moral character is that everyone has his own bag. However, the problem runs deeper than the composition of a given list of virtues and vices. Although it may be true that the notion of teaching virtues, such as honesty or integrity, arouses little controversy, it is also true that a vague consensus on the goodness of these virtues conceals a great deal of actual disagreement over their definitions. What is one person's "integrity" is another person's "stubbornness," what is one person's honesty in "expressing your true feelings" is another person's insensitivity to the feelings of others. . . . Student protesters view their behavior as reflecting the virtues of altruism, idealism, awareness, and courage. Those in opposition regard the same behavior as reflecting the vices of irresponsibility and disrespect for "law and order." Although this difficulty can be recognized clearly in college education, it is easier

for teachers of younger children to think that their judgments in terms of the bag of virtues are objective and independent of their own value biases. However, a parent will not agree that a child's specific failure to obey an "unreasonable" request by the teacher was wrong, even if the teacher calls the act "uncoopera- tive," as some teachers are prone to do (1: pp. 9–10).

Second, virtue-oriented approaches to morality cannot avoid the impor- tance of action, for action is how we come to know character. A courageous person is one who does courageous deeds, the caring person is noted for caring actions. And there's the rub, for caring impulses and habits may lead us astray. Sometimes, for example, excessive caring can suffocate, whereas "tough love" can be a cold-water tonic. The British philosopher G. J. Warnock (1971) insisted that actions are inherently more "fundamental" than character, motives, or feelings:

> [I]t is clearly not *only* actions that are ever the topic of moral thought, or moral discussion or remark. . . . But it seems reasonable to say that . . . some more or less direct reference to actions is always present, and is fundamental. A person is morally good or bad primarily at least because of what he does or omits to do. A morally bad character is a disposition to act morally badly, or wrongly. Motives typically, and feelings often, tend to issue in actions. . . . If a book could sensibly be said to be morally bad, that might be because writing or publishing it was taken to be a morally bad thing to do, or perhaps because reading it was thought liable to prompt people towards acting in morally exceptionable ways. So it seems that, when moral issues come up, there is always involved, more or less directly, some question of the doings or non-doings or rational beings (pp. 12–13) (emphasis in the original).

Hardie believes in the centrality of actions. Although also committed to virtues, character for him is made manifest in actions, not dispositions. To judge the deed, however, is not to act without compassion. On the contrary, Hardie believes, it is the overly permissive, "let's try to understand you" orientation that lacks compassion, for we *become* our deeds; it is our deeds that form us. If, controlled by an adult authority holding the line, a child does the right thing frequently enough, he will find a gratification in righteous behav- ior that is not available through the reactions of other children or talking things over. Doing right will become habitual.

## The Salience of the Actor's Feelings and Motives

Those of Maria's persuasion would look more to the motivation immediately behind the act. They would note that an act may appear benevolent (or malevolent) but take on the very opposite quality once its intention or motive is known. A child's offer to remain after class to help clean up looks less worthy once we find out that her plan was to rifle the supply closet. A student's tattling appears more benign when it is a sincere effort to stop children from hurting one another (as in the Downer scenario) than when it is self-serving. More controversially, we may excuse, or at least condemn less strongly, a student's lie when we learn that he sought to save a fellow from unwarranted abuse or faithfully preserve a secret.

An emphasis on motivation may proceed from skepticism about character-oriented, as well as act-oriented, approaches. Maria does not share Hardie's enthusiasm for character building, or rather her interpretation of character is less puritanical than Hardie's. She too cares about qualities within the person, but more important than general dispositions, she finds, is the motive of each particular act. One who is motivated to protect a secret should not be judged harshly if in certain circumstances she lies (and don't we all?). Virtues and habits, however punctilious and self-restrained, can be mindless, sometimes injurious. Indeed she is suspicious of those stiff-upper-lip folks who are dutiful, who would never cheat or lie, yet are often intolerant, and who have an almost priggish pride in their own goodness. They lack the milk of human compassion, to her a more central trait.

Good motives, of course, are insufficient. Not wanting to "get into trouble" or "make my friend mad at me" can lead one astray. The child must learn to distinguish a motive to protect his or her own comfortable status from more worthy ones. Seemingly decent motives can be an excuse for both cowardice and nastiness. We would not approve of a child who changed a grade on a paper before showing it to his parents in order to keep them happy or, wanting to be approved by the popular, consented to the order, "If you want to get into our club, you can't be friends with so-and-so."

## An Emphasis on Reason (Reflection)

For Lawrence Kohlberg (1981), who follows in the tradition of Immanuel Kant and John Dewey, morality is informed reflection on alternatives in a context of carefully reasoned voluntary choice. Moral education is a matter of teaching children how to *think* about moral questions rather than of exhortation or prescription. A person is virtuous to the extent that she or he resolves conflicting claims as an autonomous agent guided by prescribed rational principles. "I define morality in terms of the formal character of a moral judgment, method, or point of view, rather than in terms of its content" (p. 170). *Morality* is not plural (like *virtues*) but singular, and it finds its source in the child's cognitive development. The essence of morality is justice, but justice is not like the virtues advanced by character education proponents. It is not a behavioral disposition (such as caring) or an attribute of the person (such as honesty); it emerges out of impartial reasoning, through which children learn to balance their (natural) self-interest with that of others.

Note that this stance is one polar opposite of the follow-the-rules ethic to which many schools subscribe. They (and we believe it is a very large "they") are more sympathetic to the approach of Emile Durkheim (1925/1961), an early sociologist concerned with schooling, who maintained that moral behavior is quite simply complying with pre-established rules:

> To conduct one's self morally is a matter of abiding by a norm. . . . This domain of morality is the domain of duty; duty is prescribed behavior. . . . Thus, we can say that morality consists of a system of rules of action that predetermine conduct. They state how one must act in given situations; and to behave properly is to obey conscientiously (pp. 23–24).

Maria's skepticism about rule-following is similar to her skepticism about act-oriented morality. She wants her children to understand the reasoning behind rules, indeed, to do their own reasoning and formulate their own rules to fit their own circumstances. John Dewey (1908/1960) noted that rule-based habits may become perfunctory and encrusted. Under changed conditions, where reexamination is required, adherence to habit leads us astray: "The 'good' man who rests on his oars, who permits himself to be propelled simply by the momentum of his attained right habits, loses alertness; he ceases to be on the lookout. With that loss, his goodness drops away from him" (p. 132).

G. J. Warnock (1971) agreed, emphasizing the centrality of the experience of choice in moral agency:

> [T]o be a "moral agent," the kind of creature capable of acting morally well or ill, and therefore liable to moral judgement in the light of his actions, is . . . to envisage alternative courses of action in those situations, to grasp and weigh considerations for or against those alternatives, and to act accordingly. What is required are certain capacities of understanding and thought, a certain capacity of choice, and also, of course, if these capacities are actually to be exercised, alternative courses of action, at least sometimes, between which to choose (p. 144).

The salience of reflection and choice give rise to a cautionary concern, which applies more broadly than an emphasis on motivation. When an actor may be said to have lacked choice, moral blame is ordinarily withheld. One who is induced by the threat of serious physical harm to commit a wrongful act is normally exonerated. It is not easy to articulate the "certain capacity of choice" that Warnock plausibly described as the condition of culpability. Although the exoneration goes beyond threats of physical harm, it bears emphasis that loss of expected advantages, however strongly desired, plainly does *not* suffice. There is a critical difference between, "I'll beat you up at recess if you don't steal something out of that girl's book bag," and "I won't be your friend [or let you join our club] unless you steal something." The siren song of peer pressure, or the shame of failure ("I had no choice not to cheat on the examination; I needed to pass the course to graduate, and after my parents had paid all that money for my education I couldn't let them down") may ring sympathetically in the ears of many people, young and older, today, but if there is any meaning to the idea of morality as a constraint on choice, it must exclude the justification or excuse that I would have been better off by doing the wrongful act than refraining from it.

## Finding the Balance

The importance of context in one's interpretation of an action suggests to us that an exclusive focus on the *act* will often fall short of producing a sound moral judgment. When a school becomes so rule-bound that attention to a child's intention and understanding is abandoned (often because there are simply too many children breaking too many rules for a thoughtful, flexible, individualized consideration to prevail), it has a moral education program in name only.

Character, motives, and the nature of the decisional process that preceded the act should, justly, exert a greater or lesser pull on one's judgment, depending on circumstances. These features should pull as well on the further question of how best a teacher or school can influence a child whose actions are found to be morally deficient. In our judgment, however, whether one regards as primary the nature of the act, the character of the actor, his or her motives, or the quality of the thinking that went into the decision to act is not the critical factor. What is essential is that a person's preference in that regard not be so powerful as to lead him or her systematically to slight the less favored factors. As elsewhere, what is most important is that each of us be aware of, and *lean a bit against*, our presumptive choice, alert to the presence of particulars in each case that might counsel us to judge more broadly.

## Your Turn:
## Character and Motives

Schools committed to moral education are most likely to adopt a virtue education approach. As the Bonham inservice experience suggests, they either adopt virtues from existing curricula or choose their own set and "advocate" one or more for a week or month.

1. Either individually or with others design your own short "virtue" list and describe the meaning of each selection.
   a) Do you have any problems choosing which virtues to include?
   b) When moving from an abstract term to specific instantiations, do you find that the clarity of the virtue grows murkier?
   c) Can you imagine a critic of virtue education finding the virtue so vague as to be an empty container?
   d) Is there a way to resolve the dispute and maintain a virtue-oriented approach?

2. A child in your class is always "sharing," be it possessions, food, or even money. She also is the first to volunteer for chores and sometimes does them on her own initiative. She is surely kind, generous, and contributing to the class community. Yet you suspect she is trying to "buy" friendship and goodwill.
   a) Are you concerned?
   b) Do you feel justified inspecting her motives?
   c) How might you address this issue?

3. One of your students conducts herself in a loud, sloppy, disorderly manner. Her desk is a mess, she wipes her mouth with her sleeve, she stomps rather than walks, her backpack is sticky from juice stains, and she rarely emits a please or thank you. Yet she is good-natured, no one but you seems to take her behaviors amiss, and she is attentive to her schoolwork.
   a) Do these behaviors represent character flaws?
   b) If so, what virtue does she not possess?
   c) Should the situation be a concern of the teacher or the class?
   d) What would you do?

4. The principal of your school decides to experiment with a character education approach and proposes to select one virtue a month for all teachers to promote in their classroom as they see fit. The first virtue is honesty.
   a) How do you (a fifth-grade teacher) feel about getting this assignment?
   b) How is honesty now handled in your classroom?
   c) What changes, if any, might be prompted in your response to instances of dishonesty?
   d) How might you be proactive in sensitizing children to this virtue?
   e) What advice do you have for the principal?

■ ■ ■ ■ ■

# CHAPTER 5

# MORAL EDUCATION
# AND THE HOME

## *Scenario*

Aggie suggested to Connie that she open the next meeting of the planning group, since she had kept a low profile thus far. Connie readily agreed. She was attracted to the *idea* of frequent class meetings but worried that they might get out of hand. As for moral education in general, Jan Bonham's inservice presentation had merely crystallized her notion that it might undermine the customary home/school separation. Three worries topped her list:

First, personal issues, which she had always thought the province of the guidance staff, would become public. Connie realizes that censoring children's conversations is antithetical to creating class cohesion and to a shared moral mission. Space must be made available for revealing emotions and for frank collective dialogue, but even in these soul-on-your-sleeve times, a place must also be reserved for the semi-private confidences between teacher and student, and for the strictly private life of the child and family. Will facial tics and stuttering, obesity and phobias, all come under the glare of group scrutiny? Will spending habits and dress habits now be publicly reviewed?

Second, she is worried that if children talk freely about the personal, the line between home and school, admittedly permeable, will dissolve altogether. The two concerns are not unrelated. When a child's peculiar or unacceptable behavior becomes a topic for discussion, the focus turns naturally, as it did in the Downer discussion, to the home. Is a child fighting because parents encourage retaliation? Is bullying in school related to neighborhood cliques?

Connie appreciates that this is risky stuff. Children do not develop "caring" if they can't talk frankly about feelings of rejection and sorrow, often rooted in home life. One does not sort out rights and wrongs by shielding exposure of the personal, even less so by disallowing judgments on what might appear to be "personal" matters. (Is it OK to boast about your parents' purchases? Is it OK to bring an expensive electronic device to school and not share it?) Yet all manner of potential problems swarm through her head. Will the teacher need parental permission to discuss personal issues when initiated by a child? Will the teacher ask families for personal details, for example if a child is anxious over a pending divorce? Teachers, she has found, are of mixed minds when it comes to entertaining intimate revelations. The mere mention of a family incident causes some to close down talk, while a few trespass (as she sees it) thoughtlessly into family affairs. But somehow the school has managed to limp along . . . until now.

Third, dissolving boundaries works two ways; the leakage from school to home could be as much a headache as that from home to school. If we police the families, they will increasingly police us—not an attractive prospect. None of the faculty will be pleased to have their limited autonomy eroded further by more parental surveillance and interference. Already each year there were activities at school that raised the hackles of some parents.

The task, Connie ruminates, is for us to develop guidelines on how to preserve parental autonomy and privacy in life at home along with educators' autonomy in life at school, while better connecting both institutions. She imagined it would be easy to reject some personal topics having nothing to do with the moral life of school, for example, sibling relationships or family political affiliations. Others might need to be addressed if the issue spilled over into the classroom, and impinged on relationships at school, for example, divorce, illness, and disabilities. But drawing the line would be a difficult, even treacherous, undertaking. What would they do, for instance, when children, aware of the school's hostile views, wanted to talk about their parents' drinking and smoking habits?

The parental policing of school seemed to be an even tougher assignment. She knew that in the past some parents had objected to the books children were assigned, the courses they took, the extracurricular activities offered. With the additional home/school transparency introduced by moral education, how would the school respond to parent objections? Schools had in mind the best interests of *children,* whereas parents had in mind the best interest of *their child.* Recalling that Hardie had recently mentioned a problem of this sort, Connie opened the planning group's next session on home/school issues with a suggestion that they begin with his account.

Hardie was only too ready to talk. Connie had barely introduced her topic when he blurted out, "Connie, bless you for bringing this up. Against your hypothetical concerns, I've got a real one that calls for immediate action. I hadn't previously seen its relevance to our moral education assignment, but now I realize it's all about boundaries and our own professional autonomy. I'd like some advice from you folks."

"We're all ears," said Connie, delighted at the unusual prospect of a teacher asking advice from the guidance counselor.

"OK, the general topic is who decides whether we initiate a service-learning project, something I think should be core to our moral education plan. But, first, let me describe the problem as it unraveled. A few weeks ago I overheard several girls in my class planning a burial for our two recently deceased hamsters. A couple of the students, unwilling to admit their sorrow even at this age, announced it was stupid to bury stupid animals. Who cares about stupid hamsters! What they wanted in class were real animals, a dog or cat. But of course, they complained, the school would *never* give permission for that. Too much like encouraging fun.

"I decided to channel the steam by calling—Maria, please note—a class meeting. I explained to the children that although school rules almost certainly prohibit dogs and cats, and there was no point in challenging a rule that is clearly a sensible one, I knew the owner of an animal shelter next door to the school and believed he would welcome the help of a few children once a week. We kept talking as a group, not, I should add, at level 6 but very much under my guidance, and other suggestions for 'helping' were raised: Photocopying in the secretary's office, reshelving books in the library, cleaning up the yard, planting seeds, tutoring 'little kids' in kindergarten and first grade.

"I went to Fred Helter and told him the class would like to use one afternoon a week for 'helping' activities. He was enthusiastic: 'Great idea, Hardie. No other elementary school in the district has started service learning, so this project should make us look good to the super. If you begin on a small scale now, we might be able to get a little cash and make it a whole-school activity next year.' So far so good. We quickly made plans and I sent a note home *informing* the parents.

"A few parents replied with favorable comments, but most didn't answer. Then, just as we're preparing to start—trouble! A group of parents, bypassing me, protested directly to Helter. They argued that service activities are inappropriate for children, certainly for their children. Teachers should be raising math and reading scores, not wasting children's time on tutoring. Let the little kids who can't read get outside help; fifth graders need to be prepared for the more demanding academics ahead. Furthermore, if the school is to do 'moral education' it should be about building character, not shelving books in the library. They commented that I did a good job keeping the kids in line, making them courteous, and insisting they develop disciplined work habits. I should stick to that agenda and not get carried away.

"I was furious that they hadn't come to me first but I nonetheless made an effort to appease them. We met at school one evening and I asked them for alternative activities, suggested we make the service projects voluntary, offered academic alternatives for their children. Nothing doing. The parents were adamant. They stalked out of the room with the warning that if this was not resolved quickly, they would be off to the superintendent and then to the school board.

"Next day one of my students dramatically relayed his father's strongly negative reaction: 'My good tax money going to that rinky-dink school so you can care for animals? No way! I won't permit it! If I want you to shovel shit from a dog cage, that's my business. I thought better of Mr. Knox. I thought he knew shoveling shit doesn't get you a decent job.' So I wasn't surprised by the summons to Helter's office. I was surprised, however, when he told me the parents had already been to Ralph Senter, the superintendent, and that he had pretty much pulled the plug on the project in deference to the parents. 'As I see it, it's just not worth stirring up a lot of dandruff over this one,' he told Fred, 'so take another look, please.' That's where we are now. Fred wants me to get back to him on how we respond to the super and, more broadly, the role of service learning in our moral education proposal."

"Just the sort of dilemma I expected," Connie commented ruefully. "The word is out that we're into moral education, so now a field trip to the animal shelter, which previously would have been just an incidental excursion, to be finessed if some parents objected, has become a biggy. Now it is part of 'service learning,' which might be a central component of the school's central mission. If it is central, like math and reading, how can it be something we allow parents to veto? But the flip side is that as it becomes central and takes on a moral dimension, it engages parents' guts, their deep-seated, generally buried feelings about the purpose of schooling and the questionable obligations of children to others. So they will fight us on this one and the more we make it a mandatory, schoolwide initiative, the more heat we'll generate."

"This is one hell of a mess," said a clearly troubled Hardie. "I think the idea is great; that it came out of the kids' grumbling is particularly satisfying. I believe in it. So does Helter, and it fits the district's own guidelines. Parents talk about the need for discipline. Well, what takes more discipline than cleaning out one dirty cage, then another, then another? Shoveling shit; yeah, exactly. I hadn't thought of it, but it's a good idea, very character-building.

"And the parents are wrong in saying the children will get more from a few hours of additional study. They won't get more. They'll miss an opportunity to be touched by the world, of which they've experienced precious little, and to feel useful in it. As for academic loss, where's the research that shows devoting two to three fewer hours each week to fifth-grade math hurts your SAT scores?

"But I feel for Helter. Once the parents get enraged, all hell can break loose—a blizzard of press coverage, e-mails, faxes, legal threats, pressure, pressure, pressure."

"Justifiably troubled though you are, Hardie, and troubling as this mess is, I'm glad it came up," Aggie joined in. "It's just what we need as a reminder that we can't do our moral planning in a vacuum. Even in the unlikely event that a proposal of ours is acceptable to all members of the school, we require a broader consensus. Hardie, I wonder if there's some way you and Helter could make service learning a voluntary experiment for the year while we think about it together—and specifically about the role of parents—as a component of our overall moral education plan."

"That was my gut reaction, make it voluntary," Hardie answered. "But now I'm leaning against the option. The parents' resistance shows me how important it is to override their unbelievable self-interest by pushing the kids to attend to others' interests."

"Let's face it, Hardie, you're furious at the parents' incivility and audacity," said Connie. "And I understand. They might have had the courtesy to consult you. Still, Hardie, be realistic. Whatever the merits of 'service learning'—I wish there never was such a term—we can't make this mandatory. It won't sell.

"Connie, why do you, and others, think that being 'realistic' is such a trump card? Realities can change. We made health education mandatory; remember there was plenty of opposition to that. I agree, the opinions of the wider parental community are critical. But their position isn't foregone. With some carefully planned meetings, we might get their approval for kids to give a few hours of service each week. And not just for the sake of their resumes, though that is a worrisome motive. Anyway, win or lose, I don't want to relinquish the cause so quickly."

"Hardie, can we declare a truce for the moment?" Connie asked, realizing there would be no quick resolution between them, "and shift to the other side of the school/family balance—that is, us getting into their business, rather than they into ours?"

At this suggestion, Maria spoke for the first time. "Connie, I'm happy to supply an incident along those lines that's got me plenty roiled up. Maybe you guys with years of teaching under your belt won't find it perplexing, but I'm in a genuine dilemma."

"Let's hear it, Maria," said Hardie reassuringly. "Misery loves company and, easy or hard, we don't often have this terrific opportunity to share dilemmas with one another."

"It has to do with my grading," Maria continued. "There's a kid in the class, Sean, with a difficult home situation that I've taken into consideration when grading. His mother, Mrs. S., was angry when I wrote on her son's test paper that I would not count the F as part of the semester grade because I knew that he had recently taken on (actually, had laid on him) substantial domestic obligations, specifically, a lot of baby-sitting for his niece, which must have interfered with his test preparation. The mother did *not* interpret my gesture as an act of kindness; rather she accused me of holding a different set of standards for rich than for poor kids. She jumped all over me on the phone one evening: It was none of my business what her child was doing after or before school. How did I come to know about the family activities? And given that I knew, how come she wasn't consulted before I acted? How did I expect her child to accomplish anything in the world if I wasn't more demanding? Then she started in on teachers who meant well—at least she gave me a pass on intentions—but who did more harm than good by bending over backward. 'No bending,' she said. 'Stand straight with him. Tell him what he's gotta do. That's my policy, it should be yours.'"

Maria paused to scan the reactions thus far. "Maria, we all get complaints like that," Hardie said consolingly. "More often it's the opposite of yours. More 'We aren't sufficiently sensitive to the strained circumstances at home.' 'Mom was just laid off and Dad is drinking.' 'The way you should handle the whining is to . . .'"

"Just a minute, Hardie." It was Aggie interrupting. "I didn't hear Maria asking for advice just yet. We need to think more about the significance of these differences, not just how to 'handle' them."

Maria went on, "I am troubled by the parent's request that I 'toughen up.' Mrs. S. said she wants every grade to count, she wants any excuse the child gives for incomplete work to be checked with her, and she wants serious penalties when work is turned in after the due date. And she means serious: a week of detention the first time an assignment is late, two weeks the second. Now that is something I simply cannot do.

"I sympathize with this parent and others like her. They live in a harsh world, and I guess don't have much experience with any but 'tough' approaches to whatever problem they're facing. It's not that I am judging them, certainly not harshly, but I am convinced that, understandable as their attitudes might be, their solution is no solution at all. I don't think Mrs. S. realizes just how difficult it is for Sean to keep up with school given all his responsibilities, and how discouraged he'll become if I start counting F grades. I also don't think she realizes that he can't do his work well with the television blaring and lots of people around him all the time. I've broached this with her, but again she's not receptive to my 'interference,' as she calls it. How do I know what conditions are required for her son to do his work? She's got a point, and yet I am a teacher, I'm supposed to know something about learning."

"Well, Maria," said Aggie, "you've given us a tough assignment, again, just what we need. Put aside your fears that this is simple. None of us, not even Hardie, can provide you with easy solutions." Hardie let the jocular slur pass as Connie took the floor.

"I suspect that, as Maria and this mother pursue matters, they will be at odds on a whole range of issues. I've dealt with parents like this before. Maria will find much of Mrs. S's lifestyle not conducive to learning, while the mother will surely disapprove of Maria's 'soft' teaching."

"Connie, you're uncanny," Maria burst in. "Mrs. S. has already raised doubts (and I guess the doubts will soon transmute into complaints) about my habit of not answering children's questions directly but rather asking them for their opinions, or for arguments supporting other positions."

"The parent has a point," Connie resumed. "What Maria sees as *engaging* children—lots of participation, free expression of opinions, opportunities to challenge the teacher—the mother will see as *pandering* to them. She probably believes that children should respect their elders, teachers above all. How can a child respect a teacher as an authority figure and at the same time keep challenging her? That's the opposite of respect. Respect means deference, as she makes very clear when Sean tries to argue with *her* at home. Teachers are supposed to be smart, know a lot, and make sure they give knowledge *to* the kids, not try to extract it *from* them. If the kids already know enough to start arguing their points of view, why should they bother coming to school? She'll have no sympathy with Maria's ideas on children *constructing* knowledge and the value of *reflection*.

"When a poor kid living in dangerous surroundings—and the danger may come from neighbors or from cops—starts arguing with, and disobeying, the rules of adults, he may end up in real trouble. It's fine for physically secure kids to speak their minds, take risks, not be held strictly accountable. What's the harm? But there are environments where, if you take a risk, even being on the wrong street at the wrong time, you sure won't take another one very soon."

"Connie, you paint a miserably bleak picture for a new teacher. Is there some way to avoid these conflicts?" Maria asked.

"Well, there's nothing novel about them," Connie replied. "It's just that we have tended to sweep them under the rug unless there's a crisis. Now that some of them may be elevated to *moral* issues, I think we need better-articulated guidelines. Some of this, after all—like the families' religious observances or the food they eat, or even how they discipline their children (short of cruelty)—doesn't often seep into school, so we rarely need to tangle with it. But when it comes to grading more leniently because of what's going on at home, well, that does seem to be a matter of fairness on which you and your student's mother strongly disagree. So we need to address it."

"But not just now," said Aggie, conscious of the meeting time slipping away."

## TEACHERS' MUSINGS

### Connie

All this conversation about guidelines got Connie thinking about the moral constraints on her own role as a counselor. Frequently a teacher would ask her to observe or talk with a child, and occasionally a student would independently request her help. The topics were usually confined to social problems in the classroom—kids picking on each other, kids being left out, nasty gossip—but sometimes they extended to troubles in the home. She had not thought she was required to inform parents of these meetings; after all, they were few in number and did not constitute therapy, but was this an example of excessive "reaching"? Informing parents would, she assumed, severely inhibit the flow of student confidences, but might parents think it intrusive of her not to get their permission? Intuitively, she knew she didn't want to get such permission. At most, parents should be told, as presumably they already were, about her role in the school. That was enough. Once again her resistance to erosion of the school-home boundaries was reinforced. Yet she had to question whether this instinct of hers was mostly self-protective, a leave-me-alone-to-do-my-work attitude that was morally questionable.

Lately referrals from teachers were increasing. It was all this prevention talk. The school was on hyper-alert. Word had come from Senter's office that they (she) were (was) to anticipate the child who might take an overdose or walk into school with a rifle. It went further. Suggestions of depression, loneliness, anger, seen in compositions, overheard conversations, or rumors were to be brought to her attention. She was to evaluate the signs and, of course, *do something.* But how could she look at a composition and decide whether its darkness was creative or personal? And what right did she have to probe a child's inner depths without the parents', not to mention the child's, own consent?

It was all quite confusing. Yes, the school needed to be alert to troubled children but, no, it wasn't right for teachers and counselors to expose the fantasies that a child entrusted to paper. How can one ecourage "creative writing" (a curriculum objective) if a child is fearful of being exposed to others? There had to be limits to snooping and reporting. Parents and children deserved some privacy; education required trust between pupils and teachers.

## Hardie

Although bruised by his recent encounters, Hardie also was still an advocate of stiff boundaries between home and school, with parents held at bay on the school's curricular decisions. There was much that schools could do to further morality, he argued, without getting caught in the sticky matters to which they were now newly attentive. He enumerated an impressive list: The school could establish norms (rules, if you like) for courteous, kind behavior amongst the students, teachers, and staff. If those rules infiltrated life outside school, so much the better; if not, he wouldn't feel defeated as a teacher. The school could also demand that children be held responsible for their work and judged by their performance. Teachers should not give credit for sloppy, late, or forgotten work. What went on at home to encourage or discourage performance—here he agreed with Mrs. S.—was not their business. But decent social behavior and serious academic effort were insufficient. They covered only the refraining-from-harm notion of morality. He also wanted to see the kids become more responsible, what Maria might call more caring, toward others. That would require a third prong: mandatory service learning scaled to the children's developmental understanding and capacity.

Fortunately, none of these components, Hardie believed, invaded family privacy. If one child teased another about her odd ways, the nature of that child's disability didn't have to be discussed. The children should be told, firmly, to cut it out, and appropriately sanctioned if they did not. Same for bullying and rudeness. To Maria's objection that, without going further into the source and motives of the aggressor, one was only masking rather than rectifying the problem, Hardie responded that the school's role was limited. If they, the educators, wanted to be left alone to do their work, they would have to give up playing psychologists. Teachers, oriented to groups, should have straight up-and-down norms for all, with very few exceptions and those justified by an obvious incapacity in the child.

## Maria

Maria recognized that Hardie's vision would make their job, especially Connie's, a lot easier and recognized too some value in her wanting to bring families on board. But she found Connie's constantly waving the red flag of latent school/home conflicts annoying. She was unwilling to accept a business-as-usual focus on getting kids to conform to the school's norms. As a novice in the field she believed strongly, or at least had until her difficulties with Mrs. S., that collaboration was the name of the game. It made no sense to have a set of rules and commitments at school that were not accepted at home. What sort of message did you give in telling a child it's wrong to hit, tease, exclude, and so on, but that's just our view, at home it may be OK? On the other hand, she wouldn't conclude that such actions were wrong without knowing more about the circumstances. That's why before passing judgment she had to get information on what else was going on, what had been going on, what pressures were being exerted, what assumptions and traditions prevailed—all that is summed up by "context."

She now realized that discounting a student's low achievement because of his extenuating circumstances *might* not have been fair after all. Maybe she'd made a mistake. Still, what would happen to Sean's school involvement after a series of Fs? It's all well and good to talk about parity—every child judged by a set of absolute standards—but that's before the turnoff from failure becomes an impassable barrier. However, if Sean and his mother thought her unjust, there wasn't a lot of moral instruction taking place. No, morality wasn't like math; it couldn't be contained within the school walls. She was discovering that "collaboration," though nice in principle, was hard in practice.

Maybe she should concede on the grading; she could see why Mrs. S. had interpreted the gesture as patronizing, though its purpose was to prevent discouragement. But she certainly wasn't ready to concede on her teaching methods. If schools didn't engage children's active participation, then all that talk about developing *critical thinking* was just a lot of empty rhetoric. She couldn't let parents dictate to her at that level, could she? What were the limits of parental involvement? She wanted them in, she wanted the relationship seamless—or did she?

## Aggie

Aggie was absorbed by just these questions. Did moral education mean school and home would have increased bidirectional involvement, as Connie suggested? If so, how could this be conceptualized in a way that satisfied both constituencies? In their school, very mixed by income, ethnicity, religion, and politics, it would be no small challenge. There were children of corporate magnates and of the long-term unemployed. There were children of atheists and of the religiously observant. There were families with parents serving time in jail, and parents who put them in jail. There were others who probably should be in jail, and those who were victims of the jailed. Agreement on "fairness" was a pipe dream. Yet wouldn't it be a futile moral education program that sought to inculcate moral norms when students felt free to disavow them outside of school?

As she listened to Connie talk about the tension over privacy, Aggie asked herself, just what sort of animal *is* morality? Students may not take other children's things, interrupt one another, or leave a messy work area; teachers may not favor one child over another, humiliate a student, or even advance a due date on a paper. What makes those rules a matter of morality rather than simply good classroom management? What *follows* from the characterization of a precept as a moral one? Isn't the obvious answer that it should be respected in *all* similar situations? When a teacher says to a child, "I don't care who you beat up out of school, but in school we don't fight," that isn't really true, or at least it shouldn't be. We do, as citizens if not as teachers, care about how children behave when there is a serious matter at hand. We probably don't care if they wear a lot of jewelry to the movies, but we find it abhorrent if they take other people's jewels. So we need the cooperation of parents on the serious matters.

On the other hand, isn't the protection of privacy, including the privacy of a family, itself part of a moral environment? Aggie concluded that they would definitely have to sketch out, however roughly, the sort of guidelines that Connie had been pushing for.

## A DEEPER LOOK

### Reaching into Homes

Teachers control a vast array of children's behavior, from language to conduct to personal appearance, without constant regard to possible parental objections. They "weigh in" on what most of us probably consider fairly trivial ("Don't pick your nose," "Straighten your desk," "Stop running," "Keep your voice down") as well as on what most would judge as serious ("You may not exclude another student," "You must not fight," "You cannot turn in someone else's paper as your own"). The first examples, while within the proper scope of a teacher's judgment, are generally considered breaches of conventions, the second breaches of morality. The distinction between the two is important for teachers to bear in mind when considering the "reach" of their judgments, for the following reasons:

First, the breach of a convention is usually not perceived as meriting the same serious attention as a moral breach. We are more aroused by a moral infraction than by a conventional infraction. That is, we care more, and want the child to care more, when he or she has hurt another person than when he or she has, say, failed to wear some piece of the school uniform. That doesn't necessarily mean you won't exert a strong hand for a non-moral violation, but the message will be different. For example, if a child forgets a permission slip for a class trip, you may have to detain him at school, a serious consequence. But your tone in admonishing him will not be the same as if a second child took someone else's permission slip, substituted his and his parent's name for those on the original, and got to go on the trip. In both cases, you will want to know about motives. In the first instance, did the child truly forget the permission slip? Did he lose it? Were the parents negligent? In the second, did he take another child's slip simply because he didn't want to miss out on the trip, or did the other child agree because he or she preferred to remain behind? Your responses to the case of genuine forgetting and one of genuine stealing and forgery will also be very divergent. Forgetting is not a form of moral turpitude; stealing and forgery are, and the child needs to learn the distinction. In part that learning will be conveyed by the reactions of the teacher.

In the instance of forgetting you will remind the child of the rule: no permission slip, no trip. You may try to help the child develop ways of remembering; for example, adopting regular daily routines around emptying his book bag and preparing for school the next day. You will want him to develop better habits so that he is not penalized for carelessness again. You may be irritated with him, you may feel sorry for him, but your disapproval of him will be mild. In the instance of stealing and forgery, your judgment goes beyond the act to the core of the child. Why did he do it? How did he think the other child would react? What if it had been done to him? Was it fair? How can he undo the hurt he inflicted, the wrong done? You will let him know that the matter is serious, calling for extended reflection.

Gilbert Ryle (1972) has spoken wisely, in our view, of the way we intuitively make these distinctions:

> We remember how our parents reprimanded certain sorts of conduct in quite a different tone of voice from that in which they criticized or lamented our forgetfulness or our blunders. . . . [W]e remember the total difference in gravity between the occasions when we were seriously punished and the occasions when we merely paid the routine penalties for infringing school—or family— regulations.
>
> In these and countless affiliated ways we were, in a familiar sense of 'taught,' taught to treat, and sincerely to treat, certain sorts of things as of overwhelming importance, and so, in the end, taught to care much more whether we had cheated or not than whether we had won the game or lost it; to care much more whether we were hurting the old dame's feelings than whether we were being badly bored at her little tea-party and so on (p. 440–41).

A second difference is that we do not grant a norm characterized as conventional the same "reach" (into the home) as a moral infraction. Consider the difference between saying to a child, "It's permissible to wear shorts and T-shirts at home, but not at school" versus, "It's permissible to steal at home, but not at school." If the school chooses to impose a dress code that parents don't like, we have no problem saying to the child, "At school you need to follow the code but at home you dress as you and your family determine." That seems a reasonable separation of home and school, because there is no moral issue at stake. But stealing is not something we condone in any (or practically any) circumstance. So if perchance a child tells us, "My parents say stealing is OK," most of us are not willing to say, "Well, you can steal outside school, but not inside school." Again, the difference is that dress style is an arbitrary convention around which we can accept a variety of tastes and choices. Morality is not a matter of taste; it is both obligatory and universal. We are enjoined to behave morally in as well as out of school. While much of this is intuitive, the distinctions between moral and conventional, and the notion of universality, are sufficiently important and difficult that we need to look at them in more detail.

This does not mean that when a teacher finds herself in moral disagreement with a family, she should preempt the ethical high ground. As we shall see, drawing lines between moral and nonmoral offenses is no easy task and, more seriously, rightness when disputed is rarely obvious. What does seem incumbent upon the moral educator when addressing parents is to distinguish the violation of chewing gum from cheating.

## The Moral and the Conventional

Emile Durkheim (1925/1961) famously pronounced: "[T]he domain of the moral begins where the domain of the social begins" (p. xi). John Dewey (1922), though often at odds with Durkheim, agreed. Morality, he said, "is as much a matter of interaction of a person with his social environment as walking is an interaction of legs with a physical environment" (p. 318). More recently, Roger Straughan (1982) identified morality as "those situations, dilemmas, problems, decisions and choices which require the consideration of other people's welfare, interests and rights; and 'non-moral' to everything that lies outside that boundary" (p. 5).

Conventions, of course, also deal with the social, but in contrast to the moral they have no *intrinsic* effect on the well-being of others. They are cultural norms of a particular society at a particular time, and as such highly susceptible to change. For example, the conventions that males hold doors, backs of seats, and coats for women; walk on the curb side of the street; pay for their dates' meals; and initiate dating overtures are now virtually extinct.

Using these distinctions, fighting, teasing, and stealing fall into the moral realm; they are actions that hurt others. Clothes, tone of voice, and manners have an impact on others only derivatively and only in some contexts. Wearing skimpy clothes on the beach, shouting at a football game, and eating with one's fingers at a picnic are acceptable, but in school they may be perceived as disrespectful and may make the lives of others more difficult (distraction and envy of others' clothes, inability to hear when some are loud, disgust related to sloppy manners and messiness). Such acts, and most of what we call courtesy, fall within parameters that are *derivatively* moral. They take on moral coloration by virtue of how they are *interpreted*.

Calling teachers by their first names, passing notes, burping in class are hurtful acts only when interpreted by others as disrespectful. One could imagine that at a different time and in a different setting each could be interpreted as appropriate. Consider the weightier matter of premarital intercourse. A generation ago it was considered a clear moral infraction which ignited a community's moral opprobrium and the perpetrator's strong anxiety and guilt (see Kagan, 1984). Within a generation society has largely (though not completely) shifted from viewing it as immoral, to a mere breach of convention, to an accepted practice.

A convention also may be interpreted as having moral valence when, though unimportant in itself, it represents a habit indicating deference to the social order. This is Hardie's argument in favor of removing one's hat. As James Q. Wilson (1993) suggested:

> The everyday display of self-control has, in any particular case, no evident moral message. You eat politely even when it would be more convenient to snatch food up and wolf it down; you put on clothes before answering the doorbell even when it would be faster to go there naked. We cannot say that wolfing down your food or answering the door unclothed are in themselves immoral actions. But we can say that the repetition of such acts will persuade others that when moral issues are front and center you do not have the state of character to restrain you from preferring your own immediate advantage over the rightful and more distant interests of others (pp. 84–85).

The problem with the derivatively moral category is that it has no boundaries. Because the conventional can slide easily into the moral (and vice versa), often it is hard to make a distinction. For example, a child doesn't bring his pencils to school or doesn't put them on top of his desk as instructed. If the teacher *chooses* to see this as manifesting disorderly habits she may take moral offense, but when we treat the merely careless as immoral, we risk moralizing every behavior. In so doing we are likely to trivialize the moral.

The distinction between morality and convention may therefore be questioned on polar grounds: Either all behavior can be judged on moral grounds or, conversely, all is a matter of convention. The former view supports the imposition of traditional conventions on nonconformists. Its adherents would admonish teachers, schools, and school systems to uphold the moral importance of insisting on convention-respecting behavior; they do not readily find traditional conventions (such as those reflecting gender roles) morally objectionable. The latter view does not look to customary practices for moral precepts. It rather sees moral value in fostering a critical attitude toward traditional norms and developing reflective, independent thinking about matters of moral choice. It views traditional conventions not only as often lacking affirmative moral value, but also as sometimes morally objec-tionable. It seems evident that the degree of attraction (and repulsion) that one has toward each of these poles powerfully influences the way one applies the dichotomy between morality and convention. That in turn will influence how one deals with parental "advice."

Enlarging the area of convention (at the expense of the moral) makes it easier to accept differences between home and school. Maria does not like revealing clothes but recognizes that, although some doubtless feel as she does, such dressing has become quite common and many no longer object to it. That's why she is inclined to view it more as a matter of convention than morality. Although she, or others, might ask students not to wear green nail polish in front of her as a matter of courtesy, she is reluctant to forbid it. She might do so in an extreme case, say, when she finds the dress just too sexualized, but would make it clear that it was the student's indifference to offending others, and not the dress itself, that was being ruled out of bounds morally. As a result, dress is not an issue she would feel obliged to bring up with parents.

However, conduct that is viewed as truly wrongful, such as stealing, is no less so when it takes place outside school. Although in one sense a school's "jurisdiction" does not extend to conduct at home, if Maria thinks of herself as engaged in moral education, she would somehow have to enter a dialogue with the family over a child's stealing, even if, for example, they regarded minor shoplifting as harmless. This is because moral rules are generally interpreted as obligatory and universally binding.

## The Moral: Universal, Disinterested, and Obligatory

To say that an act is morally wrong is to suggest that it is wrong in all, or virtually all, circumstances and wrong for all, or virtually all, people. When we say lying and cheating are wrong, most of us mean that it is no more right to lie on a rainy than on a sunny day, to lie to the weak than to the strong, to lie for a good outcome than for a bad one. One part of Maria's struggle is that when it comes to many of the behaviors that schools forbid, for example, swearing (as opposed to lying and cheating), she is uncertain of their *universal* wrongness.

A meaning of universalizability, then, is our willingness to generalize the rightness or wrongness of the act (or belief) across similar circumstances and people. You may prefer to lie, choose to lie, or seek to justify a lie, but that does not destroy the proposition that, presumptively at least, it is a wrongful act and imposes a duty of restraint. The principle of universalizability as essential to morality goes deep in our moral tradition. Core to the ethical philosophy of Immanuel Kant (1993) is the axiom that "I should never act except in such a way that I can also will that my maxim should become a universal law" (p. 14). This is his famous categorical imperative, analogous to the religious precept: Do unto others what you would have others do unto you.

The "similar circumstance" provision mentioned above provides a bit of wiggle room to the principle of universality. Maria, for instance, might decide that it is wrong to retaliate *unless you are personally endangered*. In school a child is not endangered because adults will protect him, so fighting is prohibited. On the streets he may be endangered, so retaliation is permitted. By narrowing the rule against retaliation to include "unless personally endangered" you preserve its universality. Nonetheless, it appears that the category of "similar circumstance" is not a small or closed one, and it may be difficult to decide with finality what "exceptions" are morally indicated. Suppose, for example, one is not personally endangered but a younger friend or sibling is. Does that circumstance permit retaliation? The admission of concern for the similarity of "circumstances," while necessary to make the rule morally plausible, relativizes and threatens to undermine entirely the principle it validates.

The universalizability principle asks of a moral actor that he or she accept a *disinterested* point of view. It requires replacing one's own interests with some greater good. In ethicist Sidney Callahan's (1994) words:

> The central insight and personal commitment undergirding the moral life is that other persons and their interests are as valuable as one's own. While one's private interests are vividly experienced and of immediate concern, moral persons accept the reality that certain basic interests of others have claims equal to one's own (p. 62).

If one lived alone on a desert island there would be no moral issues, one could do as one liked (except as one considered protecting the environment and other living creatures an aspect of disinterest). But in a social world, there is bound to be a clash of interests and a reluctance, especially among the young, to value the interest of others properly. Children not only have difficulty putting aside their wants for the good of others; as often, they don't even see the needs of others. That is one of Hardie's difficulties with leaving morality up to children's own judgments. Just because of this limitation in children, to some extent morality must be imposed.

Morality is also typically regarded as *prescriptive*. It does not describe behavior, it evaluates it. Morality tells us what we ought to do and not do. *Obligation* carries with it the meaning of its Latin root, *ligare*, to bind. In the words of the British philosopher R. M. Hare (1952), "[A] moral judgment has to be such that if a person assents to it, he must assent to some imperative sentence derivable from it" (pp. 171–72). Thus, we find something wrong in the statement, "I know it is wrong to cheat, but I am going to cheat anyway because it will help me get a better job or grade," whereas we are less uneasy if someone says, "I know I shouldn't eat a lot of sweets, but I'm going to have some ice cream today." Where the wrong is a moral one, we are obliged to heed it; where the act is only one of imprudence, we condone a bit of laxity.

Morality, then, is burdensome. It requires that we sometimes resist feathering our nests; it carries prescriptive and universal weight. We cannot, should not want to, turn away from it. At the same time, we have some freedom in determining the values to which we give our allegiance. Given all that follows from classifying something as moral, how should one think about the circumstances of Hardie and Maria?

## The Moral Weight of the Teachers' Dilemmas

Hardie's claim that service learning is a valid and important part of moral education arises in part from a conception of moral action and character that goes further than simply avoiding wrongful acts. It requires devoting at least a portion of one's energies to pro-social acts, responding in some way to the needs and suffering of others as a brake on the self-regarding, "get ahead" focus of most of our efforts. Hardie values service, not only for the immediate good that it prompts but also for the prospect that children will form habits of pro-social action, that they will become accustomed to taking the concerns of others seriously in their decision making.

Beyond that, Hardie's approach has a pedagogical premise as well, a commitment to experiential learning as a necessary teaching method. Children can, to be sure, learn the value of "good deeds" by reading about moral exemplars, whether heroic figures of history or ordinary folks around them. Yet the lesson is far more powerfully brought home, proponents of service learning maintain, if they actually carry out thoughtfully designed, age-appropriate service projects *and* engage in focused reflection on the experience, the insights and perspectives it yields, and the questions it raises.

In this view, time spent in service projects is hardly "wasted," for it is as much moral instruction as reading about George Washington and the cherry tree, or even about Rosa Parks and Martin Luther King, Jr. As Jesuit teacher William J. O'Malley (1998) observed:

> Trying to make a person in a nursing home smile, or feeling the palpable need for love in an injured child, or reading to someone blind can be a more profoundly educative experience than getting through *King Lear.* It opens your horizons, which is what being human is all about (p. 18).

The answer to the "waste of time" fear implicates several central ideas about learning and achievement. There is not so tight a connection, this answer asserts, between the quantity of effort put into, say, math and the extent to which it is learned. A child whose school day is balanced among several modes of learning activity, and balanced as well between "work" and "play," will, according to this theory, learn more than one whose teacher relentlessly keeps the child's nose to the grindstone. The contemporary phenomenon of subjecting young children to an entire school day without recess for the sake of greater academic achievement is not only an atrocious restraint, but academically self-defeating as well.

Specifically relevant to the moral aspect of education is the idea that an ethical stance toward others in the world requires a certain moderation of anxiety about "falling behind" in the race of life. Unalloyed, this fearfulness is a major source of antisocial conduct. Indeed, academic values too are best served, in this view, by reining in anxiety to succeed or excel. Time spent in service learning teaches a student that he or she can do well *and* do good, that these ends are not in wholly unyielding competition.

Maria, too, grounds her approach to teaching—what Mrs. S. objects to as "soft"—in premises about the nature of moral action and about effective pedagogy. Her thinking exemplifies the concept of "disinterestedness." To her, living a moral life calls for a developed ability to exercise moral judgment, to reflect on choice and experiences, to stand outside one's own opinions and priorities and imagine how they appear to others. Texts are an excellent vehicle for such exercises. Expressing doubt, asking questions, and questioning answers are vital means of getting into the heads of others, be those others contemporaries or historical. Again, Father O'Malley:

> [H]uman life begins to die when we stop asking why. Children begin to feel it is somehow impolite to be too inquisitive. [T]hat a child . . . keeps pestering, badgering, asking unsettling questions, intruding on the lesson plan . . . is what learning, as opposed to schooling, is all about (p. 14).

Maria sees knowledge as not absolute and wholly given, but emergent and partial. "Mistakes" are an essential part of the learning process, as long as students are encouraged to acknowledge them, learn from them (and from one another), and try again. "Getting it right" is a lifelong process, not a daily pedagogical objective.

What students most need as they grow is to learn to struggle productively with hard questions. For Maria, this learning is of moral as well as academic significance. Equalizing (somewhat) the teacher-student relation encourages students to support more egalitarian relations throughout life, whether they find themselves on the "high" or the "low" end of an inequality. This is a major moral virtue to Maria, and a valid source of "respect."

Maria's commitment to individualizing expectations, another aspect of her morality-driven pedagogy, was apparent in her consideration of Sean's "F." She believes it is simply wrong in judging the work of a student to ignore that it was carried on under unusual pressures. She assumes that young children treated with empathic individualization will turn out stronger and more self-reliant than if they are made to "toe the mark" prematurely. Beyond her own moral sense, she is educating the students' moral sense as well. They learn from such experiences that an individualized view of equity is preferable to a uniform treatment. She expects her students will come to make similar contextualized judgments, will become sympathetically alert to the actual lives of those who cross their paths, those whom *they* will be judging in the future.

At bottom, however, this prediction is as much a statement of hope as of expectation. Her (and, she hopes, their) outlook is aspirational, oriented toward the world as it could be, rather than simply grounding normative directives in what is. As with Hardie, "realistic," with its connotations not to question, not to rock the (anyone's) boat, doesn't suffice as a conversation stopper. She will not allow her teaching methods to be driven by such folk wisdom as, "You've got to go with the flow," "It's results that count," "You're either a winner or a loser," or "You can't count on getting by on sympathy."

But maybe Hardie and Maria are wrong in their moral stance. Parents listen to the sounds of very different drummers when it comes to what morality consists of, what makes for good pedagogy, and how they (and their children) should deal with the imperfections of social life. In this instance, at least some parents believe it is "wrong," and it is miseducation to push service learning. Their values clash with those of the school. The question thus arises: How should a school or school system (in the case of Hardie's service-learning proposal) or an individual teacher (in the case of Maria's teaching) respond to sincerely held, and vigorously asserted, parental objections?

## Balancing Views

Faced with such conflicts, it is tempting for schools and teachers to invoke pragmatic considerations. From a strictly pragmatic standpoint, to avoid controversy Helter or Hardie might decide to accede to the parents' wishes and make service learning an extracurricular or voluntary activity. The school might offer a principled justification for siding with the parents by staking a *pluralist* claim. As distinguished from *relativism,* which contends that there is no right or wrong answer, only differing points of view, pluralism rests on the belief that there *is* a right and wrong at stake and that one may believe he or she *knows* what it is but still think it right not to *insist* on having others act in accordance with that view. A pluralist position thus recognizes significant differences in moral beliefs but does not think it appropriate to insist that *others* act in accordance with one's own moral judgment, even though one might deem that judgment correct and the others' morally deficient. (See Chapter 7 for a further discussion of these distinctions.)

Forbearance to insist on the priority of one's own moral outlook is a form of what has been termed "epistemic modesty." This phenomenon, giving rise to an obligation to respect the moral views of others, has several sources. The broadest, perhaps, is the recognition that one's judgments, however clear they may seem to their holder, might in fact be wrong, that a person with whom one is in serious disagreement might be correct. It might also rest on a recognition that, even if wrong, the other person is nonetheless to be respected, that he or she has come to a differing conclusion responsibly and with integrity. Finally, and most relevant in the present context, one might incline toward a pluralist position out of a recognition that the other person has a special stake in the answer; Mrs. S. is, after all, more intimately and enduringly responsible for her child's welfare and development than is any individual teacher.

There are obviously limits to the proper role of pluralist considerations. Although those limits differ in people's minds, it is not difficult to postulate easy cases, where *in*tolerance of another point of view is plainly called for. The torture of children to learn the location of money, for example, cannot seriously be presented as a case for not "imposing" prevailing views on nonconformists. Isaiah Berlin's (1992) words make the point well:

> [I]f we meet someone who cannot see why (to take a famous example) he should not destroy the world in order to relieve a pain in his little finger, or someone who genuinely sees no harm in condemning innocent men, or betraying friends, or torturing children, then we find that we cannot argue with such people, not so much because we are horrified as because we think them in some way inhuman—we call them moral idiots (pp. 203–04).

In a school setting, the boundaries of pluralism are neither self-evident nor clearly legislated. There is a loose, largely implicit, consensus that parents defer to educators in core matters of "schooling," while educators defer to parents in core matters of "child rearing." Thus, parents do not normally expect a school to exempt children from competitive athletics, and teachers do not ask parents to prohibit children from watching particular television programs. Both requests are "out of bounds." The division of authority between school and home may wobble under trying circumstances—if the teacher thinks the family very misguided in their child-rearing methods, if a parent strongly objects to a particular text or to required participation in after-school activities—but there is normally a mutual expectation that the domains are separate. Both teachers and parents may have to put up with what they don't like, even what they consider immoral. Yet a teacher who has good grounds to believe that a parent has physically abused a child is rightfully expected to override parental authority and intervene in some way.

The more schools are asked to take on parenting roles, though, the less discernible these lines become. This is what worries Connie. What are the limits, she asks, no matter how benevolent one's intentions, of delving into a child's psychic (and, inevitably, family) life? What child doesn't fantasize about mean parents? Cinderella has survived the ages perhaps because children sometimes see their parents as wicked. How many children think about, even contemplate, running away because they feel unloved, because their parents fight? How many dream of "getting even" through self-destruction? The revelation of such thoughts, probably cathartic for the child, generally should not trigger an intervention. To test the (possible) ill winds blowing around the home reaches too far. It is right for school to establish an atmosphere where trust and openness prevail. It is right for teachers and guidance counselors to make themselves available to children in trouble, as well as to parents troubled about their child. If the child *displays* unusual dispiritedness or irritability (doesn't do her work, acts provocatively), it is right to raise questions, but suspecting trouble when none is manifest intrudes too far into the family.

This separation of powers is a form of live-and-let-live pluralism. The boundary markers between the domains are less a wall than a membrane, permeable yet real. But a porous boundary can be the source of legitimate dispute. Suppose, for instance, that a teacher believes a parent is likely to "overreact" (but short of clear abuse) to a child's poor performance, and decides as a result to withhold the information that parents would normally receive. In this instance the parent has a real basis to object to the teacher's rejection of a pluralist response. The teacher should exhibit some "epistemic modesty," respecting parental authority to judge what is appropriate and inappropriate discipline even when she is strongly critical of its manner of exercise.

Parents too might test the boundary. For example, when a teacher's discipline is perceived as inappropriate or ineffective—either because it is too harsh or too lenient—or when a school adopts a text that is deeply offensive to some, parents may not willingly accede to the implicit boundaries. In these instances parents might object to the teacher's actions, or ask that their own child be removed from the class or exempted from reading the book, putting the teacher to the necessity of choosing between resistance and deference to parental viewpoints.

There are not clear answers to the questions raised in the preceding instances. The unpalatable reality of life is that at every level of human relationships one must, for the greater good of social harmony, sometimes put up with what one finds deeply objectionable. But it is also true (as in the instance of clear abuse) that such tolerance is not boundless. There are times when intolerance is called for.

In our scenarios, concluding that Hardie's service-learning proposal and Maria's pedagogy were clearly matters for the school to decide would require some parents to tolerate what they don't like. If they were clearly matters of parental discretion, then some teachers would have to tolerate what *they* don't like. (The first case is like math, the second akin to watching television.) As professionals, a school or school system, acting at times through teachers, may justly insist on imposing its view on the entire student body. The decision to hire Maria and Hardie bespeaks a certain (perhaps provisional) judgment as to the discretion that they should have in the form and style of the classroom; and it may be appropriate for teachers, and principals, to turn aside individual parent demands for a different approach.

## The Decision

The question in our scenario is whether the educational authorities should defer to parental objections or requests and to that extent allow the parents to make the decision. We turn first to the question of the disagreement between Maria and Mrs. S.

We suggested above that, roughly speaking, teachers have, and assert, the greater say in matters of curriculum and pedagogy but should more readily defer to parents in matters of child rearing. This principle points fairly strongly toward endorsing Maria's reluctance to defer to Mrs. S's objection to her classroom style of encouraging students to raise questions, form and express their points of view, and engage critically with what they read and hear. She has presumably come to her view as a result of study and experience, and she has concluded that it is a desirable way of teaching (in the case of this student as well as generally), at least for her. Maria should give the parents' objections a serious hearing, but she must feel free, if her professionalism is to have any salience, to follow her conscientiously considered decision. (Were the parent to take her objections to the principal, he would be obliged, we believe, to decline to overrule Maria). Beyond these matters of principle, it is not practically feasible, except at the margins, for Maria to individualize her instructional methods in the classroom. But even if feasible, she should desist.

Maria's second issue is whether she should accept the parent's earnest request not to "customize" her evaluation of a child's performance in recognition of the student's extra-home responsibilities. Here, too, there is an argument in favor of the teacher's professional autonomy. However, it is a much closer call, and we can see the rightfulness of acting in accord with the wishes of the parent. Maria's judgment is based on her perceptions of the child's domestic life, what he does and does not have time for outside of the school day. Relying on her own judgment pushes the limits of the school boundary and moves more into the parental domain. Despite Maria's belief that the parent is in error, epistemic modesty may require her to acknowledge not only that she "might in fact be wrong" but that even if she is right, the parent's "special stake" is entitled to deference. Moreover, parents may have a greater claim when asking the teacher *not* to make an exception for their child than when (as with respect to service learning) they are asking *for* an exception.

As for the service-learning issue, although wide consultation with parents and parent groups is certainly wise, in our judgment the considerations counseling *against* deference to parental opposition are decisive. Service learning seems central to a sound program of moral education; it is the major vehicle for moving a student's consciousness to a more inclusive sense of "we." Parental disagreement with the moral lessons of service learning is no more entitled to carry the day than would disagreement on the value of other curricular requirements.

Moreover, making it a requirement (with or without an "opt out" provision) does not preclude extensive parental involvement in the design and evolution of the program—how much service, what kinds, and so on. It does not even preclude an occasional exemption, but the threshold for opting out should be high, requiring a compelling individual reason well beyond the waste-of-time objection. In general, laypersons tend to be more skeptical than teachers toward many forms of experiential learning, and the idea that service learning is a diversion from "real school" will find an attentive ear at parent-teacher meetings. Yet as professionals, teachers are not only justified in "imposing" their view on the entire student body, as they do about all of the other decisions that go to make up a curriculum and pedagogy, they have an obligation to exercise their best judgment of students' educational interests.

## Your Turn
## Whose Business?

Given that morality both blurs the private-nonprivate distinction and offers no clear directives as to who prevails when, it is obviously critical to consider issues carefully as they arise. Ideally, moral clashes within a classroom will be discussed as a group, but this can occur only if the class is sufficiently and reliably caring of its members. The teacher, like the doctor, has a primary obligation not to make matters worse. Children should be protected from embarrassment and humiliation, and attention to infractions should not provoke worse ones. Consider these examples:

1. A parent writes a note, not for the first time, that her son Troy won't be in school next week, for the family is taking a trip to attend a cousin's wedding. You believe the repeated absences are harmful to the child, who is new to the school and struggling with the work. You have already raised your concerns, but the parents didn't "hear." They are telling, not asking. What should you do?

a) Tell the parents that attendance is compulsory and a cousin's wedding is not a justified absence?

b) Reiterate your concerns in more forceful terms than you did previously, and tell them that merely sending homework along is insufficient?

c) Have a conference in which you ask the parents how they understand Troy's school performance, what it means to them and to him, their expectations this year and for the future, and so on?

d) Let it go?

e) Other?

2. Bill, one of the cool kids in the fifth grade, is joined by his fourth-grade brother after school as they both wait for the bus. You are assigned to bus duty. For a couple of weeks now you've watched a crowd of student admirers surround them daily as they delightedly tell vulgar jokes—there seems to be no end to their collection. Finally, in exasperation, you tell the two boys to knock it off; that talk is offensive. They're surprised: "What's the big deal? Why are you on our case? It's OK with our parents. Whatever happened to free speech?"

a) Is this a moral issue, derivatively moral, or a breach of convention?

b) Is it something for a teacher to take on?

c) If so, how?

3. Outside school premises, on her way home, Aggie spies Melissa continuing to litter by dropping gum wrappers on the street. Aggie reminds Melissa that littering the street is as thoughtless as littering the school and asks her to stop. Melissa replies, "School is out, Ms. Cerine." She continues to move away, and now she seems to be dropping her wrappers intentionally. Consider this issue in terms of the school's "reach."

a) Is Aggie right to intervene, or should she ignore this after-school behavior?

b) Is the behavior morally offensive?

c) Supposing she had put a wad of gum into her mouth, or smeared makeup on her face, but not littered. Would that be different?

d) Given that her request was rejected, should Aggie follow up in any way? With Melissa in school? With Melissa's parents? In short, is this any of her business?

4. For her English assignments, Bertha, a sixth grader, has been writing dark stories: A girl is constantly being flogged for refusing to give up a friendship; a girl has a fight with her parents and runs away, only to end

up living on the street; a girl, very lonely, flirts with cleaning out her parents' medicine chest.

Although Bertha is rather quiet, her teacher has seen nothing amiss in her behavior. She discreetly asks the other teachers (art, gym, Spanish) how Bertha is doing. No problems have been noted.

a) Should you do anything more than grade the paper and write your normal comments?

b) Should you ask Bertha if by any chance these stories are self-referential and whether she would like to talk matters over with you?

c) Should you talk with Bertha's parents, and if so, do you need her permission first?

d) Should you make a referral to the counselor, and if so, would you need permission from Bertha? From her parents?

e) Are there others who should be notified?

# CHAPTER 6

# MORAL DISCIPLINE

## *Scenario*

While Connie was stewing over the scope of moral education, Maria was eager to give class meetings an extended tryout. Maybe they could replace the disciplining to which she had in desperation resorted but fundamentally detested. In the weeks following the Downer discussion, she invited the students to raise topics of concern to the group. No one did. Apparently, it wasn't going to be easy to make this practice part of *their* culture. Before long, however, an opportunity presented itself. The precipitating event centered on her student Tony, the boy from Chapter 2 who, you will recall, habitually withdrew with a stack of books into a remote corner, and whom classmates considered "weird" because his cap, stained clothes, and muddy shoes made him look more rural than suburban.

Under Maria's persistent but gentle prodding, Tony had begun to "socialize," but with a vengeance. A few weeks ago, trying to ingratiate himself with a couple of students, Tony began to pass notes during class, not just now and then but on a regular basis. Then, when confronted by Maria, he denied having done so. The bald denial got to Maria more than the note passing, which was annoying enough. She was at her wit's end with his constant lying, but worse than the notes and lies were the smirks and mocking looks he would now toss the other children that said, in effect, "We're in control now, she can't stop us, she can't touch us," creating a real we-against-you mentality. Yet, except to confiscate the notes without reading them, Maria largely ignored the disruption, on the assumption that the children would soon lose interest in Tony's antics. Given the nascent spirit of cooperation and goodwill, she thought she could count on her students to reject these disruptive bids. But the antics continued, so Maria decided to hold a class meeting, hoping that through a free exchange of ideas (level 5 in Bonham's model) the students would give Tony the corrective "feedback."

Maria started the meeting by noting with concern the mounting we-against-you undercurrent. Some of the kids denied it, but others, seemingly with genuine regret, gave examples of how the class was indeed deliberately obstructing Maria's instruction. Best of all, they blamed themselves, not Tony. For a few days the class's interest in Tony's notes, and their frequency, declined.

Then Tony, no longer getting the amused attention he sought, upped the ante. One morning, presumably inadvertently, he let out a loud burp that set off a paroxysm of giggles in the class. Pleased by the reaction, Tony began manufacturing burps at ever-shorter interludes. Sometimes he would go over to another child and burp in his face. It was worth annoying the few—and several children were obviously disgusted with this prank—to tickle the fancy of many. Maria's instinct was still to ignore Tony as much as possible. She reasoned that serious discipline would only rally support for him and heighten the we-against-you sentiment that Tony had again stirred, yet she was leery of attempting another class meeting. So this time she tried a light-handed use of authority. After his next loud burp she went to him in front of his classmates and said, "I know you think that what you're doing is pretty neat, Tony, but save it for after school, please; for obvious reasons, it's not permitted during class time. You need to cut it out now."

No response from Tony. After his next series of burps, Maria took him into the hall for a talk. "Tony, let's say you were teaching this class. Would you let a child burp?"

"Dunno."

"I think you do know, Tony. It's obvious to us both that I can't teach when the children are laughing at you, right?"

"Guess so."

"And maybe that's what you want: me not to teach and you to get the kids' attention."

Silence from Tony.

The talk was useless. Tony got bolder, even as Maria began giving him demerits. Added to the burping were incidents of farting and saliva bubble making. Increasingly, too, he seemed to be getting his jollies from mocking Maria. For example, he drew funny faces on the blackboard before class and on his jacket. She was pretty sure the portraits were caricatures of herself. Still the kids said nothing to Tony. They were now clearly enjoying both his outlandish behavior and his willful disobedience. Maria realized that she needed to stop it once and for all. It was either another class meeting or punishment by the principal. For Maria, an obvious choice.

She brought the class together: "I understand that you think Tony is funny," she began. "Let's talk about why he is funny to you and not funny to me." She had thought they might note that farting and burping, like all bathroom humor, are not intrinsically amusing but become so when forbidden in the classroom, and that it is this very inappropriateness, the breaking of social taboos, that makes it disrespectful to her as proprietor of the classroom. She raised this as a possibility, but the children couldn't (or wouldn't) respond, except to say Tony was just obviously funny and then giggle surreptitiously in the telling. Maria considered increasing her authority, that is, moving to a lower Bonham level, by threatening a group punishment if all this monkey business didn't stop. But no, wasn't that just what she had criticized Downer for? So, with little expectation of significant compliance, she closed the meeting, asking the children to attend to class activities, not Tony.

Maria was prepared to let events unfold a bit longer. One could look at Tony's behavior, despite its inappropriateness, as a significant bit of progress. After years of being a misfit, an outsider, he was making moves to become an insider. The class-clown routine was Tony's way, and a not uncommon way, of affiliating with his peers. He was like a five-year-old trying to score peer points by clumsily showing off ("My Dad is the strongest man in the world"). Maria still conjectured that with time these infantile bids would yield to more age-appropriate behavior. But while Tony was making halting efforts to socialize, the class was becoming desocialized, abandoning the hard-won emergent courteousness.

It was largely the disrespect that got to Maria. She had been performing somersaults for Tony because he, more than most others, triggered her sympathy. She knew what it was like to be a loner, to be rejected by peers, to be discounted. She had been a bookish-brainy nerd for years and it had cost her psyche plenty. Sensitive to Tony's unhappiness, Maria had devised numerous strategies to ease him into his peer group: pairing him off with a "suitable" buddy for various class assignments, featuring him in sharing time by asking about the birth of their calf, inviting him to be the class co-photographer and to chronicle their field trips, even preparing a unit on power tools to make Tony look "cool," as only he could explain their use on a farm. Now he was turning on her. She felt unsuccessful, unappreciated, scorned.

As Maria mused over next moves, Tony brought events to a climax. It started out as just another school day of burps and farts until suddenly, when Maria went to the board to write down some arithmetic problems, the class broke out into a hilarious bout of laughter. The indignity of being the clueless object of this raucous outbreak pushed Maria over the edge. "For God's sake," she bellowed, smashing the chalk onto the floor, "What is going on here?" The children were startled and chagrined. One of the girls blurted out, "It's your skirt, Ms. Laszlo. There's a lot of white stuff on the back of it." Sure enough, her rear was covered white. She glanced at her desk and saw that the chair, where she just had been sitting, was generously dusted with powder. She glared at Tony: "So this is your idea of a good joke?" Silence. "Are you, or are you not, going to admit to doing this, Tony?" No response. She again considered a class meeting but immediately realized that one shouldn't use them to extract information *from* children *about* children.

"OK class, this instant you are to tell me: 'Who did it?'" Silence. In exasperation, Maria asked, "Was it Tony?" After a pause, the girl who had pointed out the powder on Maria's skirt gave a shy, barely perceptible nod.

Under the circumstances it was sufficient evidence. "Tony, come up here." No movement. Maria stalked over to his chair, grabbed his arm and shoved him onto her powdered desk chair. Then she lifted him up, turned his backside to the class, and said, "Good, now you look like me." Returning him to the chalky chair she continued, "You'll sit here until recess. Don't move, don't grin, don't open your mouth. Then, at recess, you'll clean this chair spotless and every other chair in the room. What you don't finish today, you'll complete tomorrow. As for the rest of you," Maria turned to the class, "You may have your recess and then we are going to talk this matter out once and for all and put an end to it. Right now you will all sit absolutely still and absolutely silent while I get Tony the sponges and cleaning equipment he'll need."

She stalked out, adrenaline flowing, heart racing, yet knowing no one in that class would disobey her orders—not this time. When she returned quiet reigned; the kids had never looked so meek or intimidated. On her command they did the arithmetic problems faster and with more concentration than she had ever witnessed. A fleeting thought: Was there something to this exhibition of power wielding, much as it went against her grain?

When the recess bell rang, Tony, without a reminder, began his cleanup. He was good at this! Clearly a child used to cleaning. Not just wiping but scrubbing. As he worked hard first on her chair, then systematically on the others, Maria felt her old sympathy beginning to percolate, and with it regret for her actions.

Anxious to undo her assault on Tony, Maria tried another tack. "Tony, I know that not having friends in the class has really bothered you a lot. You've tried to get the kids to like you by being funny, but you just forgot that I have feelings and get hurt too. Remember how you didn't like it when the boys made fun of your clothing and hat? That hurt you. Well, when you make fun of me, drawing those chalk caricatures and now the practical joke with the powder, that hurts me—a lot. Do you understand, Tony?"

"Guess so."

"I bet you thought of how the other kids would laugh at the powder on the rear of my skirt, but did you think of how it might really upset me, even make me cry?"

"Cry? No, I didn't think of that."

The children returned from recess and Maria, more confident than before, settled them down for yet another talk. This time, however, she was prepared to descend to a level 2 or 3 on Bonham's scale.

"Look, guys," she began, "we've got to change the atmosphere around here. You've got to understand why it is not OK to mock a teacher, or to laugh at disruptions, and why it is important to police your own instincts, even sometimes for you to police each other. I won't tolerate these episodes any longer. Up to now I've not chosen a tough punishment because I wanted you to realize how unfair you've been. Since that hasn't happened, let me explain it to you now."

She started by asking them what a parent would do if one boy in the family, assigned to set the table, deliberately omitted the forks and then his sister, amused by the omission, got a bunch of forks and put them on the chairs instead of the table. Maria's students were in agreement; parents would find both kids at fault. Now, Maria hypothesized, supposing the sister had merely laughed and egged on her brother to keep setting places without forks. Most of the students still thought that the sister should get punished ("accessory to the crime" argument). Finally, Maria asked, what might the sister do that would contribute to a positive family dinnertime?

One suggested, "The sister should tell on her brother. He's goofing off."

"No," another disagreed. "It's wrong to be a tattler. She should just go get the forks herself and put them on the table where they belong."

"But that wouldn't be fair," a third jumped in. "It's not her day to set the table. It's her brother's day and he has to do it. Otherwise she is doing more than her share."

"OK, you're right," admitted the second. "How about the sister talks to the brother and tells him to stop being stupid? Doesn't he know they won't be able to eat until the table is set right and he's just making everyone suffer by being so goofy? That way there is no tattling and the brother still has to do the work 'cause it's his turn."

"And if he doesn't stop 'being stupid,' and if dinner is ready but can't be served, then what should a parent do?" Maria pressed on.

The students talked about deprivation of dinner for the kids and worse punishment.

Maria made the analogy to the current class situation. She pointed out that, in like manner, the students should try to stop Tony from pursuing his shenanigans. If their direct appeal to him was fruitless, they should tell her; above all they should not covertly encourage him by laughing. And if they or he didn't stop, it was punishment time. Fair?

At the end of the day, Maria reflected on the class discussion. True enough it was *leading,* and she dangled a threat of punishment, but the kids had followed along—genuinely, she thought—so maybe this time they would not disregard the conclusions.

## Maria Consults Hardie

A familiar rat-a-tat-tat on her classroom door was followed by the good-na-tured face of Hardie with a bag of delicious-smelling popcorn in hand. "Have you taken up permanent residence in this room, Maria?"

"Lost in thought, Hardie; sorting through a rough day. Sit down if you have the time and save yourself a long evening telephone call."

Maria described the Tony-related events in full detail, including her guilt for having disparaged Tony in front of his peers. Had she forever jeopardized the possibility of trust between Tony and herself? Would he venture forth to make friends again, or had her temper sabotaged his initiative? What a disaster that would be!

Hardie interrupted her. "Maria, how very different we are. I applaud the acts that you regret; I regret the acts that you approve. The punishment of Tony was entirely appropriate. You had tried more modest means—talking to him, holding class meetings. Given his nasty little prank, losing your temper, embarrassing him, making him sweat were all absolutely called for. My goodness, he was begging you to break into his escalating mischief. The mistake, as I see it, was in not clamping down sooner. In *my* class the first note passed would have been the last. And as for your anger, well, it's not something I'd recommend as a daily prescription, but it's good for kids to see you're made of flesh and blood just like them, that you're not some mechanical automaton—all programmed responses and no feeling.

"Forgive me, Maria, I also don't approve of all the talk that you so value. Your efforts to get to the bottom of behavior—why the kids find Tony funny while you don't, what Tony is trying to accomplish with his foolishness, whether or not this is the child's or group's responsibility—seem to me misguided. Maria, we are not in the "talking cure" business. We are educators, not therapists. Besides, you can't expect eleven-year-old children to understand the motives of their behavior and then, based on their insights, to change. Would we even expect that of one another? Your last foray, that analogy about table setting, was clever, but surely you don't think that the children will recall it when the next prank occurs. Kids aren't like that. They don't generalize from a hypothetical to a real, and only remotely similar, situation."

"Hardie, you sure are predictable. Isn't this the same conversation we've had since the first day of school? You think I'm hopelessly naïve, and I think you seriously underestimate children's capacities."

"Not hopelessly naive," objected Hardie. "Just naive."

"You need to understand," Maria continued, "that I'm an unregenerate believer in a cooperative and constructivist model of education. That means a lot of things: First, I am loath to impose rules based on the because-I-say-so rationale. Most rules should arise from class experiences and reflections (discussions) about them. They need to make sense to the children.

"Second, I do not consider a little OK. More than a little unruliness is a very high price to pay for the opportunity to work out social and moral issues collectively. I know it looks bad to see a child passing notes, worse to see him burping, but wouldn't it have been great if the kids had turned Tony's antic off, better yet if they had figured out a way to include him as a peer so that he didn't have to resort to clowning? Instead I forced obedience by shaming him. Now what does that accomplish except a deflated sense of self and the possible abandonment of any desire to affiliate? I want the children to become moral agents, not obedient sheep. That objective can be accomplished only if the kids think and talk about Tony-like incidents, both the motives behind them and their fallout.

"Also, Hardie, most interpersonal problems are collective, not individual. Tony would not have passed the notes had there been no receiver for them. He would not have mocked me if the students had been outraged. We've got a way to go; they disappointed me a lot, but Rome wasn't built in a day, as they say."

Though Hardie was straining with impatience, Maria continued. "One last word, Hardie, and the floor is yours. I do, unlike you, think talking is critical. It is by talking about what's fair that children become fair, care about fairness. I should think at least some of the kids were genuinely outraged, at least by the powder incident, but were afraid to speak out. If we don't talk these things over as a group, how can we help children develop a conscience, a conscience that will not permit them to be a bystander when others are humiliated? Just because matters went badly, yes, disastrously today, doesn't mean it wasn't one of those 'good learning experiences.' Except, of course, for my eruption. Punitiveness, shaming a child, is not growth-producing."

"Maria, that was a powerful defense of a reasonable position. Not naïve at all, but maybe wrong on the pedagogy. Let me try to explain. We're not far apart in our goals. I also want children to be considerate of their teachers and one another, and I agree that respect doesn't mean blind obedience to imposed rules, though children should favor adult judgments as the default position. And, like you, I want children to be skilled analysts of a moral situation, to figure out the just solution, to care a lot about pursuing it, and to end up responsible and respectful members of the community. Moral anesthesia may be our greatest social problem. Like you, I want children to have the guts to resist group pressure and speak out against wrongdoing.

"Where we part company is on how to reach those ends. I am absolutely convinced that 'talking through' misbehavior or, as you might further insist, talking about what behaviors constitute misbehavior, is not a useful tool to accomplish our shared goals. Children acquire virtues by experiencing rightful conduct. That means living in an ordered classroom with reasonable rules regularly enforced. We adults provide a model of fairness for them; they do not construct the model. They are just not capable of doing that. Yes, I trust them less than you. The little Tonys of the world always keep accelerating their antics, because they speak for the rebellious spirit of their classmates. The more outrageous they are, the more they successfully defy authority, the more the other children enjoy it.

"True, a few kids may be offended on your behalf (not on behalf of some moral system they've constructed), but I would never rely on that sentiment, particularly when it is a group, not a single child, you are trying to influence. Groups have a particularly nasty way of seizing on and relishing destructive behavior. Tony acts out his classmates' forbidden instinctual resistance to being contained, to being civilized. Talking over the infraction is not necessarily wrong, but it's at best unproductive and at worst will lower your rightful (indeed, required) position as classroom leader.

"As for trying to stoke empathy by telling Tony how hurt you were, to the point of almost crying, that strikes me as a clear mistake. You recognized, Maria, that Tony has no insight into his own acts, so how can you expect him to grasp the repercussion of those acts on you? My sister still complains that I just don't get her reactions, try though I do. But even if Tony did know he was upsetting you, so what? How motivating would that be? He's not your child. Teachers, even teachers as well disposed as you are, just aren't that central to kids. And it's just as well, given how we come and go in their lives. We should appeal to fairness, not feelings.

"Part of a fair, ordered classroom is making sure that all the children are well informed of the limits within which they must operate. When they test the limits, as they surely will, there have to be appropriate consequences. Moderate punishment—I like to think of it as a conscience-raising experience—will inhibit them when temptation arises again. Once they pay the price for wrongdoing, they are forgiven, and a new equilibrium has been established. That is justice. The children will never have the sense of expiation and rightful restoration of a moral order if they are simply asked what went wrong and what should be done.

"I mean, think of it! One kid wallops another. You ask him what made you do it, while the victim goes off to the hospital in an ambulance. That route just invites the perpetrator to rationalize, to disregard the interests of others, to lie in the service of himself. Justice is not an infraction followed by a series of probing questions about whys and wherefores.

"When I was in the Marines, Maria, no one gave a hoot in hell how I felt about the rules, why I sometimes broke a few, how my input would have improved them, but that didn't stop me from obeying them. And not just because of the 'or else' bit. I respected the rules, and though naturally I objected to some, I understood my objections should be overruled in the name of discipline. Well, you'll tell me school is not the Marines. And I agree. We have more flexibility, but we still require a comprehensive set of expectations designed by the adults that are applicable to all.

"What goes for correcting Tony goes for the group. I would not have them dig into familiar domestic activities and extract from them appropriate norms for a well-functioning classroom, even if they could make sense of the analogy. I'd tell them: As a group we must respect the teacher and each other. I'd elaborate on what respect means, and disrespect too. Then, having supplied the frame, I might have a group *activity*, not discussion, on the topic; perhaps I'd ask them to write an essay on respect, giving examples. Maybe I'd post the best ones, and explain why they were the best. Finally, and only after all the parameters of respect and disrespect were clear, I'd invite them to look at how respect plays out in families."

Hardie, noting his rising intensity, abruptly stopped himself, but Maria nodded for him to finish.

"Look, Maria, I understand your fear that teachers impose lots of arbitrary rules signifying nothing of moral importance. They do. We rule makers must be very careful that we select for worthwhileness, for the good of all, according to principles of justice and benevolence. Children should understand the order to which they must submit. We want their buy-in. But, Maria, they must habituate to the rules, they must feel the pinch of inhibiting themselves, feel some deprivation, be able to exercise control, get those old habits up to snuff, before they can responsibly invent and impose a moral code on themselves and their classmates."

The two colleagues looked at each other with wan smiles, silently acknowledging their mutual wish for common ground, their shared earnestness about this subject, and their exhaustion.

"Maria, we've been talking a long time and of course haven't resolved our differences," Hardie said. "How would you feel about taking this 'case' and the larger questions we've raised about authority and sanctions to our next group meeting? As part of our moral education plan, we obviously must address how we should interpret and respond to wrongdoing."

"Good idea, Hardie. I'd like to believe that the distance between us can be narrowed, or at any rate bridged. In fact, it's got to be bridged if we are ever to get this program up and running. The alternative—chuck it, agreement is too difficult—sure isn't attractive."

"I'll deliver our message to Aggie then, unless you want to, Maria."

"No, I'll leave it in your competent hands—and Hardie, thanks for hanging out with me."

"Are you kidding? This is one of the best conversations I've had since I became a teacher."

## TEACHERS' MEETING

When Hardie gave a brief account to Aggie of the Maria incident and their subsequent discussion, she readily concurred that it should be the focus of the group's next meeting. She asked Hardie's permission to invite Jan Bonham to the session, explaining that she had kept Jan abreast of their committee's progress; they were both active in the local National Education Association chapter, and Jan, currently working on the topic of discipline, had indicated her wish to be included when the topic arose, merely as a fly on the wall.

"From class meetings to discipline," a skeptical Hardie commented. "The two would seem to be odd bedfellows."

"Yes and no," Aggie replied. "As Jan laid it out, class meetings join morality at the ground level. But notions of right and wrong don't really get to kids until they step on each other's moral toes. That's when, eager to relieve the pinch, they will earnestly engage the topic and battle out competing stands. Discipline joins morality at the top. It's more about enforcing than inventing, more about policies than particular events. I'm not surprised that Jan would put them together. We know from her piece on class meetings that she understands good moral education to combine laying on the school's expectations with allowing children to help determine those expectations. As always, it's a balancing act. Under what circumstances are teachers entitled to bear down on kids, and with what sanctions?"

"Do my antennae pick up another *Six Levels of Teacher Authority*?" Hardie asked.

"Come on, Hardie," said Aggie, "let's give Bonham a break. She wants a taste of the real world, and we want—or I do, anyway—to reconcile our differences, if only a little. Maybe after hearing us out, she'll have some advice."

"Well, I suppose that prospect is worth an invitation, after we check with the others."

There was no opposition, and Jan took a seat at one side of the room. Maria and Hardie began the meeting by summarizing their prior discussion. Aggie then suggested that they concentrate on the discipline issue, obviously central to a moral education program, by thinking about it in steps: First, they needed to disentangle the strands of wrongfulness, then articulate the objectives sought through discipline, and finally consider their preferred sanctions. Aggie tackled the first matter:

"I see three sets of wrongs in Maria's story: There were the wrongs Tony did to Maria, directly by humiliating her and indirectly by seeking to ally the class against her. Then there was the wrong Tony did to the class by passing notes, burping and farting, and stirring up insurrectionist sentiments. Finally, there was the wrong done *by* the class in going along. Is that a fair account?"

Everyone, including Maria, saw merit in Aggie's divisions and agreed that the first offense was the worst, the third the least offensive. Deliberately humiliating a teacher was simply unacceptable. The class's acquiescence in Tony's behavior, while displaying a passive and overly suggestible peer-group ethos, was more or less to be expected. Kids are predisposed to go along with mischief. However, Maria wasn't so certain about Aggie's second wrong, what Tony did to the class.

"It seems to me," Maria asserted, "that burping and farting are moral offenses only if others object to them, and we can choose not to object. Yes, I was upset and angered by Tony. Yes, I exploded, but that doesn't mean the acts themselves were so awful. I wish I had reacted as if they were simply annoying distractions that I could put aside."

Hardie of course disagreed. "Burping and farting are wrong in and of themselves, Maria. Sure, they may not directly injure someone, as throwing a rock does, but they injure in just the same way as name calling. Such acts have become deeply associated with a disregard for the social norms. They express an in-your-face indifference that we cannot allow to be perpetuated."

Aggie, fearing another cycle of intractable arguments and wanting desperately to advance their mission, said: "Leaving aside the issue of burping and farting for the moment, we agree that humiliating a teacher is unacceptable, right? If that's true, then don't we also agree that our first objective is to suppress that behavior?"

For different reasons both Connie and Maria demurred. Yes, the behavior had to stop, but just charging in with a tough punishment, if that's what she had in mind, might have bad repercussions. No, they couldn't support suppression at any cost. There were the longer-term consequences to consider.

Maria asserted that in this (and most) instances of misbehavior the objective is to rehabilitate the child and to repair the relationships between the misbehaving child and herself, between the child and his classmates, and within the class. For that to happen, she wants to be a reliable, understanding presence, for if Tony comes to appreciate her goodwill, over time he will let go of his ill will. As she put it, "Deep down no one *wants* to mock, taunt, or ridicule others. We all know it was Tony's insecurities speaking. My job is to cut through the behaviors that come from his fright. I need to reach his authentic self, the part of his nature that is affection-seeking and affection-giving. Punishment is anathema to these deeper ends."

Connie expressed somewhat different concerns. "To my mind sanctions against Tony would probably be ineffective and might backfire. Getting tough with him could well increase his anger and lower his self-control. Then anything could happen. I think of Tony as a 'disturbed' child who should be referred to a specialist. The school cannot be held accountable for his behavior. This is a good example of a problem beyond our reach. He (and perhaps his family) require in-depth treatment. So I guess my most pressing objective is to get him to the right therapist."

Hardie agreed that his objective, and the purpose of sanctions, was to have Tony affiliate with the class norms. But his primary goal was more behavioral. As he put it, "I want an orderly work atmosphere restored to the class. I want the class to show that they are deserving of *my* trust—never mind *their* trusting me, that goes without saying. I want assurance that next time the other students will resist going along with a provocateur, that their loyalty to me and to decency will prevail against other temptations."

Aggie, still hopeful of reaching an accord, went on to her third question: "Can we address what sanctions, or next steps if you prefer, each of you would invoke to achieve your goals?"

Hardie seized the floor. He was more than a little irritated by Connie's dismissive rejection of a teacher's obligation to discipline Tony, and by Maria's unwillingness to ruffle feathers after the beating she had taken. "To me it's pretty simple," he said. "Tony violated important codes of behavior, for which there is a price. Punishment is a form of expiation, a way of paying one's dues. Once paid, a new equilibrium can be established, but not until there is an effort at undoing the wrongdoing."

"How is the wrong undone?" Aggie asked.

Hardie went on at some length giving a careful analysis of punishment. He was opposed to an eye-for-an-eye retaliatory stance. That was not what he meant by "payment." Because he was against humiliating Tony, as Tony humiliated Maria, he also would avoid any sort of dunce-cap action—having him sit in a highly conspicuous seat, write the nature of his offense ten times over, make a public confession, give a report to his parents. Finally, he disapproved of arbitrary punishments unrelated to the offense such as extra homework, missing recess, demerits, detentions, a report to the principal. "What I mean by undoing," he explained, "is *making* Tony (not inviting him to) engage in a series of respectful behaviors toward Maria. He should assist her in whatever might be genuinely helpful: maintain the exhibits on the walls; keep the blackboards clean; arrange the room furniture; join her in supervising lunch, recess, and bus boarding. These chores will take time and deprive him of other, preferred activities. He will find them demanding and to some extent disagreeable. And I know there is a risk that he might become resentful and turn more sharply from school, but if discipline is done in the right spirit—and we can rely on Maria to have the right spirit—it will support good habit formation and promote a spirit of respect for the teacher's role."

Maria, straining to bridge the gap between herself and others, acknowledged that Tony went too far in his disorderliness, disobedience, and disinhibition. An occasional burp or fart was one thing, practical jokes against the teacher and instigating class rebellions were another. For all their sakes, his "acting out" had to be limited. But not by Hardie's methods.

"So what methods would you use?" Aggie asked.

"I want to continue to talk to Tony about his and my reactions, though perhaps not about my rising tears. Hardie cautioned me wisely against such disclosures. Maybe I can find books that present analogies or poignant dramatizations in the lives of others. I'd like to keep searching for school activities where he can shine and win the admiration of classmates.

"What more?" she continued, despite Hardie's unconcealed expressions of exasperation. "Maybe I could write a contract with Tony. What does he think are appropriate sanctions for note passing? For egging on classmates? For taunting a teacher? If he takes his usual mute role, I could give him options and together we might evaluate each. Once we reached an agreement, I could ask the class for input. Although, as you know, I don't like generalized rules, an if-then contract, coming from the *class* on the heels of this incident, might work. The agreements would be more contingencies than rules, subject to review and revision."

More fundamentally, Maria went on to explain, she could not approve any sanctions without further class debriefing. She thought it especially important to get at the students' internal disagreements. Maria imagined that many of them harbored complaints against both her and the daily routines of school. They probably appreciated Tony for daringly acting out their own resentments. Others, she suspected, were appalled by his antics but scared to oppose him lest they look "dorky." The whole Tony affair would be a wasted opportunity for moral education unless the discontent of the complainants and the cowardice of the scared to oppose were also addressed. Maria saw no problem in unmasking internal discord. It is through discord and dialogue that children form commitments and resolves. For Maria, undoing meant having the group arrive at a better understanding of their motives and behavior. She would reinforce the new insights by role-playing possible future scenarios, and together they would plot better outcomes.

Aggie, with one eye on the prospective moral education plan and the other on her long teaching career, tried to emphasize what the teachers had in common. "Maria," she said, "I understand that while you are centered on motives and feelings, you also acknowledge that teachers are due some deference and students must accept some regulation. Behavior matters. Hardie, while you want decorum and decency in the class, I heard you say that authority must be bridled and that punishment should instruct as well as repress. And you both share the ultimate objective that Tony become a responsible and respectful member of the community."

"It occurs to me that a child's response to disciplinary measures probably depends as much on his pre-existing attachment to school, to the values of the school and teacher, as it does on specific techniques. Discipline may be less about *creating* respect, as Hardie assumes, than about *reinforcing* existing attitudes. This is something like the familiar distinction between it's not what you do but who you are. The earnestness and dedication of teachers like Hardie and Maria—their *character*, if you like—are independent of their disciplinary choices. The children notice Maria's long comments on their papers, Hardie's weekly library trips to acquire relevant and interesting supplementary reading. It is in light of such deeds that they are inspired to become more decent themselves. So here's a heretical thought: Maybe just what choices you make aren't all that important."

She went on to explain that this quasi-separation between person and pedagogy explains why the "tough" and "soft" approaches are less polarized than they may appear, and why within both camps there are teachers who succeed and teachers who fail. If Hardie and Maria are perceived as fair-minded and well-motivated teachers who make reasonable demands, the children will respond to either of their methods. If not, all disciplinary measures will be ineffective, perhaps backfire.

"If I am right," Aggie concluded, "that the techniques of discipline are secondary to a child's prior commitment to the school ethos, and that commitment relies on an abiding good faith between teacher and children, then a moral tone must be established from the outset. As part of our plan we will have to include something about moral atmospherics."

"You are good, Aggie," said Hardie, "really good. What you've done, albeit slyly, is to tell us we'd do well to mind our better selves if we want children to mind our discipline. That's a sober message to absorb until we meet again."

"You're not too bad yourself, Hardie, surreptitiously trying to end this meeting. But before we scatter, I'd like to ask you, Jan—so flylike we'd all but forgotten your presence—for comments."

"With Hardie and the others half out the door, all I want to say is thanks for letting me sit in. It has been a great hour. The talk, especially outing the discordant views, was enormously helpful to my own halting efforts. I've been trying to conceptualize a discipline approach that takes into account this spectrum of opinions. Give me a couple of weeks and I'll get you something in writing that might help, if it doesn't further provoke, in forming discipline policies."


## A DEEPER LOOK

Aggie's valiant effort to reconcile the differences between Hardie and Maria contains an important insight: The character of the teacher is an essential aspect of the viability of a moral education program. As British philosopher Mary Warnock (1992) observed: "You cannot teach morality without being committed to morality yourself" (p. 164). While in practice it may be true that children are more attentive to who you are that to what you do, Aggie is nevertheless courting disappointment if she believes that her emergent program can avoid engaging the Hardie/Maria differences. These differences emerge from discordant worldviews, which need to be inspected if they are to be respected. In what follows we examine how each "reads" Tony's manifest behavior, for it is these readings that prompt or promote their differing pedagogic responses. Specifically—and here we play out distinctions developed in preceding chapters—we examine the following relevant differences between these teachers:

their *reactions to student misconduct*
their *moral priorities*
their *notions of discipline*
their *interpretations of human nature*

## Interpreting (Mis)conduct

In *Habits of the Heart,* Robert Bellah and his colleagues (1996) tell the story of the Puritan leader John Winthrop, first governor of the Massachusetts Bay Colony, who, when informed that during an "especially long and hard winter" a poor miscreant was stealing from his woodpile, summoned the man and instructed him to take whatever amounts of wood he needed whenever he wished for the rest of the winter. "Thus, he said to his friends, did he effectively cure the man from stealing" (p. 29).

Just as removing the wood was not theft once permitted by its owner, so note passing, even burping and farting, are moral offenses only if deemed objectionable by those present. Maria, while upset and angered by Tony, and not disputing that his motive was to disrupt her class, is not willing (unlike Hardie) simply to condemn his antics as "sabotage," "insolence," or "insurrection." She has none of Hardie's moral outrage because, like Winthrop, who looked past the wrongfulness of an act to see a man pressed by hunger, Maria responds to her perception of Tony's motives, both his immediate ones—what he is trying to accomplish with his peers through these annoying behaviors—and, more essentially, his longer-term ones. She focuses on the person, more essentially on the person-in-being, less on the doing.

Given such eyes, she is relatively indifferent to the note passing (though less so to what followed). She regards the acts, or at least wants to regard them, not so much as a threat to her authority, or an effort to embarrass her, as a bid for attention. That the acts do deeply embarrass her, making her feel helpless and out of control, and give Tony undeserved notoriety, troubles Maria, but despite her explosive surge of anger she would prefer to respond to them simply as annoying distractions that she can put aside.

Beneath the mischief making, beneath what appear to be hostile, mocking acts, Maria sees a lonely boy deprived of healthy social experiences, who is struggling for the first time to earn peer-group status and friendship. Maria reacts to Tony's motives—not his acts—primarily with compassion and understanding, seeking to place in the background her moral judgment and condemnation. Doing the wrong thing just doesn't have the same moral opprobrium for her as for teachers who take primary account of, and demand accountability for, the acts students commit.

Out of this orientation emerges, as well, a fairly fluid notion of what is correct behavior and a correspondingly broader tolerance for deviance than we would find in one whose views of right and wrong were focused on acts. Maria can turn her head and disregard the note passing, not defining it as wrongful. She can ignore outspoken children, somewhat excessive noise, spontaneous outbursts, even burping. Maria wants children to enjoy maximum freedom and minimum restraint at school, for she views the class as an experimental laboratory where, through the press of social demands, children, encouraged to *be* themselves, can become better selves. She finds the usual school climate unnecessarily stuffy and too intolerant of oddballs.

Maria sees her task in dealing with this difficult student primarily in relational terms. Attracted to oddballs and lost souls, she wants to influence Tony's behavior by being what might be termed a "friendly presence" in his life at school. To be sure, she would hold out to him a standard of proper behavior toward another person and toward a teacher, but she would do it in a manner that makes clear her regard for him as a person and her concern for his emotional and moral well-being. She is not content simply to see to it that he knows what behavioral change is expected of him and suffers whatever consequences are appropriate should his responses fall short.

Maria is thus predisposed to a philosophical stance that emphasizes caring as the foundation of morality. That means withholding judgment, refraining from imposing oneself on others, stripping the teacher-student relationship of customary role constraints, maintaining "receptive attention" (Noddings, 2002). It means, in short, putting aside, at least tentatively, one's own determinations and absorbing the determinants of the other.

Maria also wants children to participate as a group in generating moral norms. It is in group situations that children collectively experiment with behaviors in a safe place; sort out together what matters to them a lot, a little, or not at all, what is tolerable and what hurtful to their mutual well-being. The feedback they offer one another and the norms they collaboratively generate are for Maria the surest ways for children to establish a moral community and their own moral identity. Values generated by children will stick because they engage their will, their deep desires, their essential sense of self; values imposed do not because they engage only children's compliance with the will of others and are likely to fade when those others vanish.

For this process to work, however, the group cannot become simply another external force imposed on the Tonys of the class. The teacher must be vigilant to guarantee the group's safety. This means that feedback cannot become ridicule or ostracism, and collaboration cannot be disguised teacher control. A teacher should not let go of the reins with one hand while tightening them with the other, as Downer was criticized for doing (see Chapter 3). The difficulty of guiding a group of children (as well as herself) to work in this way, however, does not impair Maria's belief that it is well worth the effort.

Hardie's "read" on Tony is altogether different. For him, as we have seen, conduct is core, motive incidental; adult judging is essential, understanding peripheral; and values express enduring truths rather than evolving truces worked out by a classroom group. Standards for righteousness are not, according to Hardie, the province of Tony's classmates. Values, being universal, need not be freshly minted by young children, whether individually or collectively. They come from the larger society and are instantiated by a teacher. Group-generated or -reinforced norms have utility in some contexts—for example, to rally support for established values, to infuse them with spirit, energy, and loyalty—but to extend the group's authority further is counterproductive at best. Groups of children are especially unlikely to further moral ends, impose discipline on themselves, or promote the virtues of temperance, humility, fortitude, or prudence. Indeed, it is at least as likely that groups operating mostly under their own authority will turn in very wrongful directions. Collective norms of "coolness" may include taunting the weak, cheating, stealing, lying, truancy, and the like. The chillingly murderous morality of the self-governing boys in *Lord of the Flies* may simply be gripping fiction, but its lesson commands sober attention.

If, controlled by an adult authority holding the line, Tony does the right thing frequently enough, he will find a gratification in righteous behavior that is not available through the reactions of other children or through talking things over. The respect and self-respect that emerge from doing right are in the end vastly more satisfying than the short-term group pleasure derived from mutual insurrection.

## Articulating Moral Priorities

Hardie, unlike John Winthrop, would never contextualize "stealing" and then declare it inoffensive. For him, stealing is simple: taking something for yourself that belongs to another. He will not countenance it, regardless of circumstances. Why so tough? Because Hardie is drawn to the sterner virtues: restraint, self-control, self-denial, diligence, hard work, obedience, and fortitude. These are the qualities that produce human nobility and grandeur, they are the source of human pride. But they cannot be acquired without a long apprenticeship in resisting easy satisfactions.

Raised from childhood on the teachings of Benjamin Franklin, Hardie often posts for students lists of the virtues that patriot valued: temperance, silence, order, resolution, frugality, industry, sincerity, justice, moderation, cleanliness, tranquility, chastity, humility (Franklin, 1963, pp. 90–91). Maxims such as these from Franklin's *Poor Richard's Almanac* are as relevant to Hardie today as to eighteenth-century Americans:

> He that cannot obey cannot command.
> Great good nature, without prudence, is a great misfortune.
> Blessed is he that expects nothing, for he shall never be disappointed.
> 'Tis easier to suppress the first desire than to satisfy all that follow it.
> Nothing brings more pain than too much pleasure (pp. 194–97).

Such stern and dour admonitions are not for Maria. She is attracted to the "soft" virtues that arise from our attachments to one another. These virtues include, as the English philosopher David Carr (1991) has noted, such "other-regarding" qualities as "unselfishness, considerateness, sympathy, benevolence, kindness, generosity, courtesy, respect, charity and possibly patience and tolerance . . . modesty and humility" (p. 200). What makes these virtues "soft" is that they tap the natural desire for affiliation—with one another, with a broader community.

Maria objects to the inculcation of the "hard" virtues. Contrary to Hardie, she does not view them as valuable in and of themselves, irrespective of the ends to which they are directed. Indeed, when toughness and strength are not nested in worthwhile ends they can be harmful (the courageous thief). Furthermore, there is no need to make diligence and self-discipline an object of moral education. Such virtues are natural by-products of interest and devotion. A child is enraptured by the sight of a cow giving birth. She wants to know more about the animal, study its life cycle, understand the biology of reproduction, learn to portray the scene in art and storytelling. To satisfy this curiosity requires diligence, hard work, and self-discipline. She begins to study collaboratively with another child. A caring relationship blossoms between them. Out of their affection emerges patience and a moderation in their self-serving desires. It is the interest not the inhibition, that requires stimulation.

These moral priorities are part of the teachers' worldviews. They stem from sources buried deep in the psyche, yet they go a long way toward explaining their pedagogical preferences. To develop a caring ethic, Tony must be attached to his teacher so that he can dare to attach himself to others. Maria, through her own caring, gives him the requisite ego-stamina to face social rejection. Recall our first encounter with Maria (Chapter 2, p. 13) when she proclaimed, "I'm going to be kind and caring toward the children; provide a good model; and expect them, with occasional reminders from me, to be kind to one another." She is still convinced that strict discipline, punishment, repression, and adult imposition of duties and obligations inhibit the growth of a natural, joyful, committed, caring community.

Qualities like frugality and caution have been termed by author Philip Hallie (1997) the "little virtues" that protect us from risk and keep us safe. Hallie is well known for his book *Lest Innocent Blood Be Shed* (1979), an account of the heroism of the inhabitants of the French village of Le Chambon in protecting Jews under Nazi occupation. He does not admire the little virtues; vastly superior are the "great virtues" of compassion and generosity which, though antithetical to cautious self-interest and "often impractical," are those virtues of the heart that make for true altruists (p. 40).

One such hero described by Hallie was Magda Trocmé. Such virtues as thrift and prudence hardly characterized her life. From one day to the next, the family cash box was as available as her home to anyone in need, while her repeated efforts to rescue desperate strangers were the height of incautiousness. As Hallie recounts:

> During the first terrible winter after the fall of France, the first refugee came to the door of the presbytery of Le Chambon. . . . When Magda asked the mayor to give her the necessary papers, he—quite rationally—said, "What? Do you dare to endanger this whole village for the sake of one foreigner? Will you save one woman and destroy us all? I am responsible for the welfare of this village. Get her out of Le Chambon tomorrow morning, no later."
>
> The voluble and eloquent Magda was wise enough not to argue against the little virtues. . . . From that winter's night on, she never tried to justify the saving of refugees to the custodians of the welfare of Le Chambon or of France. She worked closely only with people who had more in their hearts than protecting their hides (p. 42).

Hardie, of course, would be offended by Hallie's dismissive reading of the "little virtues." He would note that Magda's great courage was not likely to have been the result of a childhood spent in caring classrooms filled with kind classmates and teachers. No, courage is a quality attained only by those who are practiced in self-restraint, in resisting easy gratifications and the enticements of conformity. He admires Magda (as well as Ben Franklin) not for her compassionate feelings but (borrowing the famous words of Reverend Martin Luther King, Jr.) for "the content of [her] character," for her daily unflinching risk taking that resulted in lifesaving acts. As a teacher, Hardie is not concerned whether a child is attached to him or to others; nor is he much interested in the internal workings of a child's psyche (his or her self-esteem, social esteem or loving motives). It is not right relationships but right commitments that concern him, commitments that are often grounded in the "little virtues" that Hallie scorns. Self-esteem (assuming that there is such a thing) will emerge from the doing of good deeds; it will not be the source of them.

Indeed, while Hardie's priorities are no less emotionally grounded than Maria's, he is "turned off" by a focus on soothing, comforting talk. To him, George Eliot's Adam Bede had it right when he said, "I like to keep my breath for doing instead o' talking" (Eliot, 1985, p. 44). Of course by virtue of their humanity, all people deserve respect and protection from the abuse of fundamental rights, but they do not all deserve praise. Approval should be earned.

The notion of a "caring community," where care is turned inward, focused on one another, rather than turned outward to the issues of the world such as the environment, animal rights, poverty, disease, illiteracy has about it a group narcissism distasteful to those of Hardie's orientation. It is all just a little too cozy, too comfortable, too easy. This "feel good" therapeutic morality that imposes no demands beyond "being nice" makes for selves stripped barren, what Robert Bellah and his colleagues (1996) called the "radically unencumbered and improvisational self" (p. 81). If we are to care for one another regardless of performance, if our worthiness is not a precondition of another's approval, who will be motivated to take the risks of resisting injustice? The awe we feel, the inspiration we receive from greatness, is flattened by expending vast sums of approval on fairly ordinary expectable "niceness."

## Approaches to Discipline

Hardie, with his attraction to the stern, hard-to-acquire virtues, unsurprisingly finds no immorality in the judicious use of punishment and no contradiction between punishment and compassion. Tony, obedient to the strictures of a moral community, enjoys the privileges of membership; disobedient, he is punished, pays his dues, and is readmitted. As long as punishment is proportionate, that is, not too harsh or long-lasting, and clearly deserved, it serves a morally educative purpose.

Appropriate punishment is also a good psychological tool. It works. Moderate pain from loss of normal privileges, as well as feelings of shame (public embarrassment at the revelation of one's wrongdoings) and guilt (internal self-derogation for having done wrong) inhibit self-serving impulses. They are a source of moral gain—uncomfortable, yes, but not bad experiences for children.

But punishment is more than a tool, and a good outcome is not the only goal. In the Tony imbroglio, it's not merely a matter of changing Tony's behavior, but of doing justice. Guilt and remorse depend on that recognition. When a child understands the moral point of punishment, rather than seeing it as pure coercion, then, as British educational philosopher P. S. Wilson (1971) observed, "[B]eing punished for wrongdoing will seem like having the existence of a moral order of things, and of one's place in it, confirmed. *Not* being punished, in such circumstances, would lead only to bewilderment, despair or indifference" (p. 116; emphasis in the original).

The sting of pain is an essential aspect of punishment. Without it, one does not acquire the heavy-heartedness of wrongdoing. As the French writer Simone Weil (1986) has said, "The human soul has need of punishment and of honor. Whenever a human being, through the commission of a crime, has become exiled from good, he needs to be reintegrated with it through suffering. The suffering should be inflicted with the aim of bringing the soul to recognize freely some day that its infliction was just. This reintegration with the good is what punishment is" (p. 209).

For Hardie, the deliberate infliction of pain (understood in the educational context as psychological rather than physical distress) is legitimate. It is proper to turn your back (at least temporarily) on someone who has wronged you (or others). In such circumstances giving and enduring pain are justified. Wilson asks rhetorically: "[If] a group of children, for example, cold-shoulder or rebuke a member of their group who is persistently spoiling what they are doing, or if between two friends a painful estrangement occurs because of some insensitivity or misunderstanding on the part of one or the other, or if a parent smacks a child because of some willfully absurd, destructive or cruel piece of behavior, *must* we say in any of these cases that the pain was necessarily 'evil'?" (p. 114; emphasis in the original).

Maria dislikes punishing children on educational, psychological and moral grounds. Although sometimes one must force a child to "mind," as when there is a serious risk to the child or to others, necessary does not equal moral. While Hardie believes discipline increases a child's *respect* for his teacher, Maria believes it increases his *fear.* Fear may be a component of the inhibition and self-control Hardie so values, but it has no place in the open, trusting relationships with children that Maria seeks. She also discredits his notion that when a child disturbs the natural "rightful" order (itself ambiguous to her), punishment is an effective means of restitution. If a child doesn't acknowledge wrongdoing, no punishment will enlighten him; if he does, punishment is unnecessary. Did Tony, forced to clean the chairs, feel cleansed of wrongdoing, worthy of being reinstated as a citizen of the class? Unlikely. More probably he was humiliated (shamed) in front of his classmates, angry and resentful toward her.

Punishment also fails to pass muster as a justifiable psychological tool, for it suppresses not just the deed but the emerging self. Children cannot separate the "I" who is punished from the "it" to be suppressed. The punished child is less likely to be reformed than resentful, less likely to become self-directed than manipulative or passive, less likely to become identified with the class and school than to be hostile to it. As for sorrow, shame, and guilt, they cramp and distort an emerging selfhood; Maria wants no part of stoking such feelings.

The deliberate infliction of pain is to her a moral violation, completely contrary to her caring philosophy. She agrees with Nel Noddings (2002): "Much of the pain that humans suffer is neither deserved nor brought upon ourselves, and good parents have to assure children of this. Neither is there meaning in the pain itself. It is a misery to be relieved, a suffering that needs consolation" (p. 199).

In large measure the dispute between Hardie and Maria comes down to the redemptive power of punishment, particularly pain. For Maria (echoing Noddings) pain, deliberately inflicted, contradicts caring. To Hardie (who would echo C. S. Lewis, 1948), pain is a component of caring. Said Lewis:

> Kindness, merely as such, cares not whether its object becomes good or bad, provided only that it escapes suffering. . . . It is for people whom we care nothing about that we demand happiness on any terms: with our friends, our lovers, our children, we are exacting and would rather see them suffer much than be happy in contemptible and estranging modes.
>
> I do not think I should value much the love of a friend who cared only for my happiness and did not object to my becoming dishonest (pp. 40–41, 49).

## Interpreting Human Nature

We might thus summarize Maria's orientation in a word as "protective," Hardie's as "restrictive." But of what is Maria protective and Hardie restrictive? Of children's natural impulses. In unpacking worldviews, then, we must turn to their basic set of premises concerning human nature.

Maria, like the philosopher David Hume (1983), believes in our "natural sympathies." According to Hume, morality is embedded in our basic emotional responses, which enable us both to identify the good and desire the doing of it. We experience "warm feelings" of approval when we engage in virtuous acts and "disgust" when we engage in vice. The good, happiness, is promoted by our natural "tender sympathies"; the evil, human misery, meets with our natural disapproval. "It appears that a tendency to public good, and to the promoting of peace, harmony, and order in society, does always, by affecting the benevolent principles of our frame, engage us on the side of the social virtues" (p. 50).

More recently, Isaiah Berlin (1959/1992) expressed similar beliefs. Morality, he said, is "constitutive of human beings as such," part of our essential nature. Knowledge of the good and the desire to be good are as intrinsic to human nature as the ability and desire to love, or the ability and desire to communicate. Human beings commit to a common morality "as part of what in their moments of self-awareness constitutes for them the essential nature of man" (pp. 202–203). His reasoning warrants further quotation:

> [T]here are . . . certain moral properties which enter equally deeply into what we conceive of as human nature . . . [T]o speak of our values as objective and universal is . . . to say that we cannot help accepting these basic principles because we are human, as we cannot help (if we are normal) seeking warmth rather than cold, truth rather than falsehood, to be recognized by others for what we are rather than to be ignored or misunderstood (pp. 203–204).

Maria acts, or hopes to act, out of this belief that human nature inclines predominantly toward benevolence and cooperation, that it becomes corrupted when children are psychologically inhibited and socially indoctrinated by adults. Children will treat others as they have been treated. The abusing parent often has been an abused child, the loving parent a well-loved child. Bad behavior is likely the manifestation of bad treatment; it is "unnatural." This belief motivates Maria to explain carefully the reasons for specific rules and the consequences of infractions, to invite student participation in (and even student acceptance or rejection of some) significant decisions, and to maintain respectful attention to student reactions. And it strongly inclines her to keep criticism, punishment, and repression to a minimum.

In humiliating Tony, and thereby breaking faith with him, Maria believes she violated her own principles and put at risk his natural drive to affiliate. Tony's intrinsic drive to be an agent of the good, derailed due to hardships, relies on her faith in and kindness toward him. This belief in a child's natural but fragile goodness echoes another theme of Simone Weil (1986): "[W]hen a man's life is destroyed or damaged by some wound or privation of soul or body, which is due to other men's actions or negligence, it is not only his sensibility that suffers but also his aspiration towards the good" (p. 204).

Hardie's "take" on human nature is more hardened. When he looks out into the world, he sees more callousness toward others than empathy. Hardie is impressed by our "limited" rather than by our "natural" sympathies, by our willingness to abuse others rather than to satisfy them. He would find compelling the fairly dismal presumptions of Iris Murdoch (1970):

That human beings are naturally selfish seems true on the evidence, whenever and wherever we look at them, in spite of a very small number of apparent exceptions. . . . The psyche is a historically determined individual relentlessly looking after itself. . . . It is reluctant to face unpleasant realities. Its consciousness is not normally a transparent glass through which it views the world, but a cloud of more or less fantastic reverie designed to protect the psyche from pain. It constantly seeks consolation, either through imagined inflation of self or through fictions of a theological nature (pp. 78–79).

The temptation to increase pleasure is limitless—from grabbing the biggest portion of food in the cafeteria to taking advantage of others as a child to hoarding riches in later life. Resisting temptation and subjugating desire are the heart and soul of morality. If one believes human nature is disposed to "self-interested and anti-social attitudes," explained David Carr (1991), it makes sense to assert that children must be "controlled externally by imposed law or internally by the inculcation of a conscience informed by principles of altruistic self-control" (p. 185). What follows from such premises is a pedagogy of constraint, of systematically and relentlessly acculturating the young to the school's (and society's) expectations.

Thus, while Maria's values of caring and kindness promote the celebration of human passions that, if followed, will *naturally* direct us toward loving attachments, Hardie's values of restraint and self-control call for the repression of human passions that, let loose, will *naturally* destroy social well-being. For Hardie, to avoid improper behavior children must submit respectfully to those in rightful authority, among whom one's teacher tops the list. Once that respect, that leverage, is lost, a child is no longer instructable. To Maria, it is as children become sensitized to the feelings of others that their sympathies expand, they supplement self-regarding with other-regarding interests, and they come naturally to consider the needs of classmates before scooping up the most and best, whether of the cafeteria food, baseball cards, or other goods.

To us human nature is both naturally "good" and naturally "bad." "The primary impulse of each is to maintain and aggrandise himself. The secondary impulse is to go out of the self, to correct its provincialism and heal its loneliness. In love, in virtue, in the pursuit of knowledge, and in the reception of the arts, we are doing this" (Lewis, 1968, p. 115). It is the duality of our natures that lends justification to Maria's and Hardie's positions and passes on responsibility for delicately balancing our own responses to children.

How do we formulate discipline strategies that reflect this thick view of human nature, that respond to our varying moral priorities, that provide for listening to and leaning on children? We turn to Jan Bonham's reflections.

■ ■ ■ ■ ■

## A FOUR-STEP APPROACH
## TO DISCIPLINE—Dr. Jan Bonham

In an ideal school there is no discipline. Students arrive at every class on time, straining to engage their studies. They cooperate with teachers and one another, obey classroom rules (which they share in designing), do homework promptly to the best of their ability, and are loyal members of the school community. But that is not our world; witness the blizzard of rules that rain down on students (and teachers).

Well beyond requirements of study, schools have a lock on children's personal lives: what they wear, when and how they talk, where and how they sit, when and how they move, when and how they eat, even when they go to the bathroom. Teachers, too, are regimented, with administrative control (of varying degrees) over the selection of their books, lessons, tests, and discipline. Maria, Hardie, and their fellow teachers enjoy the luxury of disagreement over Tony in part because he is a fifth-grade student. Had his misbehavior occurred in a high school class, he most likely would have been reported to the vice principal and a punishment meted out according to the disciplinary code of the school (see Ingersoll, 2003).

Discipline in contemporary public schools is heavily bureaucratized, with uniform, well-publicized rules and associated sanctions for breaking them: for example, late once, a reminder; late twice, a reprimand; late thrice, a deprivation of privileges; on the fourth lateness, an in-school detention. (For a rich discussion of bureaucratic discipline, see Sergiovanni, 1994.) The impersonal sanctions look to the violation, not the violator or context. Any objective of discipline, beyond that of student control, is not readily apparent from reading a number of high school and district codes. This is true not only in schools but also in much of the school-advising literature, which since the 1950s has increasingly stressed strategies over purpose (see Butchart, 1998).

Yet order is not a self-evident justification for discipline. A quiet room with obedient children does not obviously maximize learning. As McEwan (1998) noted, "While some students may be willing to bend to the control systems practiced by educators, particularly when those practices are consonant with the homes from which the students come, there are others who will view imposed, arbitrary rules as a call to arms" (p. 143).

The debate on discipline circulates around the best methods to secure compliance. Is it through a participatory democratic approach, which minimizes coercion and encourages voluntary acquiescence? (see Glasser, 1990). Or through clear behavioral expectations that, when breached, trigger predetermined consequences? (see Canter and Canter, 1992). One camp believes that imposed sanctions and punishment devalue the child and take away his agency, the other that sanctions and punishments engender respect for rules. Both sides justify their respective approaches on grounds of effectiveness. The message is, "Buy my approach and have a smooth-running classroom."

*(continued)*

A bureaucratic approach is not without merit. One asset is its apparent fairness: Rules are transparent; violations are treated uniformly. Teachers, as equal-opportunity enforcers, cannot be accused of arbitrariness or favoritism. If a child or parent complains, there is the ready response: "Don't blame me, it's the rule." It's a "teacher-proof" system.

Bureaucratic discipline also clarifies the exact nature of the school's expectations. Rules are perceived by the authorities as not to be tampered with, acquiring almost a sanctified status: The value of the rule is the rule. As Durkheim (1961) observed:

> Doubtless when one examines the rules of conduct that the teacher must enforce, in themselves and in detail, one is inclined to judge them as useless vexations. . . . Is it not possible for a child to be good and yet fail to be punctual, to be unprepared at the specified time for his lesson or other responsibilities, etc.? If, however, instead of examining these school rules in detail, we consider them as a whole, as the student's code of duty, the matter takes on a different aspect. Then conscientiousness in fulfilling all these petty obligations appears as a virtue (p. 151).

Respect for the rule equals respect for the school, equals respect for the social moral order.

But there is a considerable downside to the bureaucratic approach. Most fundamentally, it is crude; it fails to make the critical differentiations required by moral discipline. The almost-exclusive focus on the act disregards person and circumstances. Call this *the lumping of children.*[1] Obviously the wrongness of a violation will vary depending upon the student's intention, knowledge, history, and precipitating events. Motives and dispositions matter. The difficulty schools have with individualized judgments—different strokes for different folks—is that it subjectivizes discipline, resulting in an unequal application of sanctions for the same act. Even though a disciplinary response that is properly adjusted to the situation may be equitable, it invites complaints of unfairness. Without discretion, however, the teacher's judgment and status are deprecated, the complexities of moral behavior buried. To serve an educative function, discipline, like instruction, must be subtly adjusted to circumstances.

Second, there is a compression of deed and sanction. Call this *the lumping of wrongs.* Those acts that violate conventions are lumped with those that violate morality. Wrongs are sometimes categorized by location (classroom, building, out of the building), sometimes alphabetically, sometimes by degree of disruption. The last, which might border on moral classification, still ends up listing

---

[1]There is some overstatement here. Occasionally one comes across a disciplinary code in which intention is required for a penalty (as in intentional disruption, rather than disruption alone). After looking at many such codes, however, one comes away impressed by their unfriendliness to context; the penalty typically follows the violation without further consideration.

together incompatible infractions. It is common, for example, to find a code that combines dress violations, lateness to school, and fraud, imposing a common penalty for all. In the School District of Philadelphia (2002–2003), running in the halls, persistent tardiness, and loitering are listed jointly as first level offenses along with forgery, cheating, and copying the work of another student.

A third inadequacy is *the lumping of objectives.* Typically, a code lists a hierarchy of sanctions that appear to be calibrated by the amount of pain they inflict. For example, depending only on the number of repetitions, the sanction for a given offense may be one to five days of after-school detention, then one to three days of suspension. To be sure, there are lesser sanctions such as reprimands, meetings with students, parent notification, temporary assignment to a different class, suspension of privileges; there are also graver ones such as long suspensions leading to a permanent ouster pending action by the board of education, with no distinctions in the outcomes sought.

What is problematic here is that the sanctions are all implicitly designed only to maximize compliance with the rule, that is, to make sure the behavior does not recur. The Philadelphia code states explicitly that its goal is to be "corrective, not punitive" (School District of Philadelphia, 2002–2003, p. 10). This simple dichotomy misses an important point. Absent from many of the lists is a recognition that there is a moral distinction between bad language and forgery, between tardiness and cheating. Absent, too, is any suggestion that one might have differentiated objectives beyond correction, and differentiated approaches beyond deprivations, for responding to wrongful behaviors. As Lawrence Nucci (2001) advised, responses to children should be "domain-concordant" (p. 145). If a child hits another, he suggests, it would be better to say, "John, that really upset Mike," rather than "We have a rule against hitting," whereas if a child gets up from his seat during math, it would be preferable to point to the rule rather than to the distress of others. With moral infractions, the primary objective is to change the *person* rather than, or in addition to, changing a *behavior* (see Dewey, 1991, Lecture 7; Durkheim, 1961). When a conventional (convenience) rule is broken, compliance is presumptively the primary objective; if a moral injunction is violated, compliance may be insufficient.

A sensitive moral-discipline policy will take into account the nature of the *rules* (standards), the *context* (child and circumstance) of the rule violation, the *objectives* of discipline beyond compliance, and flexible systems of *intervention* that meet the objectives. These four factors caution educators not to "manage" incidents before reviewing them. The meaning of identical acts—jostling and lateness, for example—will vary, as we have seen, by circumstances. Circumstances also affect objectives, and objectives constrain interventions. However much one might long for a decision-making tree (or a computer program!) that could thread through the variables, that longing seems doomed to frustration. A tree could never capture all the subtle inter-

*(continued)*

actions, nor the variety of individual judgments. Tardiness, for example, may result from an errant parent, absent-minded child, or deliberate disdain for a teacher; a scowl from a caring teacher may be more effective than expulsion by an indifferent one. There is no substitute for the sensitive discernment of a teacher backed by school policies that promote her discretion.

The matrix below describes an array of acts and contexts that differentially implicate the objectives and interventions appropriate to each circumstance. Following is an illustration of each point in the array.

The following situations illustrate the meaning of the several acts and context.

**Intervention as a Function of the Act in Its Context**

| | | Context | | |
|---|---|---|---|---|
| *Act* | | *Intentional* | *Extenuating Circumstances* | *Innocent* |
| A Moral Matter | | punishment, designed to change *person* | punishment (lesser) designed to change *person* | teach, without punishment, to change *act* (deter) |
| | 1 | (a) | (b) | (c) |
| Derivatively Moral | | correction, expected to change person or change act (deter) | explain, through correction, to change act *or* punishment (mild) to change person | explain, without punishment or correction, to change act |
| | 2 | (a) | (b) | (c) |
| Convention | | correction, to change act *or* change rule | explain, through correction, to change act *or* change rule | explain, without correction, to change act *or* change rule |
| | 3 | (a) | (b) | (c) |

1. A student takes a wallet
   (a) knowing it wasn't hers, intending to keep or discard it.
   (b) having been put up to it by a "club" she was anxious to be admitted into.
   (c) thinking it was hers.

2. A student says, "Screw you!" to another child
    (a) as a put-down.
    (b) because he becomes suddenly angry and "loses it."
    (c) intending to convey nothing more than "no way."
3. A student gets into line at the wrong place
    (a) intentionally.
    (b) talking with a classmate, who has a different place in line.
    (c) unaware of the rule about place in line.

## Your Turn:
## Tailoring Discipline

The varying presumptions of Maria and Hardie in their "reading" of morally significant conduct, moral priorities, disciplinary responses, and human nature at least partially explain their pedagogical preferences. Now it devolves upon you, the reader, to consider *your* premises and how they inform *your* pedagogy. To concretize these reflections we invite you to imagine the following scenarios. As you do so, consider, along with any other inputs you think valid, Dr. Bonham's analytical framework and her matrix.

1. A couple of children have been bringing copies of a major clothing catalogue, which includes topless models, to school. The teacher's attention was drawn to the "reading material" only when other students joined the "perpetrators" during recess and after lunch. So far the catalogues have not appeared during instructional time. When the teacher shares the incident with colleagues, their suggestions run the expected gamut:
    a) Forbid them from bringing such publications to school.
    b) Allow students to look at them only off school property (school bus, walking to and from school).
    c) Hold a class meeting in which all views are exposed and a solution is democratically determined.
    d) Don't do anything as long as students peruse the catalaogues only during their free time.

    Assume that the teacher explains to the class that the publications are offensive and bans them from school. After a week or so they reappear. She informs the instigators that she will now have to speak to their parents and, if the problem reappears, send them to the vice principal.
    e) Would you have banned the catalogues?
    f) Would you have made the disciplinary decision or taken a different course?

g) On what premises would you rely to explain your responses? Consider the distinction between correction and punishment.

2. A child in your fifth-grade class frequently copies the work of her neighbor. It is done so openly that you are not completely certain that she knows this is cheating. When you confront her, she denies any cheating: "Just checking my answers," she says.
   a) In dealing with this incident, do you see a role for the neighboring child? For the entire class?
   b) Imagine a conversation between you and the child: Would you want to separate the issue of copying from that of her denial?

3. Some fifth-grade girls start painting their nails despite a new policy against it. You intuitively agree with the rule; cosmetics already absorb them too much, what's the rush? They tell you their families have no objections; in fact they've been wearing nail polish to school since first grade. Why this new policy?
   a) What kind of an offense are they committing?
   b) How do you interpret the circumstances (intentions, consequences, mores) surrounding their objections?
   c) Is this a problem to be mutually resolved, or a behavior to be corrected? Should the rule be reconsidered?
   d) Is there reason to consider punishment for the disobedience?

4. Schools are increasingly adopting "zero tolerance" policies for various offenses. A senior girl had a sexual encounter with a classmate in his home, while a boy in your ninth-grade home room videotaped them through a window by prearrangement with the senior boy. The school got wind of the affair when the tape began to circulate among the students.
   a) Is this behavior deserving of punishment or only correction?
   b) If the former, what should be the proposed punishment?
   c) Assume that the school's policy calls for expulsion in such circumstances. Does that change your reaction?

■ ■ ■ ■ ■

# CHAPTER 7

# WHOSE VALUES?
# RELATIVISM
# AND PLURALISM

## *Scenario*

After their blow-up, Tony dropped his provocativeness and occasionally participated in the class meetings that Maria was now holding on a regular basis. She could barely suppress a spasm of self-righteousness these days as, walking down the hallway, she heard Hardie's stentorian voice. But this confidence was shattered when, out of the blue, she stumbled into another moral education pitfall highly reminiscent of Don Downer's troubles.

It began with Jon, a student possessed of a large weekly allowance, who came to class with a batch of baseball cards. Within days the children were pulling cards from tote bags and lunch boxes, spending every spare moment outside class time trading. The activity uncorked a torrent of competition among the students; for a fifth-grade class a great deal of money was being brought to school and spent. Maria noticed that some children were getting twenty-five dollars for a card, others no more than a few dollars. The rich were getting richer, and Maria strongly suspected that the successful traders were taking advantage of the more gullible boys. Worse, more than once cards apparently disappeared from students' desks; enraged children were accusing others of stealing. Finally, Maria began to overhear a fair amount of pretty crude language, usually directed at fellow students and muttered in low voices.

Maria was distressed by the children's emotional and social blindness, their greed and materialism, their discord and bad language, the possible stealing. But she hesitated to act on impulse and simply forbid baseball cards in class. Although she despised the acquisitiveness, the jockeying for position, the showing off associated with the trading, she understood that her reaction was probably personal, reflecting her identification with the excluded, exploited, weaker kids. She realized that trading baseball cards was a time-honored pastime—her cousin had a much treasured collection—and that it might be a natural and relatively harmless way to learn "social skills." So the kids were thoughtless and insensitive to each other. Did that require her to intervene, especially when it seemed limited to this one activity? Was this particular insensitivity any worse than teasing or gossiping? The children weren't the only ones Maria knew with a craving for making money, nor the only consumers of expensive items. Money is one of our society's highest values. So long as the card trading did not interfere with academic instruction, maybe she should let it go, even if it had some troubling fallout; see it as a craze that would dissipate over time and not the affair of a teacher or the school. For her to keep interfering whenever anything met with *her* disapproval was to alienate the kids and to make school an increasingly unnatural, then a detested, place. Stealing was another matter, but it had not been proved; she resolved to keep a sharper eye on that aspect of the problem.

As for the bad language, much as that really bothered her, it was increasingly part of many people's everyday vocabulary. With threats and punishments she could probably curtail the speech at school, but was it worth doing when they didn't swear during work time? Given that swearing was so much a part of their speech habits, and widely accepted outside school, what would she accomplish with a prohibition?

So Maria kept her own counsel, which was not difficult for her, thinking as she still did that "moral matters" were part of her job only when they kept her from doing her real job. But the sudden eruption of a large and loud fight among her students in the cafeteria lunch line brought the question to a head. While the class was waiting its turn for food service, Jon, still king of the cards, negotiated a trade with his classmate Michael, giving a Brady Anderson card in an even exchange for a Ken Griffey, Jr. Luke, a friend of Michael's, observed the transaction and vigorously took umbrage: "You can't do that, Jon; you know that's no fair. Michael, don't be a damn fool. Don't give that cheating asshole your Griffey."

Jon's anger flared up, and his voice rose. "Fuck off, Luke. Get out of his face. It's none of your damn business. Where were you yesterday, Mister goody-goody, when someone stole my Greg Maddux card?"

Luke moved menacingly toward Jon. "Go to hell, asshole! You're just a big fat bully. Leave Michael alone or I'll beat the shit out of you."

Maria was mortified. Children and teachers were watching the scene intently. Her heart racing, she moved rapidly, grabbed the cards and the boys, took them to the end of the line, and sternly commanded them to see her immediately after lunch. Jon, inflamed over the incident, muttered another "fuck" as he released his cards.

When it was time for the talk, Maria, still smarting with anger and humiliation, decided that she was in no shape to sort out her responses to the incident and the broader problem that had dramatically returned to center stage. So she simply asked the boys to think over the event and come to school the next day prepared to talk about it. She would do likewise.

Maria was slightly delayed the following morning, having stopped briefly at the front office to consult with Fred Helter. He advised her to stand firm: Listen to the boys' stories, but briefly, and give them a three-day detention. If she wanted to let them have more say, as he suspected she did, there could be some negotiation around the specifics of the detention—what they would do, where they would do it, what would be said to their parents. Maria was not thrilled with the advice. The quick resolution, the standard punishment, seemed canned.

As she entered the fifth-grade classroom, Maria's now attentive ears picked up a familiar covert buzzing, always a tip-off that there was big news. When she spied the poorly concealed gash on Jon's arm and Luke's purple, puffy eye, she guessed it. Attempting to sound casual, Maria leaned against her desk and observed, "So, there's been a fight. Would you tell me about it now before the bell rings?"

Silence.

"Look, I'm not asking you to tattle on each other; you don't even have to use names. Just let me know if it's over, or if you guys are still angry."

More silence.

With exasperation, she tried again. "Boys, I can't teach until I know we've got some peace around here."

A deepening silence.

"I thought we were building a community in this room. How can that work if we don't trust one another enough to talk over what is obviously a big deal? Jon, will you start us off?"

"No, I don't want to talk. It wasn't anything."

Maria saw that she must bide her time. At recess she put three chairs by her desk and told Jon, Michael, and Luke to stay in. Sulkily they slouched into the chairs, Jon shoving his a distance from the others.

She began, "OK, you don't want to talk. Maybe it would help if I get us started and you chime in. What I figure is that after school you were still mad at each other over the card trading that turned sour." She stole a glance at Jon. "One of you started taunting and teasing. That provoked another, and soon fists were flying. The scuffle got serious and probably more piled on. Right so far?"

"Sort of," Michael grudgingly responded. The others bored holes in the floor with their fixed stares. Maria suspected her approach was not going to yield the whole story, but she sallied forth again.

"I'm not interested in the details of who did what to whom or why, but I am interested in why you think the solution to a dispute is fighting. You know this school has a no-fight policy; you know that. We have a committee on conflict resolution that is supposed to hear from you when there's a problem. How come you didn't go to them? How come you *never* go to them"?

Jon finally broke the silence. Raising his shoulders, and moving forward in his chair, he began in a taut voice: "Look, Ms. Laszlo, with all due respect, going to committees and having meetings is not the way we handle stuff. My dad says that when someone says something insulting to me, I should stand up to him. You heard Luke yesterday, and you should have heard him sound off with my brother. We're supposed to take care of ourselves. Only a sissy walks from a fight."

Jon's word brought Luke in, taking the baton as Michael's champion. "I'm not sorry for what I said after what he did to Michael. If Jon and his brother want to fight it out, fine with me."

"But what's the point?" Maria protested (just as Downer would have). "You hit him, he hits you, more people get involved, they get hurt, it escalates, it all gets repeated again and again."

"Ms. Laszlo," Luke responded, "We just don't see it your way. You talk about respect and all that stuff. Well, we keep our respect by not letting no one take advantage of us. I help Michael out because he's not that strong yet. He helps me plenty with schoolwork. We help each other; we stand up for each other. That's respect for us."

"But don't you see how much better we would be if we all took care of one another and worked out our problems as a community?"

Luke jumped up, his initial statement having stirred up his anger: "If you don't want us to fight, why didn't you do something to stop Jon in the first place? He started the whole thing. Everyone could see he was abusing Michael."

"I don't see Jon as a bad kid."

"Come on, Ms. Laszlo, take another look. Jon wants the best goddamn set of cards in the school. He's a bully. OK. That's how he is. Lots of kids are like that. But if you want to stop the fighting, you gotta stop the bullying. Otherwise we'll take care of it ourselves. And talking it out, and going to that dispute resolution place—that's just not our way."

With this final shot, Luke pushed his chair back, and returned his eyes to the floor. Jon kept silent.

Maria realized with a start that she had become the enemy, the boys united against her. Their ethic of fair fighting, getting even, was firmly entrenched. "OK boys, I get where you're coming from. I don't agree, but we'll leave it at that for now. Around school, however, you must understand there is to be no fighting, and no cursing either. I'm going to do some consulting with other teachers before taking further action about what you all did in the cafeteria yesterday."

Before meeting with the committee, Maria tried to identify just what aspects of this complex mess called for a response and what response she should make. Although knowing that most of her colleagues would have no difficulty condemning all elements of the incident, she still wondered what exactly the offense was: Is swearing wrong in itself? Is it wrong when directed to, or at, a fellow student, or at her, in front of her colleagues? What about Jon swindling Michael? What of Jon's accusation regarding the theft of his Greg Maddux card? Was card trading itself the villain? Or was it the association between trading and money? What about the easy resort to manipulative, aggressive bargaining methods with classmates? And then this constant conflict over conflict: How much fighting, even out-of-school fighting, should she tolerate?

The answers to these questions would help her decide whether to impose a sanction, confine a discussion to the three children involved, open up the subject with all the students who traded, or engage the entire class in a discussion. They would have to examine how the trading excluded and hurt people, leading to unacceptable speech and manipulation among the students; how it accelerated into violence, perhaps even outright theft, degrading the general moral climate of the class. Until she knew what judgments to make, she couldn't even begin to think about interventions.

Maria decided that her fundamental problem was how to distinguish what was wrong for her, but not necessarily for others, from what was universally just plain wrong. With these reflections she joined the committee meeting.

## TEACHERS' MEETING

When they had gathered together, Maria opened up with a full account of the last two days. Hardie, incredulous that Maria would let matters so degenerate so soon after her experiences with Tony, tactlessly asked, "Why didn't you do what must be obvious to your sensible nonteacher self: clamp down on the card trading as soon as it got out of hand?"

"Hardie," she answered, "naturally, part of me wanted to put card trading and swearing totally off limits. You know I don't allow either during instructional time, but I'm unclear (cloudy vision, remember) whether I should put a stop to it altogether, limit it further in some way, or talk with the class about the problems it seems to have created.

"Take the swearing. No one likes to be cussed out in public. But should we try to stop all use of foul language? I don't like to hear it; to me swear words degrade the language, and the speaker too, when they become habitual. But that's me. Nowadays, it's ingrained in the talk of so many people. Is it really any worse than saying 'like' all the time or wearing revealing clothes? I guess students should realize that such things will hurt them when they get out of school and into the workplace (or higher education), but maybe the words aren't really wrongful unless they are being used to injure another person. There's a difference between swearing that is mean, directed *against* someone, or really defiant, and the talk we hear from children every day, the 'what the fuck, who the fuck, this fuckin' thing.' It matters whether you swear into the air, so to speak, or swear *at* someone else.

"As long as there are no bad *consequences*—and I see that the kids basically ignore the speech—maybe we should treat swearing as just another one of those practices that change with the times, just as pants replaced skirts in my day—to the howls of horrified adults, I might add. Suppose when trading cards Jon meant to swindle Michael but Michael actually knew the value of his Ken Griffey card. If he wasn't misled at all but didn't care because he's crazy about Brady Anderson, then perhaps Jon did no harm."

"Maria," Hardie retorted, "I am sick of making every decision on the basis of good, bad, or neutral consequences. To me it doesn't matter if people are offended only because swearing is a social (call it conventional) no-no, or if in a particular case it doesn't seem directed at anyone. Suppose there are times when it's just a tough-guy way of talking, meant to impress and not to hurt. So what? Sure, kids and a lot of adults are desensitized to swearing, but the fact remains that it degrades the classroom environment, and just ruling it out of bounds is a lot simpler than trying to explain a bunch of fine distinctions."

"The truth is, Hardie, that I'm personally much more bothered by the callous manipulations of the kids' card trading than by the swearing. To many, their classmates were just objects to be pushed around for their own self-aggrandizement. Talk about behaviors that have moral implications for later life! I saw some embryonic corporate raiders at work in my class, and that's where some moral education would make a lot more sense than imposing our cultural speech patterns on them."

"Some of those corporate raiders, Maria, are their parents, or they would be if they could pull it off. And as I recall, one of the buildings at the university where we met is named for a particularly successful and, from what I've heard about him, particularly nasty one. You'd be raising a hornet's nest, complaining about good old American initiative."

"But Hardie, everyone says moral education starts with simple things like respect for others and their feelings. How do I let the card trading pass when in its own way it's at least as unfeeling and vicious as a hearty 'fuck you' can ever be?"

"I would get at that in a little less challenging way, Maria. I teach students respect for one another with positive routines—call them rules if you want. We've been talking today more about inhibiting the immoral than fostering the moral. The point of my 'rules' is less to forbid than to cultivate 'character.' As you know, I insist on a lot of what I see as character-building behaviors. Every morning, for instance, the kids stand up and greet me, and I them. They tutor younger children, say the pledge, clean up the pets' cages, write notes to anyone who is sick, water the plants, straighten the room before lunch, and . . ."

"Let's get back on track," Maria interrupted, mildly annoyed by what she perceived to be Hardie's moral smugness. "What would you do in my shoes?"

"I'd go after the swearing and I'd let the card trading go, although if you wanted to rule 'no cards in class at any time' because they cause a lot of disruption, I'd back you 100 percent. I'd let the lecture on the ethics of capitalism go, too. Instead, pick something simple and nonthreatening that will teach them to spend a little time on someone other than number one.

"Well, no surprise, looks like we've got into another logjam." It was Aggie joining in. "If I understand you two, Maria would comfortably clamp down on the card trading because she sees the way it was done as 'really wrong'; inevitably, it produced victors and vanquished, and encouraged and rewarded antisocial behavior. Hardie would have a no-swearing rule regardless of whether swearing is intrinsically 'really wrong.' Is that about it?"

"In a way," Hardie said, "but . . ."

"It's the *but* that I want to understand," Aggie went on. "I somehow suspect it does matter to you that swearing, even if it isn't 'really wrong,' is still something that offends a lot of people and is going to get in the way of your students making their way in the world. It isn't just a matter of personal taste."

"It matters," Hardie responded, "but not to that great an extent. Even though I don't see card trading as morally offensive as long as it doesn't interfere with academic work and as long as no kid is *deliberately* swindling another, I'd still support Maria or any other teacher who wanted to stop it. Teachers' values need to be respected regardless of whether a behavior is universally seen as wrong."

"You mean to say, Hardie," Aggie continued, "that we teachers should exact conformity to our personal preferences even when the act isn't 'really wrong,' or isn't something that 'bothers a lot of people'? Isn't that what people (justifiably) call intolerance? What about the fact that I'm bothered by 98 percent of what passes for music these days? It doesn't directly interfere with my teaching, but I think it 'degrades the classroom environment,' as you would say. Do I get to tell the kids they can't listen to it, even in their free time, if I'm in the vicinity?"

"Well, let's see," began Hardie, growing thoughtful. "Clearly you've got to stop the morally impermissible; swindling is a good example. I think you should also stop that which 'bothers a lot of people.' Perhaps you should be careful about 'just a personal thing.' However, I'd probably grant teachers a pretty free hand with all three. In a sense that's what tolerance is. I mean, kids have to be tolerant of teachers' preferences just as we're supposed to be tolerant of theirs.

"Mind you, I understand Maria's concern about abusing authority—and perhaps yours and Connie's, too. If we weigh in on every bothersome behavior, how do we teach children to honor the moral *imperium*: to understand the commanding, universal quality of morality? After all, no one would say to a child, 'Stealing is wrong, but if you really like those sneakers take them,' whereas even I might say, 'Baked potatoes are better for you than French fries, but eat whichever you want.' Still, I feel a greater latitude to 'train up' the child according to my own notions than you do. That's clear."

"If I can jump in here," Connie began, "I think Hardie, self-assured though you are, could use some support. The fine lines you're trying to draw, Aggie, are just that—very trying to me. We were not charged by Helter to write an ethics curriculum but to establish a moral ed program for our school. Isn't it obvious that we need a crystal-clear policy forbidding swearing, card trading, *and* fighting in school? And if fighting occurs outside school but has repercussions in class, we must get to the parents right away about it too. That should be an up-front, spelled-out policy that's enforced by the entire faculty."

Maria thought, she's just like the principal, jumping right over the merits of the children's positions with an "obvious" policy. Yet she's highly experienced, so what gives?

"Connie," she said, "You're moving too fast for me. If you'd only heard the kids, then maybe you'd agree with me that they have a point we need to consider. There are strong friendships and strong rivalries among them, and they watch each other's backs. It works. Luke emboldens Michael; without Luke, Michael would be easy prey. He could never go up against Jon alone, never mind taking on that tight Jon-and-his-brother combination. But these coalitions are cemented by confrontation and payback. They are part of the kids' world, part of their friendship. It all makes sense to them."

"But Maria," protested Connie, "You can't be suggesting that we just let kids fight it out, that might makes right around here."

"Look, Connie, I hold strong credentials as a peace lover. Everyone has told me all my life that I've got my head in the clouds. Well, maybe they're right. Anyway, my efforts to negotiate the problems away aren't working. What the kids are saying is that life is about competition, about winning and staying on top until you're toppled. They jostle for position and power. A certain amount of aggression is part of their system.

"The truth is that's how it is in all humans everywhere, right? We're not talking about killing or knives or guns; just a limited 'fair fight.' You know, when the Bible said, 'Eye for eye, tooth for tooth, hand for hand, foot for foot, burning for burning, wound for wound, stripe for stripe,' it was outlawing excessively violent retribution, but not proportionate violence."

"Oh, great! Maria, you *are* suggesting we let kids slug it out in school!"

"No, we can't allow it in the classroom, that's clear. But," Maria persisted, "outside the classroom? Should we be down on them for it? Is this one of those universal values? It seems that the angrier they get, the more we crack down, the less they respect us. Now we don't even allow children to play dodge ball at recess; soon we won't give them recess altogether. Should we be *so-o-o* disapproving? What I'm trying to say, Connie, and Hardie too, is that though it's not my way, not your way, it's not so clearly a horrible way; there is something very natural and normal and eternal about getting even. Who am I to say it should be repressed entirely—as if it could be repressed, when that's the way they and their families, and the world for that matter, live?"

"Maria, don't give me all that relativistic who-can-judge crap. If . . ."

"Just let me finish, Connie. I'm also wondering about the price we pay working so hard to kill their form of 'dispute resolution.' There was an energy in the kids' talk about fair/unfair, getting even, that I sure hadn't seen in the negotiations we drag them to. Good solid friendships always have their share of indignation. Maybe our way isn't just naive; maybe, it's got a real downside. It flattens and stifles relationships."

Connie rose from her chair, amazed. "Maria, what world, or at least what school, allows *any* fighting?"

"For one, I've read that in Japan teachers of young kids do permit fighting," Maria rejoined. "And many of my kids' parents are advocates. They don't want their children—especially their sons—growing up as sissies. We don't prepare them for the real world by insisting that everything goes to dispute resolution committees."

"I don't get it, Maria. Aren't you bending over backward to justify something that is completely contrary to your own standards? You know that at school we do, and we must, teach children to use reason, not turn to their fists each time someone gets in their way. Unless they can subdue their anger by rational thinking, in school and out, they can't possibly grow to be decent, fair-minded people."

"I'm not suggesting we give them a free pass on violence and abandon reason," said Maria, frustrated at Connie's complacent self-assuredness. "I'm suggesting that maybe limited acts of violence have a justified place in their relationships. As you know better than I do, they and their parents certainly think so, including Jon, who was the target of the fight."

"Maria, you're playing devil's advocate with me," said Connie.

"I suppose so, given my basically pacifist leanings, but hear me out. You're right, we don't have to put up with fighting; it's not a necessity of life, like breathing. But it is an expression of authentic feeling, and I don't need to tell you that feelings are the stuff that shapes actions. I'm not so sure there isn't more honesty, more truth, more dependability in emotions (even hostile ones) than in reason. The indignation and loyalty that were behind the boys' fighting was good. The purpose of their fighting was to right an injustice, not to celebrate the glory of battle. That was good too.

"At least in fifth grade, the kids are as much physical as rational beings. Of course we have to curb their physicality; the question is how much, in what circumstances, and in what way. It's one thing to say there have to be rules to protect people from really getting injured, or to say fighting is not appropriate at school. It's another to say it's just flat-out 'wrong.' My brothers fought; they're decent, and good buddies as well. Now that I look back, I believe their fights also were usually a means to an end, and the end was often a matter of fairness, of principle."

"Maria, I can't supply a study," Connie began, "but we do know that children identified as aggressive in early life are more likely headed for later trouble than children who don't get so identified. However, I realize you're not talking about chronically aggressive children.

"I appreciate what you've 'shared,' as they say in my field. I mean that. Much of it sounds plausible, especially the thought that we'll never eliminate aggression. I do, however, think we all should do our best to stop, and persuade the kids to stop, the fighting. It's a good zero-tolerance prohibition, a good limit. The risk of injury from even minor violence is just too great for us to condone or ignore fighting, on or off the school grounds. And, not to be uppity, my guess is that after you're done with your fair-minded considerations, you'll see it my way."

"Look, guys," said Aggie. "Connie has a point. We gotta get real. Whatever the long- and short-term consequences of fighting, Helter will think we've gone nuts if we get more permissive about violence. That, however, doesn't mean we need to be centurions. A little not noticing might be good, though not explicit, policy. That's what I was hinting at in the Downer scenario. But Maria has raised a much broader and enormously tough question: How do we handle value disagreements, not just among the families but among ourselves?

## A DEEPER LOOK

In this chapter we confront head-on themes that have bedeviled the teachers on several prior occasions (see especially Chapters 3 and 5). Given the moral diversity within our schools, how do we think about our own values, and what do we do about our conflicting answers? Many will think the question is absurd; only academics would quibble over what everyone else absorbs with their mother's milk. We ask, if you are one of those, that you suspend your certainty, at least temporarily, for to us it is equally absurd that one should think the answer obvious. While every society must prescribe a set of moral imperatives, those imperatives vary. There is no getting around the fact of moral pluralism and the need for schools to confront it.

Some would resolve the conflict of values by an appeal to consequences. This was part of Maria's rationale when she pleaded with the boys to stop fighting: "But don't you see how much better we would be [read happier] if we all took care of one another and worked out our problems as a community?" Consequences were also behind her doubt as to the wrongness of swearing: "As long as there are no bad consequences—and I see that the kids basically ignore the speech—maybe we should treat swearing as just another one of those practices that change with the times." On the other hand, Hardie scornfully dismissed the appeal to consequences ("I am sick of making every decision on the basis of good, bad, or neutral consequences") as a criterion for deciding whether or not and how much to curb the boys. Guided by a consequentialist approach, the question becomes not what practice is right, but what works out best for all involved. According to such reasoning, cheating at card trading is wrong, not because it breaches some principle, but because one cannot enjoy card trading if participants cheat. It breaks the ground rules that make the activity pleasurable.

We now explore the issues of pluralism, moral diversity, and consequentialism and then refocus on how a teacher threads her way between tolerance on the one hand and moral guidance on the other.

## Pluralism and Relativism

Maria and her students have incompatible positions on a genuine moral issue. She, like many teachers and school systems, is committed to teaching and exemplifying a rejection of violence as a proper response to injury, whereas Luke, Michael, and Jon regard limited violent retribution as an appropriate response to the disrespect they experienced. It is important to understand initially that each side in this disagreement makes a *moral* claim; that is, whether right or wrong, the boys are not simply rationalizing willful behavior. Nor do they seem to be making the *relativist* claim that Maria should not judge the rightness of their actions because neither side is right nor wrong; the matter simply reflects a variation in subcultural norms. Both sides seem to agree that there is a right and wrong response to what went on the preceding day. Recall Luke's impassioned words:

> We just don't see it your way. You talk about respect and all that stuff. Well, we keep our respect by not letting no one take advantage of us. I help Michael out because he's not that strong yet. He helps me plenty with schoolwork. We help each other; we stand up for each other. That's respect for us.

A relativist claims, as we wrote in Chapter 5, "There is no right or wrong answer, only differing points of view." It is impossible to arbitrate between Maria and her students because values have nothing to do with objective truths; they are all just cultural conventions. Those with power control the mores, but they do so without any justification beyond their position of power.

A rising moral skepticism has contributed to the idea that moral relativism is self-evidently sensible. We catalogue here a few of the major changes in our modern world contributing to this view:

*philosophically,* the failed quest for universally acknowledged truth

*technologically,* the rising influence of science, the rapidity of technological change, and the rise of instantaneous global communications

*politically,* the end of colonialism and the delegitimization of racially and religiously based notions of fitness to rule

*sociologically,* the continuing secularization of American life, the accelerating presence of multiple cultures within a single society, and the challenge of post-modernist thinking

*psychologically,* a widened acceptance of the belief that the superego unduly constrains our instinctual natures and is the cause of neurotic symptoms.

Some philosophers have maintained that goodness is not an objective set of facts but a judgment we impose upon the world. To say that X, something or someone, is good is to say nothing more than, "I approve of X." Goodness is not a tangible physical object, not a physical law (gravity), not an analytic fact (2 + 2 must equal 4 because of the meanings of "4," "2," and "+"). It is not the sort of thing that can be studied by the natural or social sciences.

In this view the answer to the fundamental question of ethics, "How shall I live?" can only be, "It's your choice" (although also your responsibility). We grope in the dark. As the existentialist philosopher Jean-Paul Sartre (1973) put it, "We are alone, with no excuses" (p. 86). Values are not part of the world, but merely a reflection of an attitude toward the world; morality is not something we can discover "out there," but something we invent. Goodness is unanalyzable and lacking any external or rational authority. In the words of David Hume (1896), morality "is more properly felt than judg'd of" (Bk. III, Part I, Sec. I, p. 470). One cannot, according to the position associated with both Hume and the English philosopher G. E. Moore (1993), derive an "ought" from an "is." To attempt that is to commit what Moore termed the "naturalistic fallacy," to confuse the desired with the desirable.

Yet we resist such extreme skepticism. If morality is nothing more than an individual's or group's subjective choice, the projection of personal preferences upon the world, then neither Maria nor the boys can make a claim of rightness for their view. Their school, of course, can establish a policy, assert its rightness, and enforce submission to it; however, when Jon enters another subculture devoted to a different set of rights and wrongs, he may be obliged to govern himself by its norms. But rule by a transient, local authority lacks a credible moral foundation, it lacks any grandeur or sense of its "overrid-ingness," and it makes one's willingness to submit less a matter of conscience than of coercion. Indeed, history supports the fear that believing the good, to be enforced on all, is solely the making of one's state, one's tribe, or one's leaders is to take a fateful step along the path toward totalitarianism. Only an external standard of morality, by which the actions of the powerful may be called to account, protects us, in the view of many, from despotism.

More personally, one's beliefs concerning the right and wrong of a matter tend to be bound up in an underlying conviction that those beliefs are actually true. A person asserting that a certain act is right (or wrong) does not ordinarily appear simply to be telling us something about himself. Philoso-pher-classicist Martha Nussbaum (1994) has eloquently described the cost of a systematic refusal to view ethical judgments as anything but the expression of wholly personal preferences:

> [Such a refusal] omit[s] something very fundamental to human life, namely the disposition to make ethical commitments and get upset about them. . . . Natural human practices are full of moral argument and moral stand-taking. . . .
>
> It seems, furthermore, that we might not want to live in the world these skeptics would give us. In that world . . . there would be . . . no commitment to fight for justice against a tyrant's pressure, no commitment to engage in any sort of unpopular or radical reform, no commitment to help a friend in trouble when help would impose difficulty, and no commitment to help [another] in her struggle for survival (pp. 208–09).

These objections take us from relativism to pluralism. As we noted in Chapter 5, "Pluralism rests on the belief that there *is* a right and wrong at stake, and that one may believe that he or she *knows* what it is but still think it right not to *insist* on having others act in accordance with that view." Thus, unlike relativists, pluralists believe in the objectivity of moral truth, that values are not just a matter of taste, but simultaneously hold that those whose moral sense differs from *their* own may be morally upright people, indeed, may even come to be seen as right.

The differences between relativism and pluralism are central to our understanding of one another and to decision making in schools. We must be careful not to confuse them. For example, let us say Person A believes that homosexuals are as "morally qualified" as anyone else to teach sex education courses. Person B disagrees but would not urge a law prohibiting homosexuals from such teaching. Why? Because though *he* is clear as to the rightness of his view, the intensity and fervor of his beliefs do not warrant his imposing it on those with differing convictions. That makes him a pluralist, not a relativist. Maria, clearly a pluralist, is leery about setting up a lot of rules around which there is strong disagreement, even though she has no problem justifying her own position.

There are many practices in the world that you and I disapprove of but others hold dear. What is our attitude and behavior toward them? It's easy when they fall into the conventional realm; we can overlook our differences. Women who go about bare-breasted in the South Sea Islands get a pass from most of us today, although they did not when missionaries were attempting to convert them. But what about the practice of clitorectomy or stoning an adulteress? Do we take a relativist, pluralist, or absolutist position? The distinctions bear importantly on our action. If it's all a matter of culture (relativism), we cannot justify intervening; if a matter of absolutism we do what we can to give asylum to potential victims and make efforts to stop it; if a matter of pluralism we argue our case but do not seek to require others to live by our view.

For a relativist, there is no basis for resolving the Maria/Hardie disputes. They may as well stop talking and agree to disagree. A school committed to relativism would comfortably admit to the arbitrariness of its standards. It might tell families, "This is what we demand and insist you conform to. Do as you wish elsewhere." Alternatively, the school might give teachers wide latitude in setting up their own norms and not stake out any schoolwide values. Alas, in today's schools an implicit relativism is dominant: The only shared value, and disputably a moral one, is "excellence," interpreted as high test scores. We believe this abdication of moral positioning is an unhappy resolution of the tensions aroused by our moral diversity. Before suggesting better options, however, let us pause over the contending moral views in Maria's classroom and elsewhere by examining two forms of diversity: *instrumental* (a diversity of "getting to" a common value) and *fundamental* (a diversity of the values themselves).

## Moral Diversity: Instrumental and Fundamental

Most teachers, as we have noted, would (and do) advocate resolution of conflict through verbal rather than physical means. Maria agrees that violent retribution is a highly destructive ethic, one that separates children from one another, works against community building, and promotes aggression and enmity.

Yet it is not obvious that the opposing ethic is wrong. Luke's assertion has some intuitive moral integrity to it, does it not? Limited violence in the service of self-respect, along with codes that specify the occasions for and appropriate measure of it, has not only been an observable aspect of many cultures, it has often been regarded as appropriate. In a fascinating study, Richard E. Nisbett and Dov Cohen (1996) described the "culture of honor" as it is played out in the descendants of Scotch-Irish herdsmen now living in the rural South. For them, violence is seen as a "legitimate response to insult, as an appropriate means of self-protection, and as a justifiable tool for restoring order" (p. 32). From such a premise, violence is a relatively unproblematic method of disciplining children, at home and at school. The southern code is similar to the urban "code of the streets" (Anderson, 1999), whereby an excessively long stare is widely interpreted as a manifestation of disrespect and (like being on the wrong "turf") viewed as warranting or even provoking a violent response.

Jon's stance is a mild form of this ethic. He does not buy into the morality of turning the other cheek. Perhaps he will forgive after an apology, or after he has gotten his "licks" in, but his morality is to hang tough, to stand up for himself. Maria's appeal to him—what if everyone resorted to violence to get even?—convinces him not at all, for Jon truly believes that "getting even" is right as well as realistic. The general welfare, as it were, is strengthened when everyone gets the point, "You mess with me and you'll be sorry." For Jon, this is the essence of "respect" and the best method for keeping peace.

Within any heterogeneous school one is likely to find some students and parents who believe in the righteousness of fighting to defend oneself and others one cares for. In holding these views they do not celebrate a life of violence or want their kids prepared for a militia or vigilante group. Their ultimate ambitions for children are more or less the same as those of the school. They see in the willingness to fight—"taking care of yourself," as the kids put it—a tool for building character. Without a certain toughness, grittiness, and moral fiber, the virtues of courage and loyalty, they believe, are pretty hollow hopes. Thus the differences are *instrumental*: While there exist common fundamental values—respect, loyalty, fairness—there is disagreement on how one grows them.

In a more radical variant of diversity, which we have called *fundamental*, the values of two groups squarely conflict all the way down. An example of this is traditional culture in India. In an eye-opening study of moral development, researchers (Shweder, Mahapatra, and Miller, 1987) found marked dissimilarities (as well as some agreement) between a group of Indian and American children, aged five to seven, that increased with age. For example, Brahmin children think it right for a father to cane an errant child or open his son's letter. American children think it wrong. Brahmin adults think it right to have unequal inheritance between males and females, or for a husband to beat a disobedient wife if she goes to the movies without his permission. Americans think it wrong. Most of the Brahmin women even believe that in an ultimate choice, one is obliged to save the firstborn son over the lastborn daughter. To the Indians, it is just for a woman to sacrifice herself for her husband, because men and women are not equal, a value at fundamental odds with current American beliefs.

Whereas we can separate ourselves from Brahmin values, we cannot separate ourselves from the collision of values represented by Maria and her students. In such circumstances, what moral justifications should the contestants appeal to?

## Consequences

As we have noted, appealing to consequences is a common recourse. Consequentialist thinkers judge the morality of an act by its contribution to overall happiness or other presumptively agreed-upon goods. According to the philosopher John Stuart Mill (1979), our moral sightings should be trained neither on the act nor on the character of the actor but on what follows from an action:

> [A]ctions are right in proportion as they tend to promote happiness; wrong as they tend to produce the reverse of happiness. By happiness is intended pleasure and the absence of pain; by unhappiness, pain and the privation of pleasure.
>
> [N]o known ethical standard decides an action to be good or bad because it is done by a good or bad man, still less because done by an amiable, a brave, or a benevolent man, or the contrary (pp. 7, 19).

Reliance on consequences is, however, much disputed. A practical objection to consequentialism rests on the recognition that judging consequences is a slippery affair at best, seriously complicated by the problems of taking full account of less immediately visible costs and benefits, and of assigning quantifiable weights to them. The tendency is to accept rather casual assumptions as to the probable results of differing courses of action—in particular, those pitting long-term against short-term consequences—and to overlook less tangible consequences, those not readily expressed in terms of dollar value. Too casual a calculus of consequences reduces itself to an easy justification for unexpressed political and moral preferences, which should rather themselves be the focus of attention. For example, suppose the afterschool fighting among the boys did keep the peace and school disruptions were minimized, a good consequence. Would it then be acceptable?

An ethical failing inherent in consequentialism is its willingness simply to aggregate harms and benefits, regardless of the justification for inflicting or tolerating harms to those who do not deserve them. One example is the practice of a group punishment: imposing a sanction on a school class when a single but unknown student has done something wrong as a means either of forcing the guilty party to come forward or conscripting classmates—even as a means of fostering group consciousness—in an effort to discourage repetition. Consequentialist justifications for this act would weigh the harm to the innocent students against the good that would come from increasing collective responsibility and eliminating a repetition of the act. But how do you factor into the greater happiness calculus the possibility that some children, knowing the terms of the peace, were merely cowed, in which case their quietude represents intimidation rather than consent.

## Duty

Hardie is attracted to consequentialism's chief competitor in moral thinking, deontology, which takes a rights- or duty-based approach to moral questions. According to this approach, certain actions are wrong because they violate an obligation that we owe to others (or even to ourselves). Lying, for example, is condemned, not because without a certain measure of trust in another's word interpersonal transactions become difficult (a consequentialist justification), but because people are entitled not to be lied to. Why? One answer, derived from Kant, is that to lie to another is to treat him or her as a means to one's ends, as a thing rather than a person. Under the duty-based banner, then, no matter how much peace may ensue from the boys' fighting, it is wrong. A deontological approach says simply that it is wrong to impose a sanction on an innocent person for the sake of some greater overall good, and Luke's added justification of the friendship and mutual help with Michael, which a consequentialist might credit because both are net beneficiaries, does not alter its fundamental wrongness.

Our moral obligations, asserts Kant, consist of duties (moral law) that emanate from "pure" reason, that is, reason untarnished by any experiential considerations of personal intentions or actual consequences. Keeping a promise, for example, is a duty. Although there may be *prudential* reasons for breaking a promise—for example, to protect another from harm—to do so is a breach of one's moral duty because breaking a promise destroys the concept of a promise.

Kant's approach has generated strong criticism, on several grounds. First, it has been interpreted, although perhaps erroneously, as preferring duty over love as a moral reason for action, and as deeming duty-based action morally sufficient, even when not accompanied by caring feelings. Indeed that done through love, for example parenting a child, is regarded as morally inferior to that done out of obligation.

A second critique of Kant's reasoning focuses on the inherent vagueness of his categorical imperative, "I should never act except in such a way that I can also will that my maxim should become a universal law" (Kant, 1993, p.

14). One can agree that, as a universal law, of course nonviolent negotiation is preferable to mutual injury, but does that mean there are no circumstances in which retaliation is morally permissible? Acts are embedded, the product of personal and group histories. The question is not whether Luke, in taking on Jon, committed an abstract wrong, but whether he did so given the particular circumstances: defending a perceived wrong done to Michael.

As noted in Chapter 5, universalizing an imperative means treating *similarly situated* people alike. The judgment of rightness or wrongness is directed not to the disembodied act but to the act in context. One *could* justify the boys' behavior, without dismissing Kant's injunctions, by interpreting "similarly situated" more openly, to account for all situational factors: The aggression would not be wrong under parallel conditions, here including the swindling of a naive boy by a sophisticated one, the perceived failure of adult authority, already established loyalty patterns, and modest retribution acceptable to all concerned.

A wariness about allowing context to distinguish situations unduly would justify Maria's antiviolence ethic. Once we open the door to extenuating considerations, many of them subjective, the supposedly objective imperative of not hurting others will dissolve. Expanding or shrinking the concept of "similarly situated" suggests that pure reason, when applied to real-world issues, is as fallible a moral decision-making guide as any other. Take Kant's belief that promise breaking is wrong because if universalized it becomes a self-contradiction (there can be no promises if promises are broken). Would the prohibition include not breaking a promise to one's family to take an expensive vacation if a close friend suddenly needed help with a hospital bill? Again, reliance on pure reason does not tell us to what extent we should take account of, or ignore, context and consequences.

A final problem in applying Kantian ethics to real life is that although moral law is purportedly the product of pure reason, in fact it includes a consideration of outcomes. Before acting one must ask what would be the *consequence* if everyone always did what one now wants to do. Kant's universality and impartiality maxims do not obviate the need to consider outcomes even in his own analysis.

Those who find defects in consequentialist and duty-based moralities look to other sources for a justification of their moral codes. We discuss these fully in *The Moral Stake in Education: Contested Premises and Practices* (Goodman and Lesnick, 2001) and therefore mention here only one other, the appeal to fundamental principles.

## Three Shared Principles

In our schools probably the most fundamental moral appeal is to a set of principles upon which, it is asserted, our government derives its legitimacy.

These principles, which permeate modern liberal democracies, were well articulated by John Stuart Mill. He suggested two basic premises from which we can deduce all rights and wrongs. The first, which grounds what Kant and others call "perfect duties," is framed as a negative injunction: Do not do that which interferes with the rights of others; *do no harm*. The most fundamental human right, to Mill (1993), is the freedom to pursue one's own interests, to express one's own conscience, as long as the liberty of others is not threatened; the most fundamental wrong is the abridgement of that freedom. "The only purpose for which power can be rightfully exercised over any member of a civilized community, against his will, is to prevent harm to others" (p. 78). Individuals have the perfect right to pursue their own interests, but that right is limited by the equal right of every other person. If we interfere with a person's interests we must do so impartially; any selective distinctions in meting out rights, privileges, and punishments must be justified as relevant. To be fair is to avoid arbitrary decisions, to give those whom we do not know or actively dislike the same treatment as those we favor.

The second premise, generating "imperfect duties," is a positive injunction: Be helpful and charitable; *be beneficent*. While Mill regards this duty as important, he sees only the first, perfect duty, as morally obligatory. "Justice implies something which it is not only right to do, and wrong not to do, but which some individual person can claim from us as his moral right. No one has a moral right to our generosity or beneficence because we are not morally bound to practice those virtues toward any given individual" (Mill 1979, p. 49). Mill privileges not harming over helping because "a person may possibly not need the benefits of others, but he always needs that they should not do him hurt" (p. 58).

Mill's liberalism legitimizes societal indifference to the substantive welfare of others. Freedom to pursue one's own interests can lead to the concentration of enormous power, privilege, and cultural control in the hands of a very few. Philosopher John Rawls has argued persuasively that freedom must be more constrained to take account of the interest in *fairness*. A just society should foster some greater substantive equality among its citizens.

These three principles—doing no harm, beneficence, and justice as fairness—are widely endorsed in our tradition and consonant with our intuitive moral sensibilities, yet as critics point out, principles tend either overly or insufficiently to constrain one's choices.

Criticizing them for overspecificity (excessively constraining) are those who question the emphasis on individual rights found in liberal democratic systems. They would find some redeeming value in societies that emphasize hierarchically organized social relations, such as the traditional Brahman Indians, or our own New England Puritans. In those communities individual interests are subordinated to, or subsumed by, the interests of group harmony, which is threatened by autonomous decision making. "Interests" and morals are not to be constructed by individuals, but accepted as part of the established traditions; one inherits them as a consequence of one's role and place in society. This attitude is manifested in tradition- or community-oriented segments of contemporary society.

The critique of individualism has an egalitarian version as well. Maria, in common with teachers, seeks a fairness that is more than procedural; she wants substantive fairness, fairness that protects and ensures the welfare of everyone. She finds it unjust that in the card-trading incident a clever few accumulate money because they know how to take advantage of the naive. She wants to restrict Jon from "having it all." But Hardie disagrees. Teachers should not try to (and cannot successfully) ensure a more equal distribution of social and academic ends.

Principles may at the same time be criticized for excessive vagueness, on the ground that, absent an existing tradition that guides and limits the *interpretation* of principles, the values of no harm, beneficence, and fairness can justify widely incompatible norms. To be helpful, principles must be embedded in the purposes of a society and the social structures that support those purposes. According to Alasdair MacIntyre (1984) the practices and customs of a community, the "ways" in which we live, generate a hierarchy of virtues, which give meaning to its underlying principles. One society values courage over compassion, another the reverse; even the identical virtue finds various expressions. In an individualistic society, for example, a mistreated child may be applauded for speaking out on his own or an injured friend's behalf; this prepares him well for taking large economic risks as an adult. In a more collectivist society, the same child might win praise for accepting his loss without complaint; this prepares him for being cautious before risking the collective interest. In both cases the virtue is labeled courage. More important than underlying "principles," then, is how they surface through the "ways" we live.

Principles either lack the actual neutrality that might entitle them to near-universal approval or are sufficiently open-textured simply to defer the question of choice among plausible subjectivities. They are either grounded in customary practices, serving to rationalize the status quo or, if kept at arm's length from custom, offer scant guidance.

Like that of philosophers for numberless years, our search ends without an answer to Maria's question: how to navigate among the great diversity of values. So what's a teacher to do?

## Threading Our Way: Pluralism

Teachers must recognize the diversity of values, however difficult that is, and not move too quickly to defend or impose their own preferences. Schools in particular can be musty places, reluctant to question their traditional ways and listen closely to others. But there are limits to deference. We believe in the existence of fundamental moral truths, at least for our society at this time. The three principles enumerated above (doing no harm, beneficence, and justice as fairness) seem useful to us, despite their inadequacies.

We therefore oppose a thoroughgoing moral relativism. Such a position just does not fit our intuition that both moral good and evil *do* exist. However, lacking an omnipotent authority to set us straight, we also believe that no conscientious decision maker can resolve moral matters in a manner that ought to persuade, or is entitled to silence, another. We are thus advocates of pluralism. Pluralism, we believe, is the right approach to the question of how a society or social institution such as a school should respond to the fact that great, although not limitless, diversity of values exists among people of goodwill.

Some regard the pluralism of civil society as a regrettable circumstance necessary only until fellow citizens come to see the rightness of their positions. But another view sees pluralism as a celebration, rather than a grim and grudging acceptance, of the diversity of moral insight. As humans—and this idea can be expressed in religious as well as secular terms—we are created with the capacity and desire to seek, to know, and to follow the good. But since we are limited in all of those capacities and desires, none of us can claim to have authoritatively found the Truth. Pluralism is therefore the *only* political, philosophical, or educational stance compatible with the hope that a society will remain committed to the continuing search for moral understanding, for the good.

At times the diversity of values may reflect profound disagreement about the nature of a moral community. The morality of Indian Brahmins, for example, may be irreducibly at variance with that of the Western democracies. Individual autonomy, individual rights, and equality before the law are simply not the primary goods of Brahmin culture. We believe that a school is justified in limiting its pluralistic ethic by forbidding members of that culture to continue to live by their cultural norms when they reside *here*. Yet pluralism suggests maintaining awareness of the ways in which such a culture has an integrity of its own.

Pluralism, if it is to remain distinct from relativism, must police its boundaries. As we discussed in Chapter 5, some moral choices are not acceptable. There are actions—for example, the wanton killing of innocent people—that have been universally regarded across cultures and centuries as immoral. But that is an extreme and easy example. As an arm of a society—of this society—the school, we believe must go further. *Do no harm* cautions us against violence in general, not only when motivated by private revenge, and not just physical violence, but injury to children through invidious comparisons, shaming, and rejection. It restricts us from blocking the ambition of any child to maximize his interests unless or until his pursuits interfere with the interests of others. *Benevolence* further requires us to model and encourage generosity, compassion, and kindness. *Fairness* demands that we help each child to flourish, giving extra support to the Tonys in our midst.

Yet even if we accept these principles as absolutes, not infrequently situations will arise in which they conflict. As Isaiah Berlin (1992) famously put it:

> Both liberty and equality are among the primary goals pursued by human beings through many centuries; but total liberty for wolves is death to the lambs, total liberty of the powerful, the gifted, is not compatible with the rights to a decent existence of the weak and the less gifted. . . .
>
> These collisions of values are of the essence of what they are and what we are. . . . We are doomed to choose, and every choice entails an irreparable loss. . . . (pp. 12–14).

An example of an inevitable conflict in the school setting is freedom (do no harm) and benevolence. The demand of freedom entitles children to make close friends of their own choosing. Friendship, however, is by its very nature restrictive. Some, therefore, honoring the principle of benevolence, will object to the hurt incurred through exclusion. Freedom supports competition—to the swift belongs the race; benevolence and fairness, on the other hand, support equality, not just at the start of the race but throughout its duration. Freedom supports autonomy, benevolence community. Freedom supports truthfulness, benevolence tactfulness.

"Threading our way" requires teachers to juggle their judgments constantly: respecting the diversity of values children bring to school, yet holding tight to some "absolute" ones; balancing the tensions that arise even amongst the absolutes. Is the right of friendship trumped by the wound of exclusion? Do the needs of the majority to "get ahead" override the interests of the disabled child to get support? The answer in all likelihood is sometimes yes and sometimes no. Balance is what's called for.

How does the pluralist approach apply to Luke's justification for fighting? The answer would be easy if his notion of respect and standing up for yourself was invoked to justify a fight with knives. That would push against the do-no-harm boundary. But a limited use of fists in a constrained encounter to which all participants apparently consented, and in which they were of approximately equal strength and size, is another matter.

Yet we recognize that what is not "indisputably" wrong to one is so to another. For example, one who prioritizes "holding the line" against all violence, as Connie does, will agree with her that plainly the boys should be told what they did was wrong. Others might prefer a more "understanding" response, acknowledging the plausibility of Luke's claim but emphasizing the danger of overstepping acceptable limits by a resort to violence. Still others might let it go. These contrasting priorities will reflect in part teachers' differing levels of confidence in vigorously condemning the specific conduct in question. They will, however, also reflect differing attitudes to questions examined in Chapters 3 and 6 regarding the relative value of habituating children to rules, as against encouraging them to become reflective and responsible for the consequences of their own actions.

A school might choose to limit a pluralist response because it seeks (properly) to socialize students into attitudes and behaviors that are morally worthy (even if not obligatory) but systematically discouraged in our culture. Again, the resort to nonviolent, mutually respectful modes of settling disputes and redressing grievances provides an example. A quick outburst of violence finds daily reinforcement in the world that children observe and participate in; "talking it out," giving and receiving feedback, peer mediation, and such responses hardly have equal time in students' consciousness as they develop their own moral sense. One might justify Maria's intervention on this ground. Just as students must be required to read good literature if they are to be able to exercise informed reading choices in later life, her students must also learn about and experience *both* approaches to conflict. A truly pluralist intervention requires her to present the nonviolent option as one with which her students must engage while they are in her classes.

When the matter in question concerns the actions of students *while at school,* the case for pluralism is often overcome by the felt needs of the institution. Many would say that a school, or teacher, should not be expected to tolerate, indeed should not tolerate, even a moderate and under-standable use of retaliatory violence by a student. Others will question whether our delegitimization of nearly all manifestations of aggression in children, whether judged by the reasonableness of alternative values or by the consequences of pervasively repressing aggressive tendencies, does not go too far.

We leave this bedeviling topic with a reminder to all, ourselves as well, to keep listening, regardless of our individual tolerance toward allowing "foreign" values into school. It is critical for children to experience an open mind, even absent an open door. If they are to engage in the search for their own answers, they must witness a teacher's own pursuit of them, both her moral doubts and her moral stability. More basically, they need to experience the productiveness of moral friction. Of all principles that might claim the loyalty of educators, surely the marketplace of ideas comes first.

## Your Turn:
## Teacher Authority and Its Limits

The following incidents are designed to elicit two themes from the chapter: conflicting values and tolerance.

1. You've noticed that when Sam, a child in your class, goes to sit at a lunch table he is repeatedly rejected with comments such as, "Sorry, you can't sit here, we're saving the other seats," or "This table is reserved for our group."

   a) What would you do?
      1) Intervene by telling the children seats can't be saved; all children are welcome at every table?
      2) Hold a teacher-directed class meeting that establishes a no-exclusion rule?
      3) Hold a nondirective class meeting to air the issue?
      4) Talk privately to the excluded child about his feelings, wishes, tactics?
      5) Do nothing?
      6) Other?

   b) Does your choice reflect a bias toward equality or toward individual autonomy?

   c) Does it reflect a pedagogical belief that children need to be protected from, or exposed to, the "slings and arrows" of life?

   d) Do these beliefs rest on your view of human nature and child development?

2. You've noticed that for the past several days a group of children has been carrying on heated discussions over money while eating lunch: Who gets an allowance without having to work and who has to work? What do they do to make money and how much do they get paid? How much does each receive as an allowance and how do they spend it? Who are the rich and poor families? How can they get to be richer than their parents?

   a) What would you do?
      1) Tell the children directly that we don't talk about money?
      2) Hold a teacher-directed class meeting that establishes a rule banning talk about money?
      3) Hold a nondirective class meeting to air the issue?
      4) Talk privately to the "poorer" children about their feelings and wishes?
      5) Talk privately to the better-off children about not flaunting their wealth?
      6) Do nothing?
      7) Other?

   b) How would you explain and justify your choice(s)?

   c) Do pluralistic considerations inhibit your reactions?

   d) Do you regard this topic as less of a moral imperative for teachers than the first case, and if so, does this make it easier for you to "tolerate" rather than intervene?

3. There have been a few serious fights in your school, and a couple of children have been injured (black eyes, cuts that required stitches). They have not complained, but the principal has proposed a zero-tolerance policy: first fight, out of school detention for a day; second fight, two-day detention; and so forth up to expulsion.
   a) What is your reaction?
   b) What would you do?

4. A teacher is fairly certain that a child (C) in his class cheated on a test. He asks her best friend (B) if she knows of any cheating that occurred while he was out of the room. B says, "No, I don't." He then asks more pointedly, "I believe C copied answers from your paper; is that so?" B, who actually turned her paper for C to copy, says, "Not as far as I know."
   a) Was the teacher right in quizzing B?
   b) Was B justified in lying to protect her best friend, or should she have told the truth?
   c) What would you do and how would you justify your action? Consider the issues of consequentialism, deontology, principles, and pluralism.

■ ■ ■ ■ ■

# CHAPTER 8

# THE MORAL ENVIRONMENT
# OF THE SCHOOL

## *Scenario*

The committee continued to plug along, meeting at regular intervals despite what seemed to be frequent setbacks when, shortly before the spring recess, Principal Fred Helter asked Aggie to come by his office. She approached the interview a bit defensively, assuming he would ask her why there was as yet no preliminary report on the moral education plans.

Helter immediately put Aggie at ease by asking innocently enough how the committee's work was going, but before she had given a full answer, he broke in. "Actually, I asked you here so we could talk about an issue I've got—maybe I should say we've got—that needs some pretty prompt action. A group of sixth-grade parents spoke to me last week about having a, well, I guess you'd call it a graduation ball."

"A what?," Aggie asked with a tone of alarm.

"Well, 'ball' is my word. What they want is for us to put on an elaborate party at the end of the year that will include a dance, hired band, catered dinner, and very dressy attire."

"What did you tell them?" Aggie inquired.

"Between us, I'm not wild about the idea, but publicly I was noncommittal. I did say that I saw difficulties with their proposal and couldn't immediately approve it. They had this solicitous air about them and quickly tried to reassure me: We wouldn't have to foot the bill, they said. Each family would pay its share. We should think of this as a tribute to the fine education they had received, a celebration of their and our accomplishments. Underneath, however, I sensed a very determined set of parents, and the meeting ended with my promising to get back to them soon. I suspect that when push comes to shove they are not going to back down, and I'm not sure I want to draw a line in the sand against them on this issue."

"So where do I come in?" Aggie asked.

"Well, first of all," Fred responded, "given the complex matter I've already assigned your committee, I thought I ought to consult you guys before committing myself."

"I appreciate that, Fred," Aggie answered. "I really do, even though you may be sorry you made the gesture."

"Why do you say that?"

"I think it's likely there will be some vocal opposition about making such a big thing out of a sixth-grade graduation. If I know Hardie, he's likely to be pretty critical of the idea."

"Yes, I suppose so," Helter agreed, "and that's my second reason for consulting you.

"It turns out that Hardie is assigned this year to be chair of the Faculty Committee on Special Events and, assuming that I am going to let the parents have their way on this party idea, I would ask him and his committee to work with the parents on planning it. I know that Hardie, bless his heart, has some pretty strong ideas about what is and isn't deserving of the school's imprimatur; if he comes down against this idea, I might very well need your help in getting him to stay with his committee assignment."

Aggie's smile had a definite wry cast to it. "As the saying goes, thanks for sharing, Fred. I'll talk it over with the group and get back to you."

"I know I can count on you," Fred answered, rising to signal the end of their meeting, "to help Hardie see that this isn't something to get dug in on."

The next day, Aggie brought up the subject of the "graduation ball" with her committee colleagues. As she foresaw, Hardie's objection was strong and clear. No sooner had she mentioned Helter's report of the parents' request than Hardie broke in agitatedly, "I hope he told them that there was no way the school could support anything like this proposal."

"No, he didn't," Aggie replied hesitantly, "but he did ask for our 'input.'"

"'Input,' huh. Why didn't he ask for our position?"

"I'm with Hardie on this one," said Connie. "Undoubtedly parents got wind of the elaborate graduations, even in elementary schools, that have become very trendy in neighboring schools. Once that 'ball' gets rolling, it's hard to stop it. But we aren't like the nearby districts. We have a lot of parents who can't afford the contribution required to put on such an affair."

"True enough, Connie," Maria chimed in, "but how about having the kids raise the money? We could agree as a community that the amount spent on the party—let's at least not inflate the terminology—will not exceed the amount raised."

"Interesting idea, Maria," Connie responded, "but I have my doubts. The kids aren't going to collect the sort of funds needed for a band and catered dinner. The wealthier parents, with their demanding children, will then raise the ceiling by asking parents to chip in. That would embarrass some of the financially strapped families, not to mention the cost of gowns, shoes, flowers; you know all the paraphernalia they seem to require.

"Besides, these parties have a way of undoing all the efforts we make to delay pairing off and sex, not to mention drinking and smoking, that are just around the corner. Who gets invited by whom, who gets invited by no one, all these miserable issues will be fostered by holding such an affair."

"You guys blow my mind." Hardie was out of his chair. "Yes, the money issue is serious and problematic. The injured psyches don't bother me, call it real life. But even if we could come up with the funds, don't you see this is just one terribly wrong thing to do? What a distortion of fund-raising, Maria, to have kids spend their free time, the time we wanted them to put into service, collecting donations for their own narcissistic pleasures! The whole idea makes me madder than hell. I'm telling you right now, I will *not* go to that party, I will *not* help the kids raise money, and I will *not* let the kids believe I approve of the affair."

At this point, Aggie's concern peaked; the discussion was getting out of hand. She regretted not having told them initially that the principal was probably going to back the parents. She tried now to lower the contentiousness of the issue before informing them.

"Hardie, when it comes to moral outrage, no one's your match, but here's our chance to show Fred how we've grown more alert to the subtleties of moral decision making. Let's take two backward steps and consider this issue against others we've confronted in our committee work.

"First of all, it's clear to me that this is a moral question. Connie points out how it may hurt our less advantaged families, and I can hardly disagree with Hardie that spending time raising money for themselves, however much it might promote a certain sense of shared community goals, isn't much of a cause. Bruised psyches, to my mind, shouldn't be readily dismissed. It also, as Hardie noted, seems to fall within the school's 'reach.' I assume Fred wouldn't be consulting with us had it been a party off the premises, given by parents. But they want it here, they will want us to supervise it, and we will have responsibility for it. More important, by holding it here, we will be endorsing it. Still, it's not centrally on our turf. It's what you might call an extracurricular activity. Is that why you weren't ready to trash it immediately, Maria?"

"Yes and no. I've been bitten this year, Aggie. I've learned that if parents and kids want to do or not do something, it's pretty hard to change their minds. Even though it's not a noble enterprise, as Hardie has made crystal clear, children would at least gain increased understanding of the connection between earning (or raising) money and spending it. That might curb a bit of the materialism he so hates."

"Good point, Maria," Aggie continued. "Let's look at our options and at the moral stakes. On the one hand the school could sanction the affair and let parents pay what they can. We could set up some sort of fund— maybe a combination of money raised by students, the Home and School

Association, and school contributions. Of course, Fred could just say, 'no way, it's not part of our tradition, we disapprove and disallow it.' But . . ."

"Now you're talking," Hardie interrupted.

"Hold on, Hardie," Aggie resumed. "There are other choices. Maria's notion of limiting the spending is one, bringing together a group of teachers and parents to work on this together is another. A combined committee could put restrictions on what's allowed and that way contain the costs. Fred could punt and take the question to the super or the school board, but it's virtually certain they'd allow it, given the practice of other districts."

"Don't you see," said Hardie, now turned plaintive, "graduations are events kids tend to remember; they are not just another Saturday night. However much negative weight you do or don't give to lavish parties in general, surely you see that a culminating event like this is an opportunity to imprint upon children and families what this school is about morally. What we could and should do is ask the kids how they might make their graduation an occasion for doing something important, such as coming up with a worthwhile contribution to our school, or spending a day—perhaps several days—volunteering for Habitat for Humanity. Maybe a repre-sentative group could counter the principal and super with their (demo-cratically determined) proposal. Now that's a worthwhile topic for a class meeting, not one of those meetings that operates at Bonham's level 6, where the decision is left to the students, but a directed meeting outlining the overall idea and asking students to suggest specific activities."

"I could hug you, Hardie, but the hug might quickly turn into a strangle," Maria said. "Your kids are lucky to be around someone who has such forceful convictions. I mean that. You stand up against authority even while you're constantly exerting it. Talk about modeling.

"But there is something about your boldness that bothers me. Why must this decision be portrayed as either holding firm or buckling under? Why don't we see this as an opportunity to deal with a conflict of values? We educators don't like change. If a bowling party was good enough for us when we completed elementary school, it's good enough for our students.

"Yes, they do have more money, they spend more on entertainment, they also probably give more away. That doesn't make them heinous. Once they realize that some families can't afford a big splash for graduation, I think there's a good chance they'll want to find a tactful way of covering the costs. They might even go for kids and parents collecting recipes together and then doing the catering themselves. They want a big celebration, and all they know is what others have done. We don't have to throw cold water all over their eagerness, and I don't think we should give up on collectively coming up with suitable ideas. Maybe we could interest them, or the kids, in putting some funds aside for a gift—what and to whom they could determine."

Aggie, with a relieved glance toward Maria, took the floor: "Look, Hardie," she began, "you have to understand that Helter's between a rock and a hard place. His instincts are against granting approval. Your point about graduation being memorable and our missing a golden opportunity—that seems right. He also realizes it's one more instance of pushing kids into situations they aren't ready for and shouldn't be ready for. In some sense, as Connie has said, it feels as if we would be promoting behaviors we otherwise try to discourage—sex, drugs, excessive pairing off, 'inappropriate' behavior. So that's the stake. But he has to choose his battles, and I'm not sure he thinks, given the trends, he could win this one. Even if he could, the price might be too high."

"No, no, no!" Hardie shot back. "This is exactly the battle to take on. Don't you see how catering to the request for a ball (that's what it will be) undermines our service-learning initiative. Part of the service idea is to live with restraint, mindful of the injustice and suffering others endure. Otherwise service becomes nothing more than grudging do-goodism, like clothing drives. Saying no to this is an opportunity for us to broadcast that message. We should hold a reception after graduation and bid the sweethearts adieu.

"Besides, let's face it, Maria's compromise position isn't realistic. Maybe it's because I am *not* a new teacher, but I hold no hope that parents will modify their requests. Recipe collections! Catering! These parents, who don't show up at a meeting to discuss their own child!"

Aggie now had to take the bit between her teeth. "Hardie, you may get more of a chance than you want to test your cynicism. Fred recalled that you were this year's chair of the Faculty Committee on Special Events. Assuming he decides to let the parents go ahead, you'll have to be the point person for working out the details with the parents."

"Give me a break, Aggie! Are you telling me that I might not only have to sit idly by watching our school make a serious mistake but that I'm also going to have to make the bloody thing happen?"

"I'm not running the school, Hardie. Maybe the best thing now is for all of us to think the question over."

Hardie stalked off quickly, but Maria caught up with him and suggested that they stop for a cup of coffee. Once seated, she seized the floor. "Hardie, although we weren't exactly on the same page on the graduation ball problem, I want you to know I realize how much you would hate having to take the lead in actually implementing the party idea."

"Thanks, Maria," Hardie replied, genuinely appreciative. "I just don't think I can do it, whether or not I'm obligated by some school rule. It's just so clearly wrong and so clearly unnecessary. I mean, it's not like we'll be sued if we say no on this one."

"Well, if it's any consolation, Hardie, I'm up against a situation that isn't so different in some ways. In fact, I was hoping to get your counsel. I didn't want to mention it in our committee, because a conversation with Connie is the source of my difficulty. Now, you have your own troubles, and this might not be the best time . . ."

"No, Maria. You know that misery loves company. What's up?" Hardie inquired sympathetically.

"Well, this problem of expecting teachers to go along with parent-generated pressures is a really serious thing. I notice the message it gives the children. We read them stories about heroes, we stress the importance of doing the right thing even when it means a loss of popularity, basically we tell them to speak truth to power, but when it comes to saying no to mobilized or insistent parents, or to pressures from the superintendent's office, we are supposed to roll over and play dead."

Hardie was alarmed by the seriousness of Maria's demeanor. "Hey, Maria! You seem really upset."

"I am," Maria began, grateful for Hardie's evident concern. "You know Connie's in charge of the achievement testing. Last week she came to me with a copy of the Stanford Achievement Test that will be given to the fifth graders at the end of the year. She told me what we all know, that Helter wants the scores to go up. Apparently he wants it badly. On a list of average scores for the district, we're pretty much in the cellar, and there are rumors that if we don't improve the school may be 'consolidated' out of its present existence as the district's consolidation movement gains momentum. Now you can guess what Connie asked me to do. Maybe *told* me what to do is more accurate."

"Uh, oh."

"Yeah, you got it. She wants me to go over the questions from the test to be administered this year, and 'tutor' the kids."

"Wait a minute, Maria. Are you saying that Connie has a copy of the actual test we're giving this spring?"

"It surprised me, too. Apparently, the test booklets are costly, and they're only reissued every so many years. In between, they're kept in the guidance office of each school."

"So Connie gives you a copy of the test and you give the kids the questions and answers?"

"No, not exactly, but too close for comfort. She wants to be sure I have 'covered' all the material that they will be tested on, more or less item by item. When I objected, explaining that I've followed the curriculum guidelines and used the assigned text, she said she didn't like to ask this of me and neither did Helter, but the scores have got to go up.

"To justify the request she pointed out how awful it would be if the school were closed. She let me know what a good thing we have going here. It's one of the very few truly integrated elementary schools around. We're a model of interracial harmony, and we've taken large steps toward developing a more inclusive curriculum. We also have an unusual degree of income and political diversity. If they consolidate us with another place, all that may be lost. What she didn't say, but didn't have to, was that she and Fred might lose their jobs, or at least their status.

"Then, to clinch her argument, Connie threw in the fact that 'prepping' for achievement tests is commonplace in the district, now that scores are so closely tied to teacher, child, and school standing. That sounded a lot like a not-so-gentle reminder that my own status around here would be hurt if the kids were to perform poorly."

Hardie moaned, "And what have you thought you might do about her 'request'?"

"Thus far, I haven't gone beyond considering my options. I guess I could tell her, 'no way.' But that would have bad repercussions on my kids' scores, and as you know, I don't exactly have the cream of the crop. I understand that these scores not only go into their records, in case any of them should apply to magnet middle schools, but may well influence their opportunities for advanced work next year and beyond. You know how, once low expectations are established, it just gets tougher and tougher for them. So if I limit my thinking to the kids' (and my own) welfare, I should go along with Connie. But cheating is cheating. You can't have a rule that says, 'Don't cheat until it hurts you.'"

"So what else might you do?" Hardie asked, impressed with Maria's wrestling.

"Well, I considered fudging. Say 'yes' to Connie but just don't do the 'tutoring,' or really keep it indirect. But that's clearly a bad idea. I'd be deceiving Connie, it wouldn't help the kids, it'd wreck my spring teaching plans, and I would have run away from the issue.

"I also considered a more political approach. Maybe you were hinting at that, Hardie."

"Yeah. What were you thinking?"

"Well, we might bring the issue up for the faculty to discuss—no, we couldn't call a faculty meeting without even telling the principal; it'd have to be just getting a few folks together informally to talk over the ethics of coaching for a test. If we got enough support we could then send a delegation to Helter. At least that's what I thought until Aggie told us about his reaction to the 'ball' idea. Now I think we'd lose with Helter.

"I also thought of getting word out to the parents or even the press," Maria continued. "But I don't think we could do that. It would make the school look awful. Anyway, I'm not sure how the parents would react. Some, I assume, would be appalled at the hanky-panky; others would rather not know and let it happen; and some, I suspect, would be delighted. They'd push hard on the everyone-does-it argument. Why should their children's scores and future opportunities be sacrificed at the altar of honesty?"

"You're absolutely right, Maria."

"Right? About what? I haven't even staked out a position."

"You're right that we can't play dead. There is no way we can ask children to respect us, or maintain our own professional and personal self-respect, if we don't do something about these matters. If we bow down to Connie on the coaching, she to Helter, he to the superintendent, it's good-bye democracy, good-bye character education."

"And what, brave soul, do you think we should do?"

"It's not entirely clear to me, Maria. You painted some very unattractive but realistic options. With so much riding on scores, the long-run solution might be to have the entire testing administration outsourced. Leaving test booklets that will be reused in some building closet or file is not a tenable policy. We are just not a sufficiently honorable community. When the stakes are this high, there will be cheating—by students, by teachers, or as a matter of covert school policy."

"But that's futuristic. What about now?"

"I think we start by talking quietly to the other fifth-grade teachers, Aggie, and maybe a few other reliably strong members of the faculty. Then, as a small group, we could go privately to Helter and let him know we're serious about refusing to cheat and prepared to stand with him against pressures from 'the system.' I'm not so sure your pessimism about his reaction is warranted on this one. Issues don't get weightier than this."

"And if you're wrong? If he claims there is nothing he can do about it, that the school's scores just have to go up?"

"I wish we knew someone who could talk some sense into these guys, but we don't, at least I don't." Maria's nod signaled her joining in this acknowledgment. Hardie went on: "Maybe then it'll be time to tell him we'll have to go public, at least inform teachers—and maybe parents. He knows that although many parents would support him, once it got into the newspapers it'd be a scandal. But that's not a step I'd like us to take: It *would* be a scandal and make the school, once again, look awful. And I'd rather convince him than threaten him.

"I have tenure, Maria. You don't. I'll gladly be the heavy if one is needed, but that's a bridge we don't have to cross right now."

"I like your plan to involve others, Hardie. We teachers so rarely act as a community, though of course we preach to the kids all the time about the concept that the school is a community, that our neighborhoods are communities. Your concern about the graduation party is also about what we are as a community, and I want to see collaboration happen around that occasion. Maybe we can get the others to think about both issues that way. And Hardie, I really appreciate your standing with me, even in front of me, on this one."

## TEACHERS DISCUSS THEIR PROFESSIONAL RESPONSIBILITY

The two teachers lapsed into silence for a moment or two, each affected by their conversation. Hardie resumed in a different vein. "Maria, before I get all uppity about taking a public stand against the graduation plan, and before we make a move that might end up in a cheating scandal, let's go over our moral responsibilities here."

"Count me in," Maria agreed.

"OK, my outrage over the pending ball. The idea repulses me. I don't see what in the world these children have accomplished to deserve our—and it is us, it's our school no matter who is putting up the money—fawning on them. Even a class gift, unless the children raised their own funds, would be another ostentatious display. Events like this, and I agree with Connie they're on the rise as more folks have more money to throw around, totally undermine any notion of moral education. They promote nothing but immodesty, self-centeredness, and an unwarranted precocity. If we approve the idea, the chatter among the students over the next several months will be exclusively about who is going to the party with whom, who will wear what, who will have parties before and after. Bad enough this goes on at senior proms, but now in sixth grade!"

Hardie paused, and asked: "Still, does that make it wrong?"

"Not to me, Hardie. I think there's something going on between you and some of these parents. Maybe it comes from the trouble they gave you over service learning. You think they're forever gushing over their kids, granting their every impulse, protecting them from any adversity. I don't see it that way. These folks have money to spend. So be it. We can't make them poor. They see spending on their children—often wrongly, I grant you—as an act of love. As for the party, the parents' intentions aren't bad, there's nothing inherently evil in the act, and I don't imagine the consequences will be that disastrous. If we can't convince them otherwise, then it just doesn't do any good to flaunt our will over them. That just increases the mutual dislike we're trying to reverse. So rather than slam the door on their suggestion, I had the notion of controlling the costs and turning the affair into a collaborative enterprise."

Hardie was not placated. "Must we still make consequences the gold standard? Who knows what the consequences will be? Why won't the parents be back on our doorstep with new awful demands? Why won't the kids ratchet up their expectations for the next school event? If it's a ball this year, what will it be when they finish middle school, and imagine what they'll concoct for high school?

"But it's not really the consequences to *them* that concerns me; it's our excessive nervousness over the consequences of drawing the line with parents.

"I've watched us cave in to that sort of pressure over and over again. With each capitulation we get weaker, more deprofessionalized, less likely to return to fight another day. Our professional integrity is at stake, Maria. Keeping peace is a worthy end, but it's not the only worthy one."

"Professional integrity, Hardie? Isn't that a bit overblown? I get your disgust over extravagance—though I had better not let you see my new designer bag—and yes, you're right, in a perfect world, given the desperate needs of so many, students would not be so indulged. That's where I think we must stand firm. No one goes to the ball unless *everyone* has the option to go, and go free of any embarrassment. But once we're over that hurdle, Hardie, I think we've gone far enough. However, for sure you should be relieved of responsibility for this event. I'll go to Aggie and explain that I'd like to take your place on the committee if you're willing to take over my assignment."

"Before I jump at your generous offer, I'd better ask what committee you're offering me. And please don't say bus duty. I'll compromise all my morals before signing on to that!"

"You guessed it."

"Now my convictions are really going to be put to the test!"

"Seriously," Hardie went on, "now it's my turn to be grateful to you for your offer. But before night falls, let's move on to the cheating. Why, intuitively, does it seem to raise the question of professional integrity more centrally? After all, in both instances we're fundamentally talking about bowing to parental pressures and considering only consequences. With the party it's the consequence of making kids and parents angry; with the cheating it's also the consequence of their anger, plus bad repercussions on the status of the children and school."

"Isn't it obvious, Hardie? For one thing, frivolous spending is just not in the same league as cheating. Cheating means deception, that what the kids produce is not their own work, and there is a real injury to those who don't cheat, assuming some of them still exist. Good Lord, Hardie, I'm picking up your cynicism.

"Also, it's one thing to stand by silently and permit an activity to occur that parents have promoted, it's another to participate actively in a cheating scam."

"Good points, Maria, but I'm not sure I see it as so obvious. Look at what standing by in silence means. It's a form of capitulation; one sees corruption around, but does nothing as long as one's own hands are clean. Supposing you saw another teacher giving out answers to a test. Would you think it OK to walk away from that?"

"I have no idea, Hardie, what I would do at such a moment. Right now I'm just trying to figure out what to do with my own problem.

"Another piece that concerns me is my responsibility to Connie. She was the one who delivered the message—read "order"—to me. But I'm not sure if she was acting under a directive from Helter or merely divined something that she thought he'd approve. I suppose Helter was behind it, but shouldn't we talk to Connie before going further? If we start talking to other teachers about our concern over this 'coaching,' she's going to look pretty bad to a lot of people."

"Excellent idea, Maria. And I'm glad you said 'we.' I was pretty pissed when the parents went above my head over the service-learning proposal. Now you point out we'd be doing the same thing if we didn't start with Connie. It's important to listen to her story. However, Maria, I hope you agree that our sympathy for the bind she's in won't stop us from going further."

"Sounds right, Hardie, though I can't see that far into the distance. Much as you seem to object to the word, I need to know the 'consequences' to her and to Helter if we start a campaign against the directive. Once again, I'm less bothered about the principle of the whole thing and more bothered about our situation here and now—who will be affected and how.

"And speaking of the here and now," Maria smiled, "how about overcoming our problems with another round of coffee and each taking half of that last piece of chocolate cake on the counter?"


## A DEEPER LOOK

In this chapter we shift our focus from the moral significance of the actions and motives of students to those of teachers, administrators, and school board members. We do this not simply because they too are in the school community, but in response to our belief that their actions and perceived motives are a powerful part of the students' moral learning environment.

This is the idea of the *implicit curriculum* (sometimes referred to as the "hidden" curriculum). Its premise is that what a school teaches is more than the subjects contained in class notes, assignments, and examinations; it includes the unspoken messages about how one should live that are embedded in the way that teachers and administrators carry out their work. A teacher who is deferential to department chairs and principals but curt and dismissive with students and younger colleagues will not get very far teaching students to be respectful of others. A teacher who does not grade student work promptly and thoughtfully will not succeed at teaching students responsibility. A teacher may emphasize self-discipline as a means of teaching students to balance the interests of others fairly with their own, but students will not learn that lesson if they observe the teacher consistently placing first priority on advancing his or her career. Students have a keen, even vigilant, set of antennae for hypocrisy. The message, "Do as I say, not as I do," whether delivered explicitly or otherwise, is not likely to be heeded, for what the speaker *does* bespeaks a lack of commitment to what he or she has *said.* Education professor Gary Fenstermacher (1990) has placed this idea in context in words that bear including here at some length:

> There are several different ways teachers serve as both moral agents and moral educators. They can be quite directive, teaching morality outright—a form of instruction often called didactic instruction. When it becomes heavy-handed or highly ideological, it is often considered indoctrination. Rather than specific instruction in morality, teachers can teach *about* morality, as might be the case in courses on world religions, philosophy, civics, or sex education. A third way to undertake moral education is to act morally . . .
>
> The first two forms of moral education are generally well known and much discussed. Depending on the teacher and the content, these two forms of moral education can be powerful influences on certain children at certain times in their development. Neither of the first two forms, however, has the potential to shape and influence student conduct in such educationally productive ways as the third form. . . . Nearly everything that a teacher does while in contact with students carries moral weight. Every response to a question, every assignment handed out, every discussion on issues, every resolution of a dispute, every grade given to a student carries with it the moral character of the teacher. This moral character can be thought of as the *manner* of the teacher.
>
> Manner is an accompaniment to everything teachers do in their classrooms. Chemistry can be taught in myriad ways, but however it is taught, the teacher will always be giving directions, explaining, demonstrating, checking, adjudicating, motivating, reprimanding, and in all these activities displaying the manner that marks him or her as morally well developed or not. Teachers who understand their impact as moral educators take their manner quite seriously. They understand that they cannot expect honesty without being honest or generosity without being generous or diligence without themselves being diligent. Just as we understand that teachers must engage in critical thinking with students if they expect students to think critically in their presence, they must exemplify moral principles and virtues in order to elicit them from students (pp. 134–35; emphasis in original).

The power of the "school climate" is heightened by the implicit quality of the message it carries. Open discussion of a moral problem explicitly invites student reflection and judgment; even a fairly didactic moral lesson leaves children free to reject it. However, when the message is unspoken, it is experienced simply as background matter to be taken for granted, its truth so obvious that it is not even worth putting on the table—"*Of course,* we all look out for number one"—if indeed it is consciously noted at all.

We therefore focus our inquiry into the morality of the actions that Maria Laszlo, Hardie Knox, and Fred Helter are considering in the realization that when making and acting on their decisions, they are plainly engaging in the moral education of their students.

We begin with the teachers, Hardie and Maria. Each is experiencing or expecting some pressure from above.

In Hardie's case, it is from the parents who plan to organize a graduation party that he believes embodies a seriously flawed message to students and a gross misallocation of energy and money. Maria is being urged by a senior faculty colleague, on behalf of the principal, to teach in a way that she considers dishonest and educationally impoverished in order to help maintain her school's standing within the school system. Dishonest, because she believes that if "teaching to the test" when she knows not only the subject areas to be tested but the actual questions is morally equivalent to giving students the answers; educationally impoverished, because she believes that, since a test can address only a portion of what a student should have learned (and that portion distorted by the requirement that it be readily measurable), her students would benefit far more from spending the time in a broader or deeper engagement with the subject matter.

In each case the primary question we consider is whether it would be wrong for them to act as they have been asked, or told, to act. And if it would not be wrong, another question arises: whether the teachers not merely *may* obey (and still be acting morally) but *should* obey. In other words, would it be wrong for them to refuse the directive? In coming to grips with these questions, we encounter the concepts of *accountability* and *professionalism.*

## Accountability as an Employee

One paradigm regards the teacher as an *employee,* albeit a fairly skilled one, of the school system in which he or she works. Such discretion as Hardie and Maria have in carrying on their work exists at the explicit or implied leave of their "superiors," initially the principal, who is in turn accountable to the superintendent, an official in some ways analogous to a CEO, whose "board of directors" is the school board. "Board members are considered public school officers with sovereign power, in contrast to school employees, who are hired to implement directives" (McCarthy and Cambron-McCabe, 1992, pp. 385–86). Even the "sovereign power" of the school board exists only by delegation from the state legislature, which in turn operates under authority given it by the state constitution and the voters, in whom ultimate sovereignty resides.

Under this paradigm, a teacher may of course remonstrate, seek to dissuade the other, and the like, but obedience is not "giving in" to anything other than the proper order of things. It is a recognition of the fact that the teacher has no authority to decide a matter contrary to a lawful directive, specific or general, of the principal. It should not be surprising that this view, which reflects the prevailing consciousness of the employment relationship, is also apparent in court decisions. As one leading case put it, "a public employee generally can be discharged for refusing to follow administrative policies and directives, even those they contend are misguided" (*Cox* v. *Dardanelle Public School District* [U.S. Court of Appeals for the Eighth Circuit, 1986, p. 675]).

Our purpose in citing legal authority is not to describe the legal rights that Hardie and Maria might have should they be discharged or disciplined for refusing to do what they have been asked to do. The legal principle in our view mirrors, rather than is the source of, a societal sense of the deference owing a "superior." A teacher is, in this paradigm, *morally* obligated to carry out lawful orders of the principal; "insubordination" is not merely imprudent, it is wrong.

Character education specialists Edward Wynne and Kevin Ryan (1997) have supported this view on two counts. The first sees a moral value in hierarchy itself: "The acceptance of hierarchy has been an important theme pervading traditional values. Indeed, without appropriate hierarchy among the adults in a school, how can pupils learn to observe discipline?" (p. 192). They also rely, however, on an argument based on the accountability of the school:

> In important institutions, there must be clear points of accountability, not merely an amorphous group of faculty members. Without focused responsibility, the clarity of decision making will be greatly impaired. We do not suggest that principals, as human beings, are necessarily wiser or more moral than individual teachers. . . . Our argument is that in education, the stakes are high. There must be one person clearly in charge (p. 193).

From within this perspective, Hardie's case is a simple one. Whether his objections to the 'ball' are wise or not, he certainly should accept the principal's judgment in the matter. He is not being asked to work on anything dishonest or illegal.

Maria's case is significantly more complex. As already mentioned, she has two reasons for resisting "teaching to the test" by going over specific questions that she knows will be on it: She deems it a form of cheating and a poor use of classroom time. Questions on a test are meant merely to illustrate the learning acquired. A valid review teaches the underlying principles (for example, sentence structure, grammar, reading comprehension, etc.), using concrete examples to aid the student in apprehending, and being able to apply these principles. Recalling from memory the answers to the specific examples taken from the test offers no assurance that a student has mastered the material sufficiently to figure out solutions to a range of similar questions.[1]

In an "employee" consciousness, Maria's second ground for resistance is probably not significantly different from Hardie's position. The fact that she sincerely, and perhaps correctly, believes that the students' time would be better spent in another way does not justify her acting on that belief in the face of the principal's contrary wish. But what of her primary objection to participating in what she regards as a plainly wrongful act? Would it be plainly wrong to go over specific questions that she knows, but does not tell the students, will be on the test?

A continuum of remedies exists to improve the students' test performance in the present case: reviewing the subject matter to be covered; emphasizing the specific areas that are ordinarily given particular attention by those designing the test; reviewing specific questions in the knowledge that they *will* appear on the test; reading out to the students some or all of the questions and telling them that they will be on the test; and, finally, adding the answers that she believes best. In today's world, most people would probably regard the first and second variants as not only educationally justifiable but also morally acceptable and the last two as plainly unethical.

Maria views what she has been asked to do as morally equivalent to these last, but in an "employee" consciousness her sincere and reasonable belief would probably not suffice. The question is whether she is *right*. If so, she can claim the status of a "whistle blower," who is sometimes protected by law from retaliation and would in any event probably be regarded as doing something deserving of praise rather than blame. If she is not right, she is simply insisting on placing her own moral judgment above that of her superiors.

There are two important ways in which the conduct Maria is asked to engage in is an exercise in deception. First, those posing test questions to students implicitly assert to students, parents, teachers, and any others who are interested in the test results that doing well in the test evidences a good understanding of the area involved. As suggested above, the score of one who has gone over the specific test questions in advance does not accurately reflect his or her understanding of the subject. Moreover, in our society both the students taking a test and their teachers are reasonably understood by others to be asserting that they do not know in advance the specific questions they are being asked. Although that would be literally true in this case—the

---

[1] For example, the Stanford Achievement Test (1996) for the spring semester, fourth grade, and fall semester, fifth grade, asks students whether the sentence, "Add more spise to the soup," contains a spelling error, as an application of the ability to apply "phonetic principles" to consonant sounds; in order to test principles of grammar, it asks whether the sentence, "She soon discovered it were a bunch of rattlesnakes," is correct, and if not, whether "were" should be changed to "was" or "are," or "discovered" changed to "discovers."

students would not *know* that they know the answers—disclosure of the action that the school is contemplating would probably create something of a scandal; the "outside" world—in particular, newspapers and their readers among the citizenry—would in all likelihood quickly characterize the practice as "coaching" rather than preparation, a form of cheating not essentially different from simply supplying the answers.

Within the school system, however, and among parents, there would be a justifying impulse beyond, although probably including, that of narrow self-interest. It would be claimed that the deception was legitimated by the oversimplified, excessive use of a school's average test scores to judge the quality of the education it provides, both in absolute terms and, worse yet, in comparison with its peer schools. Accordingly, prepping students is necessary, and therefore appropriate, to protect them and the school from undeserved harm. Moreover, given the prevalence of "coaching" throughout the school system, Maria's action in acceding to Connie's request, far from giving her students an unfair advantage, would simply compensate for the advantage that others are getting.[1]

In an "employee" consciousness, it need not be established that the claim of justification *is* legitimate, only that the principal's decision to treat the act as justified is not unreasonable. A teacher should recognize that her responsibilities are narrower than the principal's and that she is not morally justified in clinging to her parochial stance. The question remains, however, whether the asserted justification is reasonable.

A "reasonableness" argument is that moral judgments regarding personal honesty and fairness may be ruled out of bounds because of the wholesale corruption of the entire process of testing students and schools. In our judgment, such a position must be rejected. It can only rest on either a self-serving rationalization or a regretful acknowledgment of an unhappy state of affairs. Whatever the legitimacy for such a stance regarding, for example, modern warfare, teaching school is a different matter. To exist as a participating citizen in today's world means one cannot resist all those actions perceived as even profoundly unjust. But in a classroom the teacher's voice is loud; hence her responsibilities amplified. A superior asking Maria to "be reasonable" is asking too much. In this context, we would assert what Supreme Court Justice Robert Jackson observed in a very different (perhaps more compelling) context: "No one can make me believe that we are that far gone."[2]

---

[1] A *New York Times* story (May 3, 2002) reported the filing of charges against a large number of teachers and principals in New York City for allegedly giving students test answers during the administration of standardized tests.

[2] *Shaughnessy* v. *United States ex rel. Mezei*, 345 U.S. 206 (1953), p. 228. The case involved national security needs at the height of the Cold War.

## Accountability as a Professional

The competing paradigm sees a teacher as a *professional*. As such, a teacher stands in a relationship of trust to his or her students, to whom primary accountability is owed, just as a physician's primary accountability is to the patient, and a lawyer's to the client. According to the codes of ethics for those professions, the fact that someone else may at times sign the check or pay the bill is not supposed to dilute that loyalty. It is only the systemic obligations of a professional that can limit responsiveness to client, patient, or student desires: For a lawyer, the obligation is to the law itself; for a doctor, to the primary principle *"do no harm"*; for a teacher, to pedagogic practices that support the intellectual and moral growth of students.

A professional can carry out these obligations only if his or her *independent professional judgment* is honored. One text expresses the idea of a profession in these terms: "By its nature a profession involves both considerable autonomy in decision making and knowledge and skills developed before entry and then honed in practice" (Goodlad, 1984, p. 194). The requisites of entry into a profession include the special knowledge, skill, judgment, and character it calls for, and which the educational and licensing requirements are meant to assure. For Hardie and Maria to be told that they must set aside their professional judgment would tend to cripple their growth as conscientious, mature, imaginative, reflective, and responsible teachers, leading them instead in the direction of becoming clock-watching, time-serving, order-taking subordinates. The conclusion of education professor Roland Barth (1989) is telling:

> Many schools perpetuate infantilism. School boards infantilize superintendents; superintendents, principals; principals, teachers; and teachers, children. This results in children and adults who frequently behave like infants, complying with authority because of fear or dependence, waiting until someone's back is turned to do something "naughty." To the extent that teachers become responsible for their own teaching, they not only help become responsible for their own learning, they also become professional. (p. 234).

To say, however, that Principal Helter and Superintendent Senter should lean toward giving their teachers responsibility for classroom matters is not to say that, even in a "professional" consciousness, Hardie and Maria are relieved from reflecting seriously on their proper course of action. They must consider, and perhaps be guided by, the unintended harms that their actions may cause others.

Hardie finds the graduation plans "repulsive," that is, morally offensive. To him, giving children such an inflated notion of their own deserts undermines the modesty and humility he tries to cultivate, while it enhances the flamboyant self-centeredness he tries to reduce. It is also "clear" to Connie "that this is a moral question"; the less advantaged families will be hurt, psyches will be bruised, and it will take time away from more worthwhile activities. This seems to us a stretch. Perhaps one could argue that the 'ball' is derivatively immoral: A graduation party is intrinsically harmless, but it might become a catalyst for bad outcomes. However, were the school to follow some version of Maria's suggestions, it could reduce the expenditure of money and time, and the anticipated social hurts. Second, while the event presses against the teachers' values, it is probably consonant with conventional community norms.

Furthermore, Hardie's stake is minimal. The event has no effect on his classroom teaching, for those involved are no longer "his" students. However sympathetic we are to Hardie's opinions (and we are), this is a decision for the administration to make in continuing consultation with the faculty and parents. It is likely that the parents have a range of views and as a group might welcome a Maria-like compromise.

But Hardie's views are not absurd; they deserve respect. Therefore, there should be no necessity for him to switch committee assignments with Maria. He should simply be relieved of the chaperoning obligation to which he was assigned. It is wrong—and here, not at all necessary—to ask a professional to do that which violates his personal conscience, and which he finds "repulsive."

Maria, for her part, needs to consider what weight she should give to the fact that, because of the likely manipulation of test scores by others, her students, and the school, may suffer undeserved harm; students in other classes and at other schools will appear, misleadingly, to be doing better. Again, that public reliance on such measures of effectiveness seriously corrupts the learning process is a fact that neither she nor her principal can change. While recognizing the corrosive effect of so smoothly adjusting to "working the system," she nonetheless must also recognize the concrete harms that might attend her refusal.

A "professional" paradigm, then, differs from an "employee" paradigm mostly in the *locus* of primary decisional authority and responsibility. A professional should certainly take counsel from the judgment of his or her peers and recognize the complexities of the dynamics of accountability. At the same time, a supervisor of one deemed "merely" an employee should permit, perhaps even encourage, the employee to remonstrate vigorously when he or she believes that important educational or moral considerations are being given insufficient weight. Each perspective has its limits of applicability: A superior order to do an act that is unquestionably illegal or, somewhat more controversially, flatly contrary to the employee's conscience carries no moral imperative; a professional judgment that is wholly impervious to the pain that its implementation is causing others, especially students, is simply a rationalization for irresponsibility.

Yet an important difference remains. A superintendent or principal can effectively choose what to expect of his or her teachers: Do as I say (and where I don't say, do what I *would* say), or develop your professional judgment as a teacher, albeit, under my general supervision. Educators, and citizens, will differ as to the correct direction in which to lean.

Where they agree, however, is in the judgment that the choice has an effect on the *moral climate* of a school or school system. Recall Wynne and Ryan's explicit avowal that a hierarchical model of principal-teacher relations has a *positive* effect on students, in light of the major role they give "discipline" as an aspect of good character: "The acceptance of hierarchy has been an important theme pervading traditional values. Indeed, without appropriate hierarchy . . . how can pupils learn to observe discipline?" (1997, p. 192). To them and like-minded others, a major justification for the "employee" model is precisely the fact that students learn what is right from observing the unspoken messages of the way in which a school is run, the influences by which their teachers are expected to guide their actions.

One whose idea of character sees "discipline" as a value that, though necessary, is dangerous as well, tends to regard this message as undermining more than reinforcing sound moral education. Students will not miss the significance of the *grounds* of the administrators' actions, and of the reinforcement of the norm requiring Maria to go along with their desires. When the "higher-ups" deny teachers the respect that their professional judgment calls for, efforts by teachers to persuade students to accord *them* proper respect will surely falter. Moreover, moral character is said to involve a fair degree of steadfastness, of courage, of willingness to risk. It is crippled by the message that, when the crunch comes (even a mild one) everyone—teacher, administrator, student—protects his or her flank, not only tacking with the prevailing winds, but not even waiting to be reasonably assured that the adverse winds will actually prevail. Moral character, all agree, is primarily about remaining honest, avoiding the temptation to lie or cheat, to gain an advantage; yet *of course* the school will cut corners and glibly embrace self-justifying rationalizations when, as with respect to its test scores, there is a benefit to be gained.

Maria's case is genuinely intractable. The true source of wrongfulness in the situation she faces lies outside the school system altogether, in the notion that educational effectiveness can be determined by quantifiable "sound bites," readily convertible to a ranking of schools. The newspapers, public officials, and the citizenry itself all bear responsibility for the corrosive effects of this impoverished notion of teaching success. For these consequences damage not only the academic enterprise of the schools but also their ability to carry on a credible program of moral education. Parents, hypersensitive to their interest in seeing their children deemed successful, are at once victims of this state of affairs and contributors to its infirmities. Victims, because as individuals they feel powerless to insulate their children from the harms done by a flawed system of evaluation and its use in a manner that magnifies those flaws; contributors because their protective responses strongly reinforce the feeling that the problem is insoluble at the systemic level, and all one can do is work the system to one's own (and one's children's) maximum advantage.

Whatever Maria's ultimate options are or should be, we can only endorse her determination to begin by seeking to consult more broadly among her teaching colleagues, rather than to see her present choices as simply obeying or placing her job on the line. For the problem is not hers alone, and even a tentative step toward encouraging her peers to recognize the dilemma they are in is a constructive move toward resisting the sense of pervasive helplessness and nonresponsibility that characterizes the mindset of all of the relevant actors—teachers, who have little power; administrators, who must please the school board and the public that elects it; newspapers, whose only accountability is to the public's asserted "right to know"; public officials, whose only accountability is to an electorate impatient with complexity and demanding simple measures to assure "better schools." No one teacher, group of teachers, or single school can turn this situation around; the more pertinent question is how these stakeholders respond to the choices that *are* present.

## Accountability as an Administrator

Maria's plight results from administrative abandonment. She is expected to execute a down-the-line decision into which she had no input. Here, as often, the school, operating on an employee model, puts the squeeze on a teacher's professional aspirations.

We have witnessed the not-so-invisible hand of the administration throughout this account—the rule against hats, the unwillingness of Downer to engage students in schoolwide issues, the conflict between Hardie and Principal Fred Helter over service learning, the tilting toward parents on the graduation ball. The climax now is over high-stakes testing. While the hand portrayed has been heavy, it need not be so. An administration can set high standards that teachers and children will strive to reach because they want to, not out of compulsion—and do so without constantly chipping away at their professionalism.

The challenge for schools is how to establish an elevated moral community while still encouraging moral autonomy in teachers and students, how to lead them and back them simultaneously.[1] How, that is, does a school inspire loyalty without strangulating dissent and independence?

---

[1] This task and possible resolutions are nicely addressed by Sergiovanni (1992), particularly in his description of leadership as stewardship.

Loyalty has its bright and dark sides. At its worst, loyalty is blind: my school, right or wrong. It falls prey easily to an us-against-them mentality. Exclusiveness, in- and out-groups, and stereotyping are its frequent by-products. But schools can as well uphold and transmit the weathered and worthy traditions of a society, without which children will feel no uplifting pride or purpose. Among the traditions, one assumes, is the commitment to revitalize and reassess those inherited traditions. An administration succeeds in creating a powerful moral atmosphere, we believe, by clarifying to all members of the community what it stands for, while providing forums to question and sometimes replace those standards.

Helter, in having teachers develop the educational plan they must in any case carry out, successfully promoted faculty autonomy. But he failed at the other half of leadership—the here's-what-we-stand-for part. Neither Connie, as the bearer of the testing orders, nor Maria as a subaltern, had a set of traditions on which to rely in framing their discussion. Absent such traditions, they had to bootstrap a solution, and inevitably they were buffeted by outside pressures. Presented with a strong moral tradition, they would have been in front of the waves.

But one is not without sympathy for Helter. He too faces undue pressure, unless backed by a superintendent willing to set standards while promoting his autonomy; and the superintendent in turn requires backing from the school board and wider community.

At a more psychological level, a school community with worthy values and practices gives children a much-sought-after chance to form a group identification. Before children can become autonomous—and one can never be so fully autonomous that group attachment is unimportant—they need to belong. While it is true that children require encouragement to resist their peer group, they also benefit from an attachment to it. One who from the outset stands outside will not develop those sympathies, loyalties, and convictions that at a later date he or she may choose to prune or discard. The more a school stands for something and instantiates that something in daily life, the thicker the child's sense of belonging.

Belonging, oddly, is the first step toward true autonomy. As American philosopher Michael Sandel (1998) has reminded us, "where the self is unencumbered and essentially dispossessed, no person is left for *self*-reflection to reflect upon" (p. 179, emphasis in original).[1] In the absence of "constitutive attachments" (Sandel's term) to others, our choices will be limited to personal preferences devoid of moral considerations. Being part of a group, caring about it, sharing its interests and values is as important to a maturing sense

---

[1] Robert Bellah and his associates also elaborated on the moral shallowness of the "radically unencumbered and improvisational self," the person who has no ties or identifications with others beyond "being nice" (1996, p. 81).

of self as the freedom to accept or resist. Adults worry about the influence of their children's peer groups, as well they might, in large measure because the group has no loyalty, institutional or otherwise, beyond its groupness. Thus, a school or a group that is mere scaffold without shape leaves its members empty and vulnerable to whatever seems cool (read "novel"). The seeming paradox here is that genuine freedom (independence) requires a persuaded belonging (attachment). Reverend Richard John Neuhaus (1984) put it well: "Beyond autonomy is the *free* acknowledgment of that by which we are bound. . . . [W]e are bound to be free in the sense that our freedom is only actualized in the free acceptance of that which authoritatively claims our assent and obedience" (pp. 18–19, emphasis in original).

## Your Turn:
## Facing the Administration

1. Hardie is confronting one of those issues that is hard to classify morally. Connie thinks it is clearly moral; Maria thinks it does not have moral valence, at least if handled carefully. We have suggested that whether you classify an incident as moral, derivatively moral, or not in the moral domain should make a difference to your response.
   a) Looking at the full context of the proposed graduation party (the role of parents, the responsibilities of the school, its effect on the students) how would you classify it?
   b) Given your classification, what would *you* suggest that the committee propose?

2. The issue of teachers cheating on behalf of students is more than theoretical. With promotions of students, careers of teachers, and the future of schools riding on test results, it is all but inevitable.
   Consider yourself in Maria's position. Let us say the principal is the source of the request to "help" students. The superintendent knows about, and has implicitly encouraged, the practice.
   a) What options do you have?
   b) How do these options fit into either an employee or professional paradigm?
   c) How might you act in the short and the long term?
   d) What do you expect to be the consequences of your actions?
   e) How will you justify them to the parties affected?

3. You are teaching a social studies class on the distribution of wealth and poverty among nations. You show a United Nations videotape that

illustrates starvation around the world. The principal hears about this lesson and tells you not to show that tape or anything like it again: too controversial, too upsetting to children, too much risk of parental complaints.

a) What is your reaction to his decision?

b) What is the proper action to take?

4. This chapter is critical of the administration for not supplying a moral canopy that protects the school environment and promotes the professionalism of teachers. Sounds good, but is it fair to ask so much of an administration?

a) Consider whether an administration can set a moral "tone" without clamping down more strongly on teachers. Specifically, how might this be done?

b) What would be the reaction of teachers and parents to such tone setting?

■ ■ ■ ■ ■

# CHAPTER 9

# THE MORAL EDUCATION REPORT: AN UNPROGRAMMED PROGRAM

## Scenario

The committee continued to meet fairly regularly, discussing incidents that arose in school, sharing ideas on how to address them, reporting on material gathered from up-and-running programs. Reluctantly, they agreed that come May, their free-flowing seminar had to end; they'd be obliged to submit their "plan."

May came. Aggie, fully aware of being controlled by the calendar rather than by a sense of closure, began their meeting.

"I know, of course, that none of us feels primed to sketch a proposal for Helter. With that in mind, I'd like us to review briefly what we've done. Then I have a suggestion to make."

Nods all around.

"As I recollect, we began this process, innocently enough, scouting for a few activities through which the school could teach morality. We quickly settled on the class meeting. It seemed just the right device for promoting thoughtful responses about ongoing moral issues as they arose in our school lives or in the books we study.

"To move the process along, you'll recall, I invented the Downer scenario. It was my assumption, frankly, that you'd all sign on to "moralizing" the class meetings and we'd promptly wrap up our recommendations for the principal. Was I ever wrong! When you folks began laying into Downer, I shredded my timetable.

"Then other possible activities emerged from our talks: selecting an existing prepackaged program from those displayed by Bonham, adopting a service-learning requirement, staking out topics that are the rightful province of school and home, determining the shape of a disciplinary code, establishing a reasonably clear set of prescriptive values to be followed, and delineating a professional morality for teachers who come into conflict with "superiors." But, every one of them became problematic, as the transition from theory to practice revealed our differences. Although we got over our hesitation about the task swiftly—Connie, I think even you came to believe it a worthy assignment—the "how to" has been more elusive than we had imagined. Why was that? Because we had no notion of just how embedded morality is in controversy, and legitimate controversy at that.

"In preparing for this meeting, it occurred to me that maybe we started out at the wrong end of the tunnel. Rather than beginning with activities, a hazard to which we teachers so often succumb, perhaps we should have asked, what's the desired outcome of a moral ed program? That is, what would *success* look like? So now that May has rolled around and the end of the year is looming, rather than submit a slapdash job, I took it upon myself to ask Helter if we could have a few extra weeks right after school closes to hold some intensive meetings to formulate our recommendations. He agreed and ponied up funds for us and for Bonham, whom he suggested we consult. If you're willing to go the distance, I thought that today we'd take a stab at outlining our objectives. Think of it as writing one of those goals statements we always see in reports. What do you think?"

After the usual skirmishing over what they would have to produce, in how many hours, for how much pay, the group agreed, as Aggie had been confident they would, to her suggestions. Hardie began the discussion.

"I know selecting a set of virtues doesn't thrill you guys, but since Bonham first unveiled them I've been attracted to the Six Pillars (see Chapter 4). Besides being unambiguous, they'd give the program a high visibility that would surely appeal to our principal and school board. Parents could walk into a school and see displays on the wall advertising the virtue of the month; they'd go from class to class and observe what was being done to promote that particular virtue. Children would be articulate about what they were to accomplish. Lots of accountability all around. So remind me why we shouldn't go that way?"

"Hardie," Aggie answered, The problem with virtues, or at least a potential problem, is that they represent free-floating qualities that can't be evaluated without contextualization. As we've noted [Chapter 4], responsibility by itself is neither good nor bad without asking, responsible to whom? For what? The same is true of other virtues such as courage, persistence, loyalty, caring: All can be devoted to good or bad ends. So I asked myself, if virtues alone don't work, where do we go? We've already dismissed specified activities as an appropriate goal. We might select measurable objectives such as no (or less) cheating, stealing, fighting; more acts of kindness. The . . ."

"Tell us what's wrong with that, Aggie," Hardie interrupted, "for I can see you're about to trash it."

"Well, it's not terrible, and schools often do use behavioral criteria, but as we've noted, an excessive focus on behavior is as bad as an excessive focus on virtues. We've recognized that motives cannot be excluded from actions [Chapter 4]; intentions are central to morality. "With a little help from Dr. Bonham, whom I called last week, I've hit upon a broad goal that I think might appeal to all of us. Succinctly put, it's the establishment of *moral identity*."

"Sounds promising," said Maria, "but isn't that a virtue?"

"I don't think so," Aggie replied. "I mean it's a different sort of quality of a person. To me moral identity is a process, a continuing search, the cultivation of a sensibility that grounds the development of virtues.

"To spell it out just a bit more, having a moral identity means being alert to moral issues and dilemmas as they occur—you could call that the development of *moral sensitivity*. It means seriously analyzing those issues in all their ambiguity and complexity—call that the development of *moral reasoning*. It means taking responsibility for making moral choices and living with your decisions—call that the development of *moral action*. It means making morality a high priority even when it isn't easy—call that *moral will*. It means filtering decisions through a moral lens—call that *moral direction*. And it means experiencing indignation, sorrow, forgiveness, restitution, and resolve—call that the development of *moral emotions*. But it doesn't mean a particular set of behaviors or qualities."

Hardie was all smiles. "Speaking of nimble, I see why Helter gave you this job. Moral identity. It just might work."

"You know, Hardie, I actually got the idea from thinking about why I'm so relaxed about the differences between you and Maria. Both of you, I realized, are deeply moral people. Why does Maria spend several evenings each week dining with her cranky widowed mother? Why do you, Hardie, volunteer each weekend at a homeless shelter? Why are you both so reliable and steadfast? Though your judgments may differ, it's your moral identity that transmutes the judgments into a sense of obligation and wills you into action. You cannot be true to yourself, cannot respect yourself, and at the same time be morally blasé. That moral core drives you; more than that, it's your master control system around which all else gets organized.

"Quiet Connie over there is the same. Why does she spend multiple evenings, heck, weekends too, calling up parents, making referrals, even doing that old-fashioned thing called home visits? I've seen her at it when she herself was ill and should have been home in bed and, I might add, when no higher-ups were around to give credit. You could call it being a professional, but it goes so much further. She just constantly puts the interests of others above her own, an exemplar of benevolence."

"Wily Aggie," Connie replied. "She strews roses in our path and leaves us speechless. Flattery aside, Aggie, it's a great objective, and I see we all agree on that. Now let's distribute tasks for the next meeting and get out of here."

Much to their delight and somewhat to their surprise, the committee members succeeded, in a few more meetings, in drafting their report.

■ ■ ■ ■ ■

## REPORT TO PRINCIPAL FRED HELTER
## BY FACULTY COMMITTEE ON MORAL EDUCATION:
## AGATHA CERINE, CONSTANCE COMFORT,
## HARDIE KNOX, MARIA LASZLO
## IN CONSULTATION WITH DR. JAN BONHAM

We start by thanking you, sincerely thanking you, for inviting us to grapple with the issue of moral education. What a surprising journey it has been! As you undoubtedly heard, we did not greet this assignment with enthusiasm. Here was yet another demand (so we thought) to fix a problem not of our making and not our affair. We saw no need to challenge the assumptions upon which we had always operated:

1. Children's moral improprieties—that's how we conceived of morality, as "bad" behaviors—should be managed by teachers, using the disciplinary powers available to them. When "problems" were beyond our purview or power to correct, they should be turned over to parents or "experts." Parents and religious institutions train children in morality, we train them in academics. We should stick to our expertise.
2. We thought of classroom morality, when we thought about it at all, as instrumental to teaching and learning, not a goal in itself. Children should be orderly, do their homework, be prompt, not interrupt, not pass notes, and listen to one another because not doing so was incompatible with our job and theirs: to teach and learn.
3. We took for granted that children are entitled to rough equality. All of us, therefore, prohibited bullying, fighting, and nastiness in general; and we allotted our attentions evenly, perhaps occasionally favoring the weaker.
4. From time to time we invited "experts" to talk about moral issues: good and bad touching, the wrongness of tobacco and drugs, and tolerance for diversity. In the spring each year we should have a food and clothing drive for the homeless. That was about it, and that was enough.

The shallowness of these notions became apparent early on. But admitting our shortcomings was a lot easier than formulating a program. We battled mightily over what more we might consider; agreement was elusive. However, our conversations did yield a few unanimously endorsed innovations. We offer them here in the form of seven recommendations: The first three are orienting positions, the second two are pedagogic, the last two are role-related.

**Recommendation 1: Morality should be a key component of our educational curricula to which teachers, children, parents, staff, and administrators all contribute. It should be pursued primarily by grappling with the moral aspects of everyday events, treated not as**

**a separate subject but as the surround of all subjects and of all our dealings with one another. And we should "do" moral education in the absence of knowing precisely what we mean by "doing" and by "it."**

The group's initial insight, fundamentally altering our understanding of the moral education task, was the recognition that daily life in school is suffused with moral issues; we had simply been blind to what now seems so obvious. Simple behaviors such as the disposition of Kleenex, classroom seating arrangements, appropriate and inappropriate topics for class discussion, all are moral occasions. Every time we tell a child what is expected, what is forbidden, and how he or she should act, we exercise a moral judgment. Yet our responses to such incidents were on automatic pilot, derived from school traditions, habits, and momentary intuitions. We weren't attending to the waters we swam in; that seemed irresponsible. Like it or not, we were "doing" moral education, and therefore should do it with forethought.

But we found deeper justifications. In failing to tangle with this topic we send our children a message of extreme moral relativism: It's not for us to judge moral questions, it's all a personal matter. By rejecting our educational responsibility to engage, we imply that moral decision making is entirely discretionary and arbitrary, that the realm of values is not amenable to rational examination and to the formation of communitywide norms. We create an amoral atmosphere at school, allowing children to believe that loyalties and commitments need not go beyond one's present best buddy, nor be any more lasting. We abandon those families who struggle against the pernicious influences of the wider culture, and we leave many of our students entirely defenseless. By abdicating the moral realm, we suggest to children that what matters is how well you do, not who you are. We erode further the notion that morality has any special overriding obligatory claim that merits investment by our schools, and we lend support to the widespread moral indifference that now afflicts us. So tangle we must.

**Recommendation 2: A moral education program must maintain a sensitivity to legitimate societal disagreement over values and pedagogy even as it clarifies the incontestable values of the community. Children should become skilled at "critical thinking" about morality, appreciating how others think even as they make (or others make for them) hard decisions by which they stand.**

Our second insight was that solutions to "moral occasions" are thick with complexities. One could make a big deal out of dropping Kleenex in the halls, or ignore it. There are legitimate arguments on both sides, and we disagreed as to the right answer. Even when we reached consensus on the seriousness of an offense, we were at odds over the best response, especially over how tough to be with the offender. Should we take a "disciplinary" or "understanding" posture, and why?

*(continued)*

We now know that educators have varying views on the nature of morality, the objectives of moral instruction and how to teach it. The differences largely parallel the stand-off between "conservatives " and "liberals" in public life. A school, institutionally dependent upon the consent of its constituents, cannot opt for one side. It must be hospitable, although not infinitely so, to a host of competing values. One of the core values that create a community and bind its members is, paradoxically, receptivity to disagreements.

Furthermore, it seems right, not just pragmatic, to preserve the disagreements. For some twenty-five centuries philosophers have disputed every aspect of morality: the nature of a moral value; the instantiation of morality in acts, motives, and consequences; the justification for placing one value over another; the prerogatives of those who judge; the methods of cultivating morality in the young. We recognize that moral values inevitably conflict—justice with mercy, discipline with freedom, honesty with loyalty, persistence with compromise. It would be unfaithful to the depth and richness of the topic if, in the name of utility and practicality, we lost sight of just how uncertain the practice of moral education can be.

A good program will appreciate that morality "is conduct to which there is an alternative" (Oakeshott, 1962, p. 60). When making choices it is therefore critical to remain alert to the alternatives rejected. Maintaining awareness of alternatives, though burdensome, emancipates the decision-making process from overly swift reflexive responses and is essential to a thoughtful tolerance.

Nonetheless we were frustrated, sometimes confused, sometimes despairing over the lack of consensus and the absence of "answers." But this discouragement too was finally overcome. We came to another realization: More critical than the right answer was struggling over the questions. However much we disagreed over what to do about improperly discarded Kleenex, we agreed that it, and other seemingly perfunctory occurrences, were anything but perfunctory. The very process of raising and probing such questions, we noted, was sensitizing our moral antennae. Not a day passes now that we don't look over our shoulders watching the moral decisions we make. As a result of *our* enhanced self-consciousness, we naturally alert students to *their* morality. Going forward, we (students and teachers) are confident that, as the faculty grows more vigilant, primed, interested, and attached to the moral realm, so too will the school become a more moral community.

Not all discussions need to end in a resolution. There is a substantial yield, as Robert Nozick (1981) pointed out, and we discovered, simply from airing issues:

> To engage in a moral dialogue with someone is itself a moral act, whose moral character does not lie solely in being an attempt to get at the moral truth. . . . Rather, (sincere) engagement in moral dialogue is itself a moral response to the other's basic moral characteristic. . . . It itself is responsive to him; perhaps that is why openness in moral dialogue, considering carefully and responding closely to the concerns of the other, so often is an effective means toward resolution of conflict.

When each is aware that the other is responsive to his or her own (valuable) characteristics in the very act of discussion and in the course the discussion takes, then this noticing of mutual respect is itself a force for good will and the moderation of demands (p. 469).

Children, too, need opportunities to discuss moral conflicts and their own moral difficulties. Even young children can grasp the conflict between what they want to do and what they should do, the problem of dual loyalties, and the plurality of values among people. Support and openness are required for such talk, whether the conflicts arise from invented moral dilemmas, literary or historical texts, or the children's own lives.

**Recommendation 3 : Schools should help children develop a moral core that will become central to their self-definition. While this responsibility is shared with families and other institutions and is a complex and lifelong enterprise, the school can and should have a formative influence. That influence is directed less to the moral content of the identity than to its centrality in a worthy life.**

A third conviction settled upon us late in our proceedings. We had been so focused on the immediacy of the task, as we suspect is true at most schools, that the long-term goal was neglected. This was a mistake. The destination one is headed toward modulates here-and-now responses in two respects: It serves as a criterion by which to evaluate decisions, and it encourages long-range planning. The destination of a moral education program, we agreed, should be the development of a strong moral identity. Schools are centrally in the business of self-construction. We want children to like themselves. Teachers try to build their self-esteem. But if a positive self-image is limited to seeing oneself as cool, popular, and with it, or even smart, knowledgeable, athletic, and influential; if it doesn't include some aspiration to a useful worthy life, to becoming a good, as well as a competent and successful, person, then surely we have sold our kids short.

Moral identity goes beyond the cultivation of good habits, compassion, and reflection. It is partially captured by words like will, resolve, and aspiration. It is as much searching and striving as coping and adapting; it is a *way of being in the world* rather than just a *response to the world*.

Moral identity shares features with our other identities, such as being an athlete or a mother. It is true of at least our positive identities (and each of us has many) that we are *preoccupied* by them, that we *monitor* their adequacy, and that we *resist* challenges to them. For example, someone with a genuine athletic identity, as compared to someone who merely enjoys exercise or engages in sports for the adulation or profit it brings, is on the look-out for opportunities to play his sport. He expresses his athleticism off as well as on the field by staying in shape and avoiding unhealthy temptations. He monitors his skill level and seeks to improve. Faced with a setback, such as an injury, he goes through rehabilitation eagerly and earnestly. Someone with a maternal iden-

*(continued)*

tity, as compared to someone who just happens to be a parent (even a conscientious one), steals time from nonmaternal activities to be with her children. She thinks about mothering when not doing it, watches others, and compares her style to theirs. She monitors and evaluates her skills, trying always to do better. When she makes a mistake or is rejected by her child, rather than withdrawing, she redoubles her efforts. Similarly, someone with a strong, as compared to a weak, moral identity is alert to opportunities for expressing moral statements and actions, sees the moral implications in seemingly neutral situations, questions the adequacy of her responses, and courageously resists invitations to act amorally or immorally, despite the cost to her self-interest (as perceived by others).

In schools we ask children to resist powerful moral counter-pulls from peers and the larger society—pulls toward simple pleasures, popularity, power, material goods, and unhealthy indulgences. They can do so only if they treasure their moral identity so highly and find its pursuit deeply gratifying. Since everyone wants to be successful and well liked, they will have to withstand these strong temptations. A major challenge for schools is how to implant *within* children the moral autonomy that allows them to question, monitor, judge their acts (and failures to act), and if necessary stand apart, while simultaneously grafting from *without* the enduring wisdom of our moral heritage.

**Recommendation 4: Every moral education program should provide opportunities for student deliberation and student decision making. This participation must be developmentally staged: less for the younger child, in whom the cultivation of habits and compassion takes center stage; more for the older child, who can override self-interest in deference to the greater good and appreciate the importance of altered contexts to moral rules.**

We have avoided recommending a particular pedagogical style, recognizing that good teaching comes in many forms and that teachers have strong allegiances to their preferred approaches. To be an effective moral educator, we are persuaded, depends more on commitment than method. Moral identity is fostered by the teacher who rules the roost as well as by the one who "co-constructs" with children. Most teachers, in any case, will draw (properly so in our view) from both ends of the spectrum. Yet we will go this far: If children are to develop a moral identity they must be active participants in their moral community; they must have a voice in establishing and enforcing the morality to which they are subject. How strong a voice? At what ages? In what circumstances? Again, there is disagreement.

To some, including at least one of us on the committee, the teacher's task—to encourage children's social sensitivity, social responsibility, moral determination, and substantial self-governance—is best fulfilled by creating many situations for cooperative teacher-student decision making. The primary method for this is the class discussion—teacher with student, student with student, students together in formal and informal groups.

Entrusting substantial responsibility to children for governing their lives strikes others (again, including at least one among us) as irresponsible. Children are much too immature, self-centered, inconsistent, and irrational to be given grave decision-making responsibilities. If we refuse children a wide latitude in deciding matters of curriculum, or even the foods they can eat and the television programs they can watch, why do we think they can determine the moral rules that should govern them? To grant such an allowance is to trivialize morality.

Every school must decide upon the extent and form of children's input. Schools will vary on both dimensions. For some, decisions on all rules will be a joint undertaking. Others will invite participation only on peripheral issues, or only by older students. Children's input may range from voicing an opinion to sharing in decisions to exercising decisional authority. A good school policy will make clear, in advance of open discussions, the extent of student determinations on rules and should review its policy periodically. The guide presented by Jan Bonham on *Six Levels of Teacher Authority* (see Chapter 3, p. 41) is a helpful aid in making those decisions.

Children should also have some role in policies of enforcement and the consequences of transgression. Again, their role can range from expressing a viewpoint to the teacher, class, or representative governing body (which itself can have a small or large student voice) to more decisive authority. Whatever the students' role, they are likely to learn, simply from the act of participation, to temper their often harsh judgments and demands for retribution with a measure of understanding and forgiveness.

What is essential is that children grow as moral agents. To that end, they must feel they have a voice, and in fact do have a voice, in matters of importance to them. At the same time, they need to become attached to our common values. That means accepting certain norms and practices as inviolable and, at least in the higher grades, understanding why this is so.

**Recommendation 5: In addition to class meetings (the from-below component) every moral education program should institutionalize a moral discipline policy (the from-above piece). Such a policy will severely limit automatic sanctions that are insensitive to the moral dimensions of school rules and the context in which they are broken.**

Schools need to resist uniform sentencing. In the management of large, impersonal organizations, a society can perhaps do no better. But even then the charge of "unfair" is legitimate. Take traffic violation penalties: Instead of merely checking speedometers, would it not be fairer to distinguish between a man speeding to the hospital where his wife had just delivered a baby and an adolescent putting his car to a road test? How much more unfair, then, is a

*(continued)*

one-size-fits-all policy in the more intimate setting of schools! The accidental shove, the retaliatory shove, and the malevolent shove are three very different happenings, and they should be treated as such. Thus, fairness requires an inquiry into the dispositions of those involved in an offense as well as their interpretations of the act and its consequences.

But moral discipline is not just a matter of doling out fair sanctions. It can and should be a conduit for moral instruction. That goal requires teachers, and school policies, to differentiate as far as possible the conventional rules that uphold classroom order—working quietly at your desk, retaining papers in your desk, keeping gum off your desk—from those that protect fundamental human rights and social obligations—no cheating, no stealing, no bullying. We recognize also a large gray area of behaviors, the derivatively moral, that are hard to classify: eating with your fingers, belching, calling a teacher by her first name, wearing a hat. Such acts become moral rather than conventional wrongs when, but only when, they sincerely offend others, intentionally or heedlessly. There is nothing intrinsically "wrong" (no one is hurt) with finger feeding or using first names; both are often appropriate and welcomed. But when designed to insult, and in fact do insult, they slide into the moral realm. School personnel then have the freedom either to de-moralize them, by not taking offense, or to treat them as moral wrongs. These opportunities provide a necessary and welcome elasticity for teachers and schools, without courting the specter of relativism.

The distinction in rules should be matched, we are persuaded, with a distinction in disciplinary objectives. If a conventional rule is broken, the objective is largely compliance. The teacher asks herself, "How do I get Johnny to hand in his papers on time?" She considers: Monitor him closely, have a friend remind him, tie a string around his finger, ask him what would help, give him remembering awards, make him stay after school to redo papers. Or, another option: Drop the rule. Perhaps I am expecting too much; let him turn in papers as he completes them. Perhaps he is embarrassed by his work; I shouldn't force him, just yet, to expose his papers.

It is different with a moral violation. In such instances, there is no possibility of dropping the rule, and simple compliance is too meager. The objective now is to convince the child that he was wrong, that he can be better. There is a shift in the teacher's tone, from problem solving to disappointment and disapproval. She clarifies the importance of preserving the moral order and the seriousness of breaching it, using those sanctions necessary to be convincing. For moral violations, but *not* for conventional ones, it is appropriate for the child to feel remorse and guilt.

We thought of stopping at this point. If a school, if this school, adopts our five recommendations—the significance of moral education, the complexities of determining answers, the centrality of moral identity, the importance of children's participation, and the establishment of moral discipline—it will be well on its way toward having a moral education "program." However, we determined, a school's commitment must go further if recommendations are to be more than window dressing. We turn then to the responsibilities, as we see them, of the key players.

**Recommendation 6: Rather than viewing themselves as cogs in a disciplinary machine, mere moral monitors, teachers should take on the greater challenge of considering seriously their own values, those expressed or implicit in the texts they use and in the wider society. This ongoing exploration should be shared with colleagues and reflected in classroom practices.**

"You can lead a horse to water but. . . ." is an aphorism particularly relevant to moral education. The linchpin for the undertaking, we have no doubt, is the commitment of teachers. Coaxing, even demanding, compliance from above will be to no avail if the enthusiasm of teachers is not engaged. The commitment must have at least these spurs: attentive inspection of their own values (content) and how they are projected to children (method), attentive inspection of the moral issues that lace the curriculum, and attentive instruction in the core values agreed upon by the school community.

To be credible to children, teachers must attend first to their own morality. As Robert Coles (1987) has witnessed:

> [T]he child is an ever-attentive witness of grown-up morality—or lack thereof; the child looks for cues as to how one ought to behave, and finds them galore as we parents and teachers go about our lives, making choices, addressing people, showing in action our rock-bottom assumptions, desires, and values, and thereby telling those young observers much more than we may realize (p. 5).

It is true of morality, as it is of literature or math, that one is forever an apprentice in search of deepening awareness. How does a teacher model that awareness so it is accessible to children? We believe that children catch their teacher's values by experiencing the fair, sometimes firm, sometimes fun-loving, sometimes forgiving, always caring manner he has with them; by his conscientiousness in preparing instruction and responding to student work; by his alert listening to their thoughts; by his genuine interest in their families and extended lives; by his attentiveness to the special circumstances of individual children; by his efforts to foster supportive relationships among students. We add to this list the imperative that teachers reveal, to themselves as well as to their students, their *moral mistakes*. If the growth motif is to control the educational process, as with any form of growth, we must look to false starts, errors, and backsliding for instruction. A teacher who can share wrongdoing and weakness in the context of renewed effort is, we believe, a powerful moral force for children.

Teachers need also to find moral "lessons" (questions as well as answers) in the curriculum. This may be a simple matter of self-consciously exploiting what already exists. As Purpel and Ryan (1976) pointed out, the ordinary curriculum is morally laden: from debates about abortion in biology to the

*(continued)*

justification for insurrection in history to career education programs (pp. 44–54).[1] Theodore Sizer (1984) elaborated on the thought:

> What a teacher selects to "tell" in a class is an exercise in values. If one refers in a social studies lesson to Native Americans as "them" and implies that the first settlers of the American West were Europeans, one is saying a great deal. Describing the Indians as the (likely) first of many human immigrants to these continents sends a quite different message. The way a biology teacher treats life in class—whether, for example, live frogs are purchased and pithed in quantity for students to dissect—signals important values. Mocking the squeamishness and reserve of students who do not want to kill frogs can deeply affect a young student. . . . Can I take this frog's life so that I can learn about reptilian innards? The adult who impatiently rejects the legitimacy of a student's confusion teaches a value. One cannot teach at arm's length: the world does not allow it. The issue of life is in the middle of every biology class, and most other classes too. To pretend it is not there is to say something about it; in that sense is the vacuum dangerous. Value issues infuse every classroom (p. 123).

Some teachers will rely on "moral moments" that occur spontaneously in the lives of children—a fight, a theft, an exclusion, an opportunity to help. Still others may prefer to turn to one of the published moral education programs. These programs range considerably in the values covered and the explicitness of the teaching. Considered as resources, they are valuable, often (for busy teachers) invaluable. But whatever the merit in such material,[2] there are dangers when a "moral curriculum" is based wholly on externally generated material. One danger is the likelihood that teachers, relying on packaged curricula, will defer to the "manual" rather than think hard (with their students) about the matter at hand. Another danger is that reliance on "lessons" from a book will undermine teachers' sensitivity to the moral moments in the school day and the imperative to resolve them thoughtfully.

The extent to which teachers lean on existing curricula or forge their own is less critical than that they be given the authority to select. Too much management by higher-ups of what to teach and how to teach weakens the likelihood that the lessons will enter the lives of teachers and therefore of children—at school and beyond. Without their signature on the instruction, success as we've defined it is unlikely.

Nonetheless, fundamental normative expectations, those common moral values that constitute the backbone of the community, must be made clear to children and clearly enforced. Robert Howard (1991), a Kohlberg-trained elementary school teacher, called them the Big Rules:

> I had certain "Big Rules" that were nonnegotiable and not subject to the will of the class. These rules, including "We will treat others as we would like to be

---

[1] See also Benninga, 1991; Jackson, Boostrom, and Hansen, 1993; Lickona, 1991; Ryan and Bohlin, 1999.

[2] For the teachers' reactions, see Chapter 4, p. 64.

treated," "People are safe in this classroom," "Property is safe in this classroom," and "People are treated with respect in this classroom," were distributed to and signed by both students and parents at registration on the first day of school. . . . The existence of the Big Rules in combination with the social contract that the students and parents had entered into [through signing onto the rules] gave me the opportunity to exercise a veto if the students wanted to create a class rule or establish a punishment that I felt violated the Big Rules (p. 61).

So, when a class democratically decided that the suitable punishment for one child who spat on another was for the class to circle around the offender and everyone spit on him, the Big Rules provided grounds for a veto.

It is crucial not to obscure or minimize the Big Rules by adding to them what are merely school-based conventions. Equating Big Rules with fundamental moral values implies that they are universalizable to all (or mostly all) human encounters and obligatory as a matter of morality. They form the community's backbone; other values stem from, and are justified by, them. To attach to this spine rules of convenience, as some codes do—not chewing gum, not bringing portable CD players to school, not running in the halls—is to blur important distinctions. School-based conventional rules such as these may require adherence and enforcement, just as traffic laws do, but the scale of approval and disapproval for obeying and disobeying them should be distinguishable so that children learn that moral rules occupy a higher status.

**Recommendation 7: The task of administrators is to facilitate the difficult work of moral education for teachers. What teachers need from administrators is less a central control over content and pedagogy than the establishment of a moral tone, public advocacy for the centrality of this work, and a real commitment of resources to training and support. Teachers cannot be expected to rise unaided to the challenge.**

In a decentralized program, as suggested here, the principal task of the administration is to seek, and prove able to tap, the teachers' aspirations, however much they may have become obscured by the many dispiriting aspects of daily life in the classroom. Implementation of even the soundest program is not a ministerial act. It cannot be wholly scripted, for it cannot displace the need for individual teacher judgment and situation-sense in response to the varying dynamics of individual classroom moments. Genuine respect for the professional discretion and judgment of individual teachers in carrying out the program should therefore be built into the design of the program.

To accomplish this end, it is necessary for the central administration to strengthen its *supportive* and lighten its *prescriptive* input. As mentioned, we have found that the meetings of this committee were significant opportunities to learn from and support one another. We also found benefit in contact with experts and serious inservice work. Administrators must secure the time, space,

*(continued)*

and resources for teachers to become conversant with the moral aspects of their pedagogy.

A good administrator will, however, realize that more is needed than time and space for talk. The atmospherics of meetings are dicey: We do not have an educational culture that relishes unanswered (often unanswerable) questions or searching self-criticism. Resources and encouragement may not be effective unless all—but most especially those "above"—share their moral assumptions and then their moral uncertainties. A good principal will make clear that she values (and will herself exemplify) such disclosures.

The administration must be concerned, not just with the atmospherics among teachers but also with the general moral tone of the school. To create a moral community requires engagement of the entire staff—including secretaries, bus drivers, food preparers, custodians, and maintenance workers, who may be in the school very little. They should have some input into, and responsibility for, the program. Children should make the effort to know the staff by name, know their responsibilities and their contribution to the operation of the enterprise, perhaps even working with them at times as quasi-apprentices. When a child drops Kleenex on the floor, she needs to understand (feel) what that means to the custodian who must pick it up, and perhaps know it by serving alongside that custodian.

In assuming a moral mandate, the school will want to encourage a spirit of collective responsibility. A child sees a paper on the floor and automatically picks it up: He doesn't want *his* school to be littered. A child is swamped with homework but comes to choir practice anyway: He doesn't want *his* group's performance to suffer. A child takes umbrage when *his* classmate is subject to ethnic slurs: *He* feels insulted. In his school and with his friends, he does what he would do in his home and for himself. According to Durkheim (1956), it is affiliation with a community "that draws us out of ourselves, that obliges us to reckon with other interests than our own, it is society that has taught us to control our passions, our instincts, to prescribe law for them, to restrain ourselves, to deprive ourselves, to sacrifice ourselves, to subordinate our personal ends to higher ends" (p. 76).

To establish those "higher ends" without bearing down on those "below" takes dexterity. Through public statements, public documents, symbols, and rituals, but most of all through visible daily conduct, administrators set the parameters of the desirable and the impermissible. It is critical that they do so because, within limits, restricting the scope of a student's (and teacher's) autonomy is, oddly, essential to it. Without clear and convincing restrictions a child will flounder in a sea of endless choices, not knowing what she wants or how to decide what she wants. She becomes, as Harry Frankfurt (1993) has put it, "volitionally debilitated" (p.17). Continuous uncertainty, particularly in the young child, will diminish the construction of a moral identity, which requires reflection on executed choices.

Another task for the school administration (including the school board) is to make known to parents and the wider community that its commitment to moral education is serious. Schools, fearing a backlash, are often reluctant to go public with such a commitment. This is a mistake. Rather than hiding behind euphemisms like "social skills" training," cooperative learning," and "citizenship," schools should out the "m" word so that parents are well informed from the moment they register their child. Administrators need to share candidly with parents the moral stances they advocate and invite families to bring objections and suggestions to the table. Parents are the primary moral educators of their children; schools can disagree with them and can try to reach accommodations with them, but they cannot ignore them. Without open discussions aimed at a shared language of the good, schools may become insulated moral islands. Children, then, will dismiss school standards as soon as they are dismissed or, worse, come to believe that morality is nothing more than arbitrary rules devised by "interested parties" to control them. The school must therefore also reach out to the community for its contributions.

Everyone calls for more "parent participation"; few get it. Because of their divergent interests—the parent in her child, the teacher in all the children—a subtle hostility between them is not unusual. Rare is the parent who will subjugate the "interest" of her child (seen narrowly as self-interest) to that of the greater good. If her child's scores will improve more by studying than service learning, her child should be excused from the requirement, never mind the antigroup spirit of this request. The tension between parent and teacher must be overcome, we believe, if moral education is to have any real teeth. When parents, representatives of the "real world," do not moderate a single-minded interest in their child's race to the front, the school is impotent. Moral education depends on a group consciousness, on parents *wanting* their children to consider the needs and rights of others as equivalent to their own.

Raising this social consciousness, rather than monitoring the particulars of moral curricula, is the primary task for school boards, state and national agencies, and opinion shapers in general. A call for character education limited to the abolition of guns and knives, or even to ending cheating, will not arouse the sort of commitment we seek. The outside call, like the inside one, must be to build the moral identities of children, however much that goes against the grain of the political milieu in which school boards, superintendents, and departments of education find themselves.

In the end, however, primary responsibility goes back to the individual teachers who, often harried by the multiple demands upon them and struggling with issues of "burnout" and related ills, must rise to the occasion, take seriously the goals and demands of moral education, and resist the ever-present voice that would mock a positive response to that aspiration.

### End/Beginnings

As individuals, we who worked together on this committee differ significantly in our priorities and dispositions. One tends toward the didactic and prescriptive, a second toward the ambivalent and interactive, a third toward minimalism driven largely by a sense of irony, a fourth toward impatience with what appears impractical. What we learned in listening to one another was . . . to

*(continued)*

*listen* to one another: to listen for the concerns, even the fears, that our favored approaches generate in others; to listen for the emergent response that seeks to meet those concerns while holding faithfully, if a little less tightly, to our own priorities; to resist the temptation to caricature, even demonize, the priorities and concerns of people with views different from ours. William Damon's (1995) insight regarding school reform generally bears keeping in mind as we think about moral education:

> [T]he oppositional ethos of many current school reform efforts has [worked] against [a] bridge-building sort of effort. When reformers argue about the virtues of play versus drill, phonetics versus whole language, encoding versus comprehension, self-esteem versus mastery, or school-as-fun versus school-as-work, they are standing on one side of the gap and placing their opponents on the other. If we are to help all our children realize their full academic potential, we must design school programs that build bridges across such gaps (p. 155; emphasis omitted).

The urge to polarize, to oversimplify, to latch on to those approaches that one finds most appealing, to "get on with the job so we can turn to other things," must be resisted. But the integration of views is more than aggregation, and it is important that moral education not be approached as giving contending approaches a "turn." No amount of integration can possibly wring out of a sophisticated program the variations that inevitably will, and in our view *should*, arise in both conception and application. The brute fact of differing views must be respected. But a program that tilts a bit too much in one direction is a far better program than one that takes even a more balanced direction and then runs downfield with it, inattentive to differences among children, schools and communities, or teachers.

Listening and balancing are not signs of "giving in" to all contending political constituencies in the field, but rather a genuine commitment to the complexity of morality, to the truth that all sides have some portion of the truth. This insight is reflected in the wisdom of Simone Weil (1986a) who eloquently reminded us that there is no real liberty without obedience, no deserved honor without discipline, no genuine submission without resistance, no legitimate authority without equality, no lasting security without risk, no authentic autonomy without belongingness. We end with her words:

> The human soul has need of equality and of hierarchy. Equality is the public recognition, effectively expressed in institutions and manners, of the principle that an equal degree of attention is due to the needs of all human beings. Hierarchy is the scale of responsibilities. . . .
>
> The human soul has need of consented obedience and of liberty. Consented obedience is what one concedes to an authority because one judges it to be legitimate. . . . Liberty is the power of choice within the latitude left between the direct constraint of natural forces and the authority accepted as legitimate. . . .
>
> The human soul has need of truth and of freedom of expression. The need for truth requires . . . that in the domain of thought there should never be any

physical or moral pressure exerted for any purpose other than an exclusive concern for truth. . . .

The human soul has need of some solitude and privacy and also of some social life. . . .

The human soul has need of punishment and of honour. Whenever a human being, through the commission of a crime, has become exiled from good, he needs to be reintegrated with it through suffering. The suffering should be inflicted with the aim of bringing the soul to recognize freely some day that its infliction was just. This reintegration with the good is what punishment is. Every man who is innocent, or who has finally expiated guilt, needs to be recognized as honourable to the same extent as anyone else.

The human soul has need of disciplined participation in a common task of public value, and it has need of personal initiative within this participation.

The human soul has need of security and also of risk. The fear of violence or of hunger or of any other extreme evil is a sickness of the soul. The boredom produced by a complete absence of risk is also a sickness of the soul (1986, pp. 208–09).

## Supplementary Statement of Dr. Jan Bonham

It was a privilege to be permitted to participate in the deliberations of this group. In my view, the *source* of the proposals contained in this report is as significant as its *content*. Principal Fred Helter deserves great credit for recognizing the talent and commitment of his colleagues, and for giving them the support needed to allow them to engage with one another long enough for their differences to become a basis not of simple declamation and counterdeclamation, but of collective wisdom and sophistication.

While the authors of this careful, thorough, and sophisticated treatment are entitled to great credit for the abilities they brought to the job, it is important to realize that talents and motivations like those exhibited here are replicated in thousands of schools across the country. These four came to their task with differences in perceptions, priorities, and perspectives like those we find mirrored in every sector of contemporary society. I believe that it was from their immersion in the daily lives of their students in the classrooms and hallways of their school, from the accumulation of incidents demanding a response, from their witnessing the range of variations in those responses, that they "got" the complexity and grittiness of the problem. It was this process of constant learning that aided them in making their presuppositions a point of departure, viewpoints to be listened to and reflected on, rather than banners to be proudly flown, firmly implanted, and fiercely defended.

Too often we read that teachers are the source of the problem. This report demonstrates that teachers are rather those to whom we should turn for informed and constructive responses to the vexing and important problem of moral education.

# REFERENCES

Anderson, Elijah. *Code of the Street: Decency, Violence, and the Moral Life of the Inner City.* New York: W.W. Norton, 1999.

Aristotle. *Nichomachean Ethics,* trans. J. E. C. Weldon. New York: Prometheus Books, 1987.

Barth, Roland. "The Principal and the Profession of Teaching." In Thomas J. Sergiovanni and John H. Moore (eds.), *Schooling for Tomorrow: Directing Reforms to Issues That Count,* Boston: Allyn & Bacon, 1989.

Bellah, Robert, and Richard Madsen, William Sullivan, Ann Swidler, and Steven Tipton. *Habits of the Heart.* Berkeley: University of California Press, 1996.

Benninga, Jacques S. "Moral and Character Education in the Elementary School: An Introduction." In J. S. Benninga (ed.), *Moral, Character, and Civil Education in the Elementary School.* New York: Teacher's College Press, 1991.

Berlin, Isaiah. *The Crooked Timber of Humanity: Chapters in the History of Ideas.* New York: Vintage Books, 1992.

Brennecke, Fritz. *The Nazi Primer: Official Handbook for Schooling Hitler Youth.* Trans. Harwood L. Childs. New York: Harper & Brothers, 1938.

Butchart, Ronald E. "Punishments, Penalties, Prizes, and Procedures." In R. E. Butchart and B. McEwan (eds.), *Classroom Discipline in American Schools: Problems and Possibilities for Democratic Education.* Albany: State University of New York Press, 1998, 19–49.

Callahan, Sidney. "Self and Other in Feminist Thought." In Courtney S. Campbell and B. Andrew Lustig (eds.), *Duties to Others.* Boston: Kluwer Academic Publishing, 1994.

Canter, L., and M. Canter. *Assertive Discipline.* Santa Monica, CA: Canter & Associates, 1992.

Carr, David. *Educating the Virtues; An Essay on the Philosophical Psychology of Moral Development and Education.* New York: Routledge, 1991.

Coles, Robert. *The Moral Intelligence of Children.* New York: Random House, 1997.

Damon, William. *Greater Expectations: Overcoming the Culture of Indulgence in America's Homes and Schools.* New York: The Free Press, 1995.

DeRoche, Edward F., and Mary M. Williams. *Educating Hearts and Minds: A Comprehensive Character Education Framework.* Thousand Oaks, CA: Corwin Press, 1998.

Developmental Studies Center. *Ways We Want Our Class To Be: Class Meetings That Build Commitment to Kindness and Learning.* Oakland, CA: Developmental Studies Center, 1996.

DeVries, Rheta, and Betty Zan. *Moral Classrooms, Moral Children: Creating a Constructivist Atmosphere in Early Education.* New York: Teachers College Press, 1994.

Dewey, John. *Human Nature and Conduct.* New York: Henry Holt & Co., 1922.

Dewey, John. *Lectures on Ethics 1900–1901.* Carbondale, IL: Southern Illinois University at Carbondale, 1991.

Dewey, John. *Theory of Moral Life*. New York: Holt, Rinehart & Winston, 1960.

Durkheim, Emile. *Moral Education*. Glencoe, IL: The Free Press, 1961.

Durkheim, Emile. *Education and Sociology*. Glencoe, IL: The Free Press, 1956.

Egan, Kieran. *Primary Understanding: Education in Early Childhood*. New York: Routledge, 1988.

Eliot, George. *Adam Bede*. New York: Penguin, 1985.

Fenstermacher, Gary. "Some Moral Considerations on Teaching as a Profession." In John I. Goodlad (ed.), *The Moral Dimensions of Teaching*, San Francisco: Jossey-Bass, 1990.

Foot, Philippa. *Virtues and Vices and Other Essays in Moral Philosophy*. Oxford: Blackwell, 1978.

Frankfurt, H. "On the Necessity of Ideals." In G. G. Noam and T. E. Wren, *The Moral Self*. Cambridge, MA: Massachusetts Institute of Technology, 1993, 16–27.

Franklin, Benjamin. *Autobiography and Other Writings of Benjamin Franklin*. New York: Dodd, Mead, 1963.

Glasser, William. *The Quality School: Managing Students Without Coercion*. New York: Harper Collins, 1990.

Goodlad, John L. *A Place Called School: Prospects for the Future*. New York: McGraw-Hill, 1984.

Goodman, Joan F., and Howard Lesnick. *The Moral Stake in Education: Contested Premises and Practices*. New York: Longman, 2001.

Hallie, Philip. *Lest Innocent Blood Be Shed: The Story of the Village of Le Chambon and How Goodness Happened There*. New York: Harper & Row, 1979.

Hallie, Philip. *Tales of Good and Evil, Help and Harm*. New York: HarperCollins, 1997.

Hare, R. M. *The Language of Morals*. Oxford: Clarendon Press, 1952.

Howard, Robert. "Lawrence Kohlberg's Influence on Moral Education in Elementary Education." In Jacques S. Benninga (ed.), *Moral, Character, and Civic Education in Elementary Education*, New York: Teacher's College Press, 1991.

Hume, David. *A Treatise of Human Nature*. Ed. L. A. Selby Bigge. Oxford: Clarendon, 1896.

Hume, David. *An Enquiry Concerning the Principles of Morals*. Ed. Eric Steinberg. Indianapolis: Hackett, 1983.

Ingersoll, R. M. *Who Controls Teachers' Work? Power and Accountability in America's Schools*. Cambridge, MA: Harvard University Press, 2003.

Jackson, Philip, Robert Boostrom, and David Hansen. *The Moral Life of Schools*. San Francisco: Jossey-Bass, 1993.

Kagan, Jerome. *The Nature of the Child*. New York: Basic Books, 1984.

Kant, Immanuel. *Grounding for the Metaphysics of Morals; Within a Supposed Right to Lie Because of Philanthropic Concerns*. 3rd ed. Trans. James W. Ellington. Indianapolis: Hackett, 1993.

Kaestle, Carl. *Pillars of the Republic: Common Schools and American Society, 1780–1860*. New York: Hill & Wang, 1983.

Kohlberg, Lawrence. *Essays on Moral Development. Vol. 1, The Philosophy of Moral Development*. San Francisco: Harper & Row, 1981.

Kohn, Alfie. *Punished by Rewards: The Trouble with Gold Stars, Incentive Plans, A's, Praise, and Other Bribes.* Boston: Houghton Mifflin, 1993.

Kohn, Alfie. *What to Look for in a Classroom: And Other Essays.* San Francisco: Jossey-Bass, 1998.

Kupperman, Joel. *Character.* New York: Oxford University Press, 1991.

Lewis, C. S. *A Mind Awake: An Anthology of C. S. Lewis.* Ed. C. S. Kilby. London: Geoffrey Bles, 1968.

Lewis, C. S. *The Problem of Pain.* New York, Macmillan, 1948.

Lickona, Thomas. *Educating for Character: How Our Schools Can Teach Respect and Responsibility.* New York: Bantam Books, 1991.

Lickona, Thomas, Eric Schaps, and Catherine Lewis. *Eleven Principles of Effective Character Education.* Washington, DC: The Character Education Partnership, 1997–1998.

MacIntyre, Alasdair. *After Virtue: A Study in Moral Theory.* 2nd ed. South Bend, IN: University of Notre Dame, 1984.

McCarthy, Martha, and Nelda Cameron-McCabe. "The Legal Foundation of Public Education." In Mark G. Yudof, David L. Kirp, and Betsy Levin (eds.), *Educational Policy and the Law.* 3rd ed. St. Paul: West, 1992.

McClellan, Edward. *Schools and the Shaping of Character: Moral Education in America, 1607–Present.* Bloomington, IN: ERIC Clearinghouse of Social Studies/Social Science Education, 1992.

McEwan, B. "Contradiction, Paradox, and Irony: The World of Classroom Management." In R. E. Butchart and B. McEwan (eds.), *Classroom Discipline in American Schools: Problems and Possibilities for Democratic Education.* Albany: State University of New York Press, 1998, 135–155.

Midgley, Mary. *Can't We Make Moral Judgments?* New York: St. Martin's Press, 1991.

Mill, John Stuart. *Utilitarianism.* Indianapolis: Hackett, 1979.

Mill, John Stuart. *Utilitarianism, On Liberty, Considerations on Representative Government.* Ed. J. M. Dent. London: Everyman's Library, 1993.

Moore, G. E. *Principia Ethica.* Rev. ed., Thomas Baldwin. Cambridge: Cambridge University Press, 1993.

Murdoch, I. *The Sovereignty of Good.* London: Routledge, 1970.

Neuhaus, Richard John. *The Naked Public Square: Religion and Democracy in America.* Grand Rapids, MI: Wm. B. Eerdmans, 1984.

Nisbett, Richard E., and Dov Cohen. *Culture of Honor: The Psychology of Violence in the South.* New York: Westview Press, 1996.

Noddings, Nel. *Starting at Home: Caring and Social Policy.* Berkeley: University of California Press, 2002.

*New York Times,* May 3, 2000, Sec. B, p. 4.

Nozick, Robert. *Philosophical Explanations.* Cambridge, MA: Belknap Press, 1981.

Nucci, Lawrence P. *Education in the Moral Domain.* Cambridge: Cambridge University Press, 2001.

Nussbaum, Martha. "Valuing Values: A Case for Reasoned Commitment." *Yale Journal of Law and the Humanities* 6 (1994): 197–218.

Oakeshott, Michael. *Rationalism in Politics.* New York: Basic Books, 1962.

Oliner, Samuel P., and Pearl M. Oliner. *The Altruistic Personality.* Glencoe, IL: The Free Press, 1988.

O'Malley, William J. "Curiosity." *America,* October 3, 1998, 14–19.

Peters, Richard Stanley. *Psychology and Ethical Development: A Collection of Articles on Psychological Theories, Ethical Development and Human Understanding.* London: Allen & Unwin, 1974.

Piaget, Jean. *The Origins of Intelligence in Children.* New York: International University Press, 1952.

Plato. "Meno." In Edith Hamilton and Huntington Caims (eds.), *The Collected Dialogues of Plato.* Princeton, NJ: Princeton University Press, 1961.

Purpel, David E., and Kevin Ryan. "It Comes with the Territory: The Inevitability of Moral Education in the Schools." In David Purpel and Kevin Ryan (eds.), *Moral Education . . . It Comes with the Territory.* Berkeley, CA: McCutchan, 1976.

Rawls, John. *A Theory of Justice.* Cambridge, MA: Harvard University Press, 1971.

Ryan, Kevin, and Karen E. Bohlin. *Building Character in Schools.* San Francisco: Jossey-Bass, 1999.

Ryle, Gilbert. "Can Virtue Be Taught?" In R. F. Dearden, P. H. Hirst, and R. S. Peters (eds.), *Education and the Development of Reason.* London: Routledge and Kegan Paul, 1972.

Sandel, Michael. *Liberalism and the Limits of Justice.* New York: Cambridge University Press, 1998.

Sartre, Jean-Paul. "Existentialism and Ethics." In Barry I. Chazan and Jonas F. Soltis (eds.), *Moral Education.* New York: Teacher's College Press, 1973.

School District of Philadelphia. *Code of Student Conduct for the School Year 2002–2003.* Philadelphia: School District of Philadelphia, 2002.

Sennett, Richard. *The Corrosion of Character: The Personal Consequences of Work in the New Capitalism.* New York: W. W. Norton, 1998.

Sergiovanni, Thomas J. *Building Community in Schools.* San Francisco: Jossey-Bass, 1994.

Sergiovanni, Thomas J. *Moral Leadership: Getting to the Heart of School Improvement.* San Francisco: Jossey-Bass, 1992.

Shweder, Richard A., Manamohan Mahapotro, and Joan Miller. "Culture and Moral Development." In Jerome Kagan and Sharon Lamb (eds.), *The Emergence of Morality in Young Children.* Chicago: University of Chicago Press, 1987.

Sizer, Theodore R. *Horace's Compromise—The Dilemma of the American High School.* Boston: Houghton Mifflin, 1984.

Sizer, Theodore R., and Nancy Sizer (eds.). *Moral Education.* Cambridge, MA: Harvard University Press, 1970.

Stanford Achievement Test. Reviewer's Edition. 9th ed. San Antonio, TX: Harcourt Brace, 1996.

Straughan, Roger. *I Ought to, but . . . A Philosophical Approach to the Problem of Weakness of Will in Education.* London: Windor, 1982.

Supreme Court of the United States. *Shaughnessy* v. *United States ex rel. Mezei,* 345 U.S. 206 (1953).

United States Court of Appeals. *Cox* v. *Dardanelle Public School District.* 790 F.2d 668 (8th Cir., 1986).

Warnock, G. J. *The Object of Morality.* London: Methuen & Co., 1971.

Warnock, Mary. *The Uses of Philosophy.* Oxford: Oxford University Press, 1992.

Weil, Simone. "The Needs of the Soul." In Siân Miles (ed.), *Simone Weil: An Anthology.* New York: Weidenfeld & Nicolson, 1986a.

Weil, Simone. "Draft for a Statement of Human Obligations." In Siân Miles (ed.), *Simon Weil: An Anthology.* New York: Weidenfeld and Nicolson, 1986b.

Wilson, James Q. *The Moral Sense.* Glencoe, IL: The Free Press, 1993.

Wilson, P. S. *Interest and Discipline in Education.* London: Routledge and Kegan Paul, 1971.

Wynne, Edward A., and Kevin Ryan. *Reclaiming Our Schools: Teaching Character, Academics, and Discipline.* 2nd ed. Upper Saddle River, NJ: Merrill, 1997.

# INDEX